Weaving Women's Spheres in Vietnam

The Intimate and the Public in Asian and Global Perspectives

Editorial Board

Danièle BÉLANGER (*Laval University*)
Fran BENNETT (*University of Oxford*)
Mary BRINTON (*Harvard University*)
Melanita BUDIANTA (*University of Indonesia*)
CHANG Kyung-Sup (*Seoul National University*)
Harald FUESS (*University of Heidelberg*)
Barbara HOBSON (*University of Stockholm*)
Shirlena HUANG (*National University of Singapore*)
ITO Kimio (*Kyoto University*)
Barbara MOLONY (*Santa Clara University*)
OSHIKAWA Fumiko (*Kyoto University*)
Rajni PALRIWALA (*University of Delhi*)
ITO Peng (*University of Toronto*)
Carolyn SOBRITCHEA (*University of the Philippines*)
TSENG Yen-Fen (*National Taiwan University*)
Patricia UBEROI (*Institute of Chinese Studies, Delhi*)
Thanes WONGYANNAVA (*Thammasat University*)

VOLUME 9

The titles published in this series are listed at *brill.com/ipap*

Weaving Women's Spheres in Vietnam

The Agency of Women in Family, Religion, and Community

Edited by

Kato Atsufumi

BRILL

LEIDEN | BOSTON

Cover illustration: Women in Hanoi and Hội An, Vietnam (2005).
© Kiely Ramos (www.kielyramos.com).

Library of Congress Cataloging-in-Publication Data

Names: Kato, Atsufumi, 1975- editor. | Luong, Hy V. Gender relations in
   Vietnam. Container of (work):
Title: Weaving women's spheres in Vietnam : the agency of women in family,
   religion and community / edited by Kato Atsufumi.
Description: Leiden : Brill, [2016] | Series: The intimate and the public in
   Asian and global perspectives, ISSN 2213-0608 ; volume 9 | Includes
   bibliographical references and index.
Identifiers: LCCN 2015039036| ISBN 9789004251731 (hardback : alk. paper) |
   ISBN 9789004293502 (e-book)
Subjects: LCSH: Women--Vietnam.
Classification: LCC HQ1750.5 .W43 2016 | DDC 305.409597--dc23
LC record available at http://lccn.loc.gov/2015039036

ISSN 2213-0608
ISSN 978-90-04-25173-1 (hardback)
ISBN 978-90-04-29350-2 (e-book)

This publication has been typeset in the multilingual "Brill" typeface. With over 5,100 characters covering
Latin, IPA, Greek, and Cyrillic, this typeface is especially suitable for use in the humanities.
For more information, please see www.brill.com/brill-typeface.

Copyright 2016 by Koninklijke Brill NV, Leiden, The Netherlands.
Koninklijke Brill NV incorporates the imprints Brill, Brill Hes & De Graaf, Brill Nijhoff, Brill Rodopi and
Hotei Publishing.
All rights reserved. No part of this publication may be reproduced, translated, stored in a retrieval system,
or transmitted in any form or by any means, electronic, mechanical,photocopying, recording or otherwise,
without prior written permission from the publisher.
Authorization to photocopy items for internal or personal use is granted by Koninklijke Brill NV provided
that the appropriate fees are paid directly to The Copyright Clearance Center, 222 Rosewood Drive,
Suite 910, Danvers, MA 01923, USA.
Fees are subject to change.

This book is printed on acid-free paper.

Printed by Printforce, the Netherlands

Contents

Preface   VII
List of Figures   X
List of Tables   XII
List of Contributors   XIII

Weaving Women's Spheres in Vietnam: An Introduction   1
   Kato Atsufumi

PART 1
Gendered Structure and Reframing It from within

1. Gender Relations in Vietnam: Ideologies, Kinship Practices, and Political Economy   25
   Hy V. Luong

2. Rethinking Vietnamese Women's Property Rights and the Role of Ancestor Worship in Premodern Society: Beyond the Dichotomies   57
   Miyazawa Chihiro

3. Divorce Prevalence under the Forces of Individualism and Collectivism in "Shortcut" Modernity in Vietnam   81
   Tran Thi Minh Thi

4. Negotiating with Multilayered Public Norms: Female University Students' Struggle to Survive the Đổi Mới Period   116
   Ito Miho

PART 2
Transgressing Boundaries, Weaving Alternatives, and Putting Down New Roots

5. The Limit of *Chia Sẻ* (Compassion): Interpretative Conflicts in the Collectivity of the Vietnamese Women's Union   141
   Kato Atsufumi

6   Living in Intimacy: A Case Study of Women's Community at a Caodaist Temple in Hanoi   166
    Ito Mariko

7   Imperious Mandarins and Cunning Princesses: Mediumship, Gender, and Identity in Urban Vietnam   193
    Kirsten W. Endres

8   The Blessed Virgin Mary Wears *Áo Dài*: Marianism in the Transnational Public Sphere between Vietnamese Catholics in the U.S. and Vietnam   218
    Thien-Huong T. Ninh

    Index   233

Preface

This volume explores how the dichotomy of public and private has affected the construction of gendered agency in the Vietnamese social context by examining case studies in the realms of family, religion, and local politics through historical, anthropological, and sociological perspectives.

I hope this volume will have a wide audience, from people who are interested in contemporary Vietnam to scholars who are engaged in comparative studies on gender issues in Asian and Southeast Asian societies as well as theoretical reflection on the concepts of public and private in the Asian context. Two groups of primary readers were especially in my mind when I was editing this volume. The first group is those who are interested in measuring the usefulness of the ideas of public and private in the analysis of Asian societies. In this respect, this volume is resonant with the literature of the Subaltern Studies Group. Dipesh Chakrabarty ([2000] 2008) demonstrated epistemological changes in Indian peasants and intellectuals under the colonial rule that were brought about by Western modern ideas, such as capital, labor, the public, and privacy. At the same time, he also tried to "provincialize" these modern ideas by revealing the formation of these ideas as particular historical processes which originated in Europe and expanded to the world, instead of describing them as the development of universal scientific ideas. This volume also tries to show that the Western ideas of public and private have penetrated into the matrix of reality in Vietnamese society to the extent that we cannot describe local people's experiences without these terms. At the same time, we also bring attention to the fact that these ideas are "provincial" concepts which have regional origins and can never cover up people's lived experiences, which means that academics need to realize that people may live their everyday lives in the world without the distinction between the public and private. "Provincializing" the ideas of public and private is different from "localizing" these ideas. We do not aim to adjust these concepts to the Vietnamese context for better use, nor to introduce another set of public and private in a Vietnamese style. Instead, we try to investigate how the dichotomous structure of public and private, in various fashions, has repeatedly affected the social construction of reality in the Vietnamese context. In this sense, we also need to "provincialize" the Chinese concepts of public and private by putting them back to the historical context of their development, which makes Vietnamese case studies more complicated.

The second group of readers is those who seek solutions to the predicaments of gendered agents in Vietnam and elsewhere, as well as seeking to empower their potential for autonomous agency. Arguments about the predicaments and possibilities of gendered agency often bring us to focus on the boundary between the public and private, mentioned above, which regulates this gendered agency. Meanwhile, discussing how the boundary works often leads us to recognize the horizon of the life-worlds in which the agents interweave their lives by transgressing the boundary, intentionally or unconsciously. The boundary between the public and private has actual effects that have regulated gendered agency, but it is also an imagined "gate of law," in Kafka's allegory (cf. Butler 1990), an effect of convention that works when people believe it is there. This gate is difficult to go through, but if people do not care about it, it is just nothing. Some people even utilize the gate to make their lives easier to endure. Academic discourse on the public and private can become complicit with people in confirming this imagined matrix of social reality when we exaggerate the effects of the boundary. The chapters in this volume try to avoid committing this kind of fault by continuously reexamining the ideas of public and private, in both the academic and local contexts, to get close to the lived experiences of ordinary people.

Vietnam is on the crossroads where East Asia meets Southeast Asia, where the legacy and aftereffects of socialist modernity meet the revival of tradition and the transnational trend toward a market economy, which makes the cases in this volume more complex and therefore more typical of our experiences of tradition and modernity in Asia. We hope that the arguments in this volume go beyond the Vietnamese context and undermine conventional frameworks such as the Chinese tradition, Southeast Asian flexibility, and modernity.

This volume resulted from two workshops organized by the Next-Generation Research Group in the Kyoto University Global Center of Excellence for the Reconstruction of the Intimate and Public Spheres in 21st Century Asia (hereafter the GCOE program). One workshop, entitled "Alternative Intimate Spheres for Women in Vietnam," was held at the Faculty of Letters, Kyoto University, on December 17 and 18, 2011. Another seminar, entitled "Current Anthropology on Vietnam," was held the next day at the National Museum of Ethnology in Osaka, with collaboration from the museum.

We would like to recognize the GCOE program for supporting the workshops and for its further support for the subsequent book project. Especially, our gratitude goes to Professor Ochiai Emiko, the leader of the GCOE program, for participating in the workshop in Kyoto on both days and encouraging us to publish this book. We thank Professor Matsuda Motoji for supervising our research unit. We would also like to express our gratitude to Professor Tamura Katsumi at the National Museum of Ethnology for supporting the seminar at the museum. We thank Professor Shimao Minoru of Keio

University for reviewing the English translation of the Chinese documents in Miyazawa Chihiro's chapter. We also thank the anonymous reviewers. We express special thanks to Paul Norbury, Nozomi Goto, Jennifer Obdam, Thalien Colenbrander, Leo Aoi Hosoya, Lil Wills, and Yamamoto Kohei for all their efforts in editing, and Song Mi Bang, Takata Shoko, and Sakai Yoko for their special support in accounting and other general affairs.

Earlier versions of some chapters of this volume have been published elsewhere. Hy V. Luong's chapter is a revised version of "Gender Relations: Ideologies, Kinship Practices, and Political Economy" in *Postwar Vietnam: Dynamics of a Transforming Society* (edited by Hy V. Luong, Rowman & Littlefield, 2003), and Kirsten W. Endres's chapter is a revised version of "The (Gendered) World of Mediumship," chapter 5 of *Performing the Divine: Mediums, Markets and Modernity in Urban Vietnam* (Kirsten W. Endres, NIAS Press, 2011). We appreciate the publishers' permissions.

Kato Atsufumi
Hanoi

References

Butler, Judith. 1990. *Gender Trouble: Feminism and the Subversion of Identity*. London: Routledge.

Chakrabarty, Dipesh. [2000] 2008. *Provincializing Europe: Postcolonial Thought and Historical Difference*. Princeton, NJ: Princeton University Press.

List of Figures

Hy V. Luong
1.1 Percentages of Women in People's Councils, 1989–2011   31
1.2 Voluntary association membership: number of memberships per 100 residents above the age of 16   45

Tran Thi Minh Thi
3.1 Typical divorce procedure   90
3.2 Number of divorces in Vietnam, 1965–2010   91
3.3 Marriage duration in years by rural/urban differential, 2000–2009   95
3.4 Percentage distribution of initiating spouses in divorces by rural/urban differential, 2000–2009   97
3.5 Percentage distribution of initiating spouses in divorces by year, 2000–2009   97
3.6 Reported reasons for divorce, 2000–2009   98
3.7 Divorce reasons by year, 2000–2009   99
3.8 Divorce causes by year by rural and urban residence, 2000–2009   99
3.9 Divorce reasons by wealth, 2000–2009   100

Ito Miho
4.1 Gender gap of university students by major, 1975–1976   121
4.2 Number of university and college students from 1976 to 2010   123
4.3 The gender gap of students in postsecondary education from 2001 to 2010   124
4.4 Female university students studying Japanese studies   129
4.5 A newly married couple in Yên Bái province   131
4.6 A female teacher giving a lecture for elementary students at temple of literature (Văn Miếu) in Hanoi   132

Kato Atsufumi
5.1 Repairing footpaths between rice fields   142
5.2 Taking attendance at the harvesting of the organization's rice field   149
5.3 The Thạch Châu Commune office of the women's union on a loan registration day   149

LIST OF FIGURES   XI

Ito Mariko

6.1   The Caodaism Hanoi Temple   167
6.2   Participating in a ritual in the Hanoi temple   172
6.3   Women gathering at Priestess Hoa's preaching   178
6.4   Participating in a ritual in the Hanoi temple   181
6.5   Praying widows   185
6.6   Volunteer cooking activity   186

Kirsten W. Endres

7.1   Altar dedicated to the pantheon of the Four Palaces   194
7.2   Ritual embodiment of Saint Trần by a female medium   198
7.3   The *đồng cô* are perceived as particularly talented ritual performers   207
7.4   Preparations for the Mông Sơn Ritual   212

Thien-Huong Ninh

8.1   Our lady of Vietnam (completed in 1995, Santa Ana, California)   226
8.2   Our lady of Lavang as a Vietnamese woman (completed in 1998, La Vang, Vietnam)   228

List of Tables

Hy V. Luong
1.1 Gender and education in Vietnam in 1989 and 2009 in percentages   29
1.2 Percentages of women in the Vietnamese National Assembly   30
1.3 Percentages of women in leadership positions in the Vietnamese Communist Party and local governments   37
1.4 Division of domestic labor in percentages   42

Miyazawa Chihiro
2.1 The Testament of Lê Khắc Địch and Đỗ Thị Sâm   63
2.2 Kỵ Điền of Phạm Gia An in his testament   69
2.3 Donations to the worship hall for Phạm Quang Nguyên in 1886 by Phạm lineage   73

Tran Thi Minh Thi
3.1 Crude divorce rate and general divorce rate in Vietnam, 2000–2010   92
3.2 Mean of marriage duration by year by rural/urban differential, 2000–2009   96

Ito Miho
4.1 Increase in the number of university students (long term) and percentage of female students from 1960 to 1969   120
4.2 Family expectations regarding children's employment (Data from Bình Lục District, Hà Nam Province, 2008)   125

Kato Atsufumi
5.1 List of interviewees   158

List of Contributors

Kirsten W. ENDRES
is head of a research group at the department of "Resilience and Transformation in Eurasia" at the Max Planck Institute for Social Anthropology, Germany. She has conducted research in Northern Vietnam since 1996, focusing on social-cultural transformation processes that arise from the dynamic interplay between state, society, and the market. Her publications include *Performing the Divine. Mediums, Markets, and Modernity in Urban Vietnam* (NIAS Press, 2011) and *Engaging the Spirit World. Popular Beliefs and Practices in Modern Southeast Asia* (co-edited with Andrea Lauser, Berghahn Books, 2011).

ITO Mariko
is a part time lecturer at Kyoto University of Foreign Studies, Japan. She has been conducting anthropological field research on religious communities and the lives of single women in urban Vietnam since 2000. She earned her Ph.D. in literature from the Graduate University for Advanced Studies, Japan.

ITO Miho
is a lecturer at Kanda University of International Studies, Japan. Her recent publications include *Education for Minorities and their School Choices: Identity Politics of Ethnicity in Vietnam* (Kyoto University Press, 2014, in Japanese). She has been conducting sociological research on ethnicity and educational policies in Vietnam since 2001. She earned her Ph.D. in arts and sciences from the University of Tokyo, where she wrote a dissertation entitled *Boarding School for Ethnic Minority Students in Northern Vietnam* (2011, in Japanese). Her research projects focus on family, gender, and identity politics and strategy formation through the daily activities of ethnic groups.

KATO Atsufumi
is a project assistant professor at the East Asia Liberal Arts Initiative (EALAI) at the University of Tokyo, where he is responsible for the Zensho–UT Japan Studies Program at Vietnam National University, Hanoi. He has been conducting anthropological field research on local governance in contemporary Vietnam since 2002. He earned his Ph.D. in Human Sciences from Osaka University. His research projects focus on the ideology and practice of participatory democracy through case studies of Alternative Dispute Resolution (ADR), Rotating Saving and Credit Associations (ROSCAs), and village conflicts

over the selection of poor households. He has also been interested in gender, elderly care, and the family in Vietnam. He recently co-edited a volume entitled *Rethinking Representations of Asian Women: Changes, Continuity, and Everyday Life* (Palgrave Macmillan, 2015).

Hy V. LUONG
is a professor of anthropology at the University of Toronto. His recent publications include *Tradition, Revolution, and Market Economy in a North Vietnamese Village, 1925–2006* (University of Hawaii Press, 2010), *Urbanization, Migration, and Poverty in a Vietnamese Metropolis: Ho Chi Minh City in Comparative Perspectives* (National University of Singapore Press, edited volume, 2009), *Hiện Đại và Động Thái của Truyền Thống ở Việt Nam: Những Cách Tiếp Cận Nhân Học* (*Modernities and the Dynamics of Tradition in Vietnam: Anthropologically Approached*, two edited volumes, National University of Ho Chi Minh City Press, 2010), and *The Dynamics of Social Capital and Civic Engagement in Asia* (Routledge, 2012, co-edited with Amrita Daniere). Luong is currently working on gifts, social capital, rural-to-urban migration, and socioeconomic transformation in rural Vietnam.

MIYAZAWA Chihiro
is an associate professor at Nanzan University, Nagoya, Japan. He has been conducting anthropological field research on the village structure of Northern and Central Vietnam since 1991. He earned his Ph.D. in anthropology from the University of Tokyo. His dissertation is entitled *The Historical Change of Village Structure in Northern Vietnam (1907–1997)* (in Japanese). His most recent publication is *The Diary of Nishikawa Hiroo in Sai Gon: From September 1955 to June 1957* (Fukyosha 2015, in Japanese). He has also been interested in popular religion and the history of Japan-Vietnam relationships in the twentieth century.

Thien-Huong T. NINH
is a lecturer in the Department of Social Sciences at California Polytechnic State University, San Luis Obispo. Her research and teaching interests include international migration, Diaspora, racial and ethnic relations, and global Christianities. She received her Ph.D. in Sociology from the University of Southern California (2013) and was a Gaius Charles Bolin Fellow in the Department of Religion at Williams College (2012–2014). More information about her works can be found at www.thninh.com.

TRAN Thi Minh Thi
is the head of Department of Women's Studies and the deputy director of the Institute of Family and Gender Studies at the Vietnam Academy of Social Sciences. She also holds a faculty post in the department of sociology at the Graduate Academy of Social Sciences. She has been conducting sociological research on family, gender, health care regimes, and social stratification in Vietnam since 2001. She earned her M.A. in sociology from the University of Washington, USA, and obtained her Ph.D. in sociology from Kyoto University. Her most recent publication is *Model of Divorce in Contemporary Vietnam: A Socio-Economic and Structural Analysis of Divorce in the Red River Delta in the 2000s* (Social Sciences Publishing House, 2014).

Weaving Women's Spheres in Vietnam: An Introduction

Kato Atsufumi

Vietnam and Beyond

This volume examines the complexity and potential of the agency of women in the Vietnamese context by focusing on the effect of the public/private divide. We analyze the agency of women and the representation of womanhood in the realms of the family, local community, and religious activity from historical, anthropological, and sociological perspectives. Our aim is to contribute to a comparative study of the reconstruction of the public and private spheres in Asian perspectives. The chapters in this volume compare Vietnamese cases with gender issues in other societies regarding, for instance, women's status in traditional East Asian societies, the effects of socialism and industrialization on women's education, the effect of modernist discourse on marriage, the effect of socialistic collectivization on the reconstruction of women's community, as well as the experiences of diaspora and their struggle to reconstruct an ethnic identity.

Vietnam is a junction of various values, ideologies, and systems, as the locus where East Asia meets Southeast Asia. More specific to this volume's context, Vietnam is where the East Asian male-centered patrilineal family system meets the comparably flexible Southeast Asian bilateral-kindred system. Historically, Vietnam has experienced drastic social changes common among developing countries, including colonization, struggles for national independence, total wars, socialistic reforms, and national divisions. Further, Vietnam experienced an "uncertain transition" from a socialist regime to a libertarian one (Burawoy and Verdery, eds. 1999) right in the middle of the extreme historical time of the "short twentieth century" (Hobsbawm 1994), though at the periphery of the world system.

This work provides an analytical description of the agency of Vietnamese women in order to understand how people at the crossroads of often contradictory values and institutions have struggled to interweave, or in some cases have unconcernedly interwoven, their lives and places of belonging. In this respect, this volume serves not merely as an introduction of intergrading between East Asia and Southeast Asia, nor does it describe *the* Vietnamese culture and women's status in it.

The key focuses of this volume are the agency of women and the effect of the public/private divide on gendered practices. The volume's most important contribution to gender studies is to shed light on the dynamics of women's agency that enable them to interweave their lives between various public norms and institutions, particularly between the official realm of the public sphere and the informal realm of the private sphere. The chapters in this volume reveal how the distinction between the public and private spheres has maintained existing gendered structures and has regulated women's lives, how the agency of the symbolic representations of womanhood problematizes this divide, and how gendered agents' practices of appropriating and transgressing the divide have reconfigured the boundary of the dominant, often repressive, gendered structure and interwoven alternative spaces for living between these boundaries. The chapters in this volume focus on the suppressive family structure upon Vietnamese women and the active agency of women appropriating and transgressing the structure. The volume also reveals the possibility of other institutions outside the family, such as school, religious organizations, and mass organizations, as a basis for mutual support and for women to actively reconnect themselves to society, ethnicity, and national identity.

Necessarily, what is described in this volume is not a static picture of women's status in Vietnam, but a more dynamic potential of women's agency. To approach the topic, this volume describes concrete cases and life stories of Vietnamese women rather than general trends regarding women's status in Vietnam. While several chapters refer to grand narratives, such as the conflict between the modernizing process of women's liberation and traditional norms obstructing this trend, most of the chapters concentrate more on case studies in which people assemble the fragments of plural norms from tradition and modernity, East and Southeast Asia, and public and private spheres.

The Agency of Women

In this volume, we use the phrase "the agency of women" in a wider sense. The concept of agency basically indicates individuals who have the capacity to act effectively on the world and their lives. However, agency can be embodied not only by persons but also by nonhuman things and symbols. In this volume the contributors consider not only the agency of individual women but also that of symbolic representations of womanhood, such as gender-transgressive males (or male spirit mediums) who embody female deities (Kirsten W. Endres's chapter), and the Vietnamization of statues of Virgin Mary (Thien-Huong Ninh's chapter). I use the concept of agency to refer to the potential of individuals and symbols that behave as active actors but are influenced by other actors around them. For instance, a woman may act on behalf of her family's will and, at the same time, appropriate the family structure that regulates her subjectivity so as to activate her own agency, freeing herself from the family. The ritual embodiment of a female deity may rescue a person from identity crisis and empower him or her to reconnect to society, but performing womanhood may reinforce existing gender ideologies.

The literature on the agency of women in the Third World provides us with a framework for this volume. It reveals how processes of modernization have liberated women as well as regulated them by "remaking women" (Abu-Lughod 1998) as subjects of nation-states, laborers in the capitalist economy, and wives in patriarchal households. Women in the Third World have been given roles of representing national, ethnic, and religious identities for local people to resist colonialism, capitalism, and globalism (cf. Chakrabarty [2000] 2008). Women's resistance against this imposition, however, often ends up reinforcing the structure, as in the case study by Lila Abu-Lughod (1990) on Bedouin young women who were captured by the capitalist commercial cosmetic culture when they tried to liberate themselves from the patriarchal family ideology by practicing romantic love. In this respect, we have to be cautious not to get caught up in the "romanticization of resistance" when we describe Vietnamese women's active agency against the existing gendered structure.

The literature on Vietnamese gender issues has also debated the ambivalent status of women between suppression and autonomy. In recent years, especially, the main interest of gender studies on Vietnamese women has been shifting from the status of women in a relatively static social structure to the dynamics of women's agency acting among this structure. Western feminists first developed an interest in Vietnamese women because the revolution and socialism seemed to realize women's liberation and gender equality. Then their interests moved to the cruel sides of the revolution and war, such as analyzing the mobilization of women for military service and militarism and sex workers in South Vietnam (see Werner and Bélanger 2002a, 13–14). There are also historical works on women's agency in premodern state institutions (Taylor 1983), the status of women in the family before the revolution (Yu 1990; Tran 2006), and women in colonialism (Marr 1981, 190–251). In recent years, many works have appeared on the sociology of family and studies on micropower relations around womanhood, such as family planning as an intervention into women's bodies (Gammeltoft 1999), girls' socialization and moral education (Rydström 2003), women in the revival of the family after the Đổi Mới (Renovation) policy (Pham Van Bich 1999; Werner and Bélanger eds. 2002b; Bélanger and Barbieri eds. 2009). Most recently, for example, Iwai Misaki argues for Vietnamese women's active agency in chain migration from northern villages to southern settlements and the construction of mutual associations there (Iwai 2012, 422–27).

These works not only describe the negative aspects of the gendered structure and the passive subjectivity of Vietnamese women, but also emphasize the potential of their positive agency, which means that a double-acting approach is necessary to describe the reality of the predicaments and potential of Vietnamese women. On the one hand, a cautious attitude that recognizes the deep-rooted gender inequality in Vietnam will help us to keep our eyes on the difficulties facing women. On the other hand, an optimistic attitude will empower Vietnamese people and bolster their potential to cope with their difficulties. Although the contributors to this volume cannot reach a consensus about the status of women in premodern and contemporary Vietnam, this disagreement allows the volume as a whole to reveal that Vietnamese women have been acting in this ambivalent situation between subordination and autonomy to enable their way of living and the lives of people around them.

The Public and Private

The dichotomy of public and private is foundational to investigating the difficulty and potential of Vietnamese women's agency. As seen in other Asian societies, in Vietnam, the public/private divide overlaps with the ideological divide of masculinity and femininity. For instance, the public domain of the political arena is often seen as a masculine sphere, while domestic work is seen as women's domain. Furthermore, men's interests and responsibilities are often conceived as "big issues" (*việc lớn*), while women's duties and interests are often perceived as "small issues" (*việc nhỏ*) (Bergstedt 2012, 124; see also Hy V. Luong's chapter in this volume). This divide has limited women to the domestic realm and systematically underestimated women's contributions, while this gendered divide also allows women to exercise their freedom within certain spaces.

In this volume there is a wide range of approaches to the terms "public" and "private." Some use these words as "experience-distant" (Geertz 1983) concepts based on academic discourse, while others close up on "experience-near" local conceptions associated with the ideas of public and private through analyzing their practical use in everyday language. This swinging back and forth between the experience-distant and experience-near is, in fact, inevitable in approaching the ongoing process of reconstructing the public and private realms in contemporary Vietnam and its effects on Vietnamese women's agency.

Several chapters in this volume use the terms "public" and "private" as universal concepts to indicate official institutions and personal lives, such as the arena of political deliberation versus the domestic realm of family life (Luong's chapter) or the secular state versus the freedom of inner life regarding religious activities (Ninh's chapter). This analytical framework is effective when we problematize issues such as the gendered asymmetry of the two realms, which has systematically enclosed women in the domestic realm, or draw an unexpected connection between the private realm of religious activity and the public representation of national and ethnic identities.

On the other hand, we can reduce the distance between the analytical concepts of "public" and "private" and the practical framework of ordinary people's recognition by using terminology much closer to local people's lives, though we must sacrifice these terms' sharpness as analytic concepts to some extent. The division between the public and the private can be understood differently when we use the ideas of *công* and *tư* in the Chinese-Vietnamese context. In Vietnamese language, these terms, which originate from Chinese characters, roughly mean "public" and "private," respectively. There are many compound words which use *công*, such as *công an* (public security), *công văn* (official documents), *công dân* (civics), *công lý* (principles), *công bằng* (fairness), *công cộng* (public space), *công khai* (openness), *công viên* (park), and *công điền* (publicly distributed agricultural land). Most of these words are related to the state as the guarantor of official principles. Some of these terms are related to law and justice. There are also several terms related to open space accessible to everyone, to which we do not refer in this volume. However, *tư* is not as widely used as *công*. There are only a few compound words which use *tư*, such as *tư nhân* (private company), *tư sản* (bourgeois), and *vô tư* (impartial, "no problem, easy matter").

In the Chinese-Vietnamese context, the idea of *công* includes not only the "public" sector but also several kinds of "private" realms, as long as they are justified and rationalized by the "heavenly principles." It may be difficult to grasp the connection between "public" and "heaven" if public is understood as a very secular, nonspiritual concept not connected to relations with the heavens. In Confucianism, however, the legitimacy of an imperial court as the guardian of secular social justice was established by the mandate of the heavens as a sacred order. In this context, the public is related to the heavens' providence, which always looks fairly on the earth world. The public sphere, in this sense, is a realm in which people are accurately protected by universal principles and the heavens' consideration. Under the protection of the public, good people are rewarded and people suffering unreasonable misfortune are protected. For instance, there are expressions in Vietnam such as, "If we always live honestly, the heavens will open the door for us" (*Mình cứ ăn ở hiền lành, rồi cũng có ngày trời mở cửa cho*, Ngô Tất Tố [1937] 2007, 105): the heavens (i.e., the legitimate public authority) will help good people. It should be noted, however, that, in Vietnam, fairness in public does not mean applying the same rules to everyone. Rather, public authority is expected to consider the particular circumstances of particular people and moderate rules flexibly for their sake. In this respect, as David Koh (2005) argues, for ordinary people a good governor is an official who protects ordinary people's lives by ignoring laws and rules if necessary.

If the public is understood as the embodiment of heavenly principles, it cannot be exclusively embodied by the state authority. For example, Miyazawa Chihiro (in this volume) pays attention to the public dimension of the traditional family. The family, regulated by Confucian ideology as well as village authority, can be seen as a realm regulated by a heavenly principle that is not merely arbitrarily adopted. Religion can also be understood as a public realm. In addition, public norms cannot be reduced to a single set of principles; there can be multiple, even conflicting, principles in one realm, such as the case of the conflict between the male-centered family ideology and the state ideology of gender equality in education and marriage in Tran Thi Minh Thi and Ito Miho's chapters.

The realm of *tư* (private) is, on the other hand, often negatively defined as an obscure sphere hidden from the heavens' light. Of course, Vietnamese people act in their own private interests, but these behaviors are seldom acknowledged, still less admired. Private motivations are often evaluated as individualistic (*cá nhân*); individualism is seen as immoral not only in the official socialist ideology but also in the everyday lives of ordinary people. A person standing alone is seen as eccentric. Living alone is often understood as being miserable. Also, private issues are evaluated as trivial. Therefore, when we use *công* and *tư* as analytic terms, we should be cautious that the dichotomy is asymmetrical, with the private less valued than the public. This asymmetry has meant women's activities in Vietnam are unfairly looked down upon, since women's sphere is often associated with private and domestic issues. Therefore, private actions often appear in association with public norms. The other problem is that these ideas are still distant from the everyday lives of ordinary people. For instance, it may sound strange to ordinary Vietnamese people to call the family a *tư* (private, individual) realm.

Several alternatives are much more neutral and nearer to ordinary language, such as *trong* (inside) and *ngoài* (outside) or *chung* (general, for everybody) and *riêng* (particular, separate). For instance, the inside space of one's house is considered a private space, while the outside world is the public space which is visible to neighbors and strangers. People talk about society as the outside world (*ngoài xã hội*), distinguishing it from the inside space of the house (*trong nhà*). The line between inside and outside is drawn not only on the threshold of the house but also, for example, on the border of the village community. In these two spaces, Vietnamese people often feel and behave differently.

The term *thân mật* (intimate) could be also another alternative. Ito Mariko (in this volume) explains how female laypersons in the Caodaist Hanoi Temple use the term *thân mật* to describe relationships among peer members, in which they talk freely about personal matters. These women use this term to express egalitarian, sisterly relationships, in contrast to the hierarchical and identical familial solidarity enforced by the female chief priest of the temple. By referring to the revival of Hannah Arendt in Japanese academic literature in recent years, she argues that these female laypersons attempt to reconfigure their temple as their own place of belonging, their place of alternative intimacy. Though her argument is unquestionably meaningful in understanding an alternative sphere for women in Vietnam, it is debatable whether it is common to use the term in this fashion in Vietnamese society. *Thân mật* often implies external affairs in Vietnamese, and expressions like "intimate relationships in the family" (*quan hệ thân mật trong gia đình*) sound somewhat awkward. That is why we do not use the word "intimate" as an umbrella concept or as a technical term in this volume.

Specifically, this volume seeks to reveal the asymmetrical relationship between the public—the positive realm of the heavenly principles—and the private—the negative realm of hidden, individualistic, and even isolated lives that affects the agency of Vietnamese women. In doing so, we can analyze more clearly the agency of women that interweaves alternative spheres, including the realm of intimate relationships.

Family and the Agency of Women in Vietnam

The family is the primary research field to investigate the agency of women in the realms of public and private in the Vietnamese context.

The status of women in the premodern Vietnamese family is one of the most important topics on gender issues in Vietnam and has been studied mainly in relation to whether Vietnamese society belongs to an East Asian patrilineal or Southeast Asian bilateral-kinship pattern (see Werner and Bélanger 2002a, 17–18). The premodern Vietnamese family seems to have been similar to the East Asian family in having a male-centered, patrilineal family system influenced by Confucianism, with women having lower status. Vietnamese women's self-determination was restricted, though they were quite active in running small businesses (see Luong's chapter). At the same time, the premodern Vietnamese family seems to be similar to the Southeast Asian family in several points, such as the flexible nexus of kindred spreading on both the father's side and the mother's side, wives having their own property rights in the family, and the convention of daughters' responsibility for taking care of their parents even after marriage. The literature on Vietnamese family (Yu 1990; Bélanger and Barbieri 2009a, 11) emphasizes that the premodern Vietnamese family had a bilateral character within which women enjoyed a relatively independent status. By analyzing women's legal rights in inheritance and marriage contracts as written in the state laws and testaments, these authors found that women were able to receive inheritance in the form of agricultural land and other assets; in the absence of a son, daughters could even practice ancestor worship and continue their fathers' family line.

However, we should be careful when we argue about the high status of women in the premodern Vietnamese family. First, it might be a "myth" (Tran 2006) created by French colonialists and Vietnamese patriots, to invent Vietnamese identity in contrast to the Chinese male-centered kinship system by emphasizing a vernacular bilateral-kinship system. The contributors to this volume also avoid exaggerating the high status of women in the premodern Vietnamese family as a unique feature of Vietnamese culture (see Miyazawa's chapter for further discussion).

Second, given regional and ethnic diversity, it is inappropriate to suppose a monolithic premodern Vietnamese family. While the family in Northern Vietnam had been exposed to Chinese culture for many years and was deeply influenced by Confucian family ideology, the family in Southern Vietnam was similar to other Southeast Asian families in which patrilocal and matrilocal residence were selective (Bélanger 2000). However, there is a different view that the bilateral character of families in the South is not the remains of Southeast Asian vernacular culture but that the Vietnamese family in the South re-attained a bilateral character through the influence of ethnic groups such as the Khmer and Cham (Iwai 2012, 411). Several scholars (see Werner and Bélanger 2002a, 18) even argue that the family in the South was greatly influenced by authentic Confucian ideology because of Ming Dynasty migration into Southern Vietnam in the eighteenth century.

Third, it is quite difficult, perhaps impossible to draw a consistent picture of the Vietnamese family system. It is, in fact, an assemblage of fragments of uncertain origins. In recent years, anthropologists have pointed out that the Southeast Asian bilateral family model, characterized by a lack of structure and permanence, is constructed as a reverse image of the unilateral closed-kinship model. As Yoko Hayami argues, it is even misleading to depict Southeast Asian families, whether traditional or modern, as a closed unit (Hayami 2012, 12). Hayami suggests the idea of the "family circle" to describe open, flexible familial relationships in Southeast Asian societies instead of relying on the notion of a closed unit comparable to the modern family model (12–13). In this respect, it might be inappropriate, after all, to understand Southeast Asian families (and to a lesser extent Vietnamese and East Asian families) as any kind of enclosed unit, whether they are bilateral or unilateral.

Vietnamese culture's inconsistency, however, like that of any other culture, has helped women in Vietnam to find chances to appropriate and escape from the seemingly seamless gendered structure around them. It is true that women in the premodern Vietnamese family were regulated by the idealized, male-centered family ideology of East Asia as an authentic norm, but this system also had room for women to perform their positive agency by appropriating the bilateral features of the family. The task of our academic inquiry, therefore, is to reveal how they have managed their lives by moving around these multiple and unfixed norms, instead of drawing a hybrid but consistent model of the Vietnamese family. In this respect, the fact that academics cannot give a consistent answer to the status of women in traditional and contemporary Vietnamese family does not mean that Vietnamese studies have fallen behind, but that Vietnam is a suitable place to practice describing the agency of women in nonidentical cultural circumstances.

Let us turn to the issue of womanhood in the family in contemporary Vietnam. To study women's lives in contemporary Vietnam, it is necessary to focus on strong familialism as an obstacle to, as well a basis for, women's agency. Vietnamese society ascribes a high value to having and maintaining a family. Though the marriage age is rising, building a family is still the norm, and once people have a family they are unlikely to divorce. The divorce rate in Vietnam is much lower than other Asian countries (Ochiai 2011, 224), although separation without legal divorce and cohabitation with a second wife are often socially recognized. As Tran's chapter in this volume describes in detail, the procedure for divorce is complicated and mediators are only allowed to conciliate to get the couple back together again.

It is reasonable to compare Vietnamese familialism with cases of Southeast Asian countries in which vernacular family models have been institutionalized along with the search for national integration (Hayami 2012, 2, 7). Familialism in Vietnam, as in these countries, is a product of the struggle against colonialism and for national independence. A difference between the two, however, is that while the ideal vernacular family model in other Southeast Asian countries is the extended family, in Vietnam, the nuclear family or patrilineal, multigenerational family are seen as the authentic and modern family model.

Vietnamese familialism is also comparable to that of mainland China, where the liberation of women was accelerated by socialist modernity, and then the traditional value of domestic women was revitalized to reinforce industrial productivity under the centralized regime (Sechiyama 2013) as well as to create autonomous socioeconomic units under the market economy. In this respect, the arguments in this volume contribute to the comparative gender studies of so-called "transitional" societies in Asia, where people have struggled to adjust to post–Cold War conditions by negotiating with the legacies of traditional values and socialist modernity. However, what distinguishes the Vietnamese case from that of China is that, while the construction of the Chinese socialistic family was an ideological program, in North Vietnam (the Democratic Republic of Vietnam) the construction of the modern family was necessary to meet the practical needs of production and reproduction during war.

It is also necessary to compare the formation of familialism in modern Vietnamese society with that of East Asian countries from the perspective of "compressed modernity" (Chang 1999). Compressed modernity is marked by the simultaneous progress of Ulrich Beck's "first modernity," characterized by the emergence of industrial capitalism, the nation-state, and the welfare state, and the rapid reconstruction of this "first modernity" in the process of "second modernity," marked by a rapid decline in birth rate, the collapse of the nuclear-family model, and the individualization of personal lives in the catching-up process (Ochiai 2010, 2). Compressed modernity forces people to experience the accelerated assemblage of the modern family and welfare state as well as their rapid collapse under the pressure of the neoliberal global economy. These countries first try to empower the family as a social unit responsible for taking care of its members. In this context, familialism is emphasized by countries that cannot afford to construct welfare systems because of the shortage of wealth and time (Ochiai 2013, 27). Responding to such socioeconomic pressure on the family, people often attempt to create alternative nexuses for mutual support by extending familial and kinship relations or strengthening religious associations, social networks, and neighborhood community (Ochiai 2010, 6–7). This process has brought about profound changes in welfare regimes in these countries (Ochiai 2009). Vietnam has also been experiencing the emergence of industrialization, the construction of the nation-state, a rapid decline in birth rate, and the emergence of an individualized rather than a communal society. It is leaping to the second stage of modernity without having the chance to pass through the first stage, and is struggling to construct a welfare state under the great ongoing pressure of the neoliberal global economy. This results in heavy pressure on "modern" women in the realm of care work and other domestic work under familialism, and a lack of efficient support from the welfare state.

In Vietnam, the image of domestic women in the modern family was first constructed during the colonial period. French administrators and some Vietnamese intellectuals tried to "remake," liberate, and modernize Vietnamese women by promoting literacy and education. Meanwhile, Vietnamese nationalists circulated conservative ethics books for women in order to create domestic housewives who would embody Asian values and to create a patriotic Vietnamese nation through the analogy of women's faithfulness to their husbands (Marr 1981, 199–214). This process is comparable to other East Asian societies that constructed images of the traditional family for their own cultural identities by appropriating Western images of Asian families and even the image of European conservative culture resisting Western liberalism (Ochiai 2013, 25, 27).

The socialist state established after the Independence Revolution in 1945 also sought to remake women and reconstruct the family in its own way. The state promoted gender equality and free love; women's right to autonomy was improved (Bélanger and Khaut 2002). However, socialist reforms and total mobilization also regulated women in a different way. The Women's Union, an official mass organization, launched a campaign for "three responsibilities" (*ba đảm đang*) that encouraged women to devote themselves to the family, the war, and society. In fact, conservative norms requiring women to be sexually pure, faithful, and devoted were strongly emphasized under the socialist revolution and the total war (Pelzer 1993; Gammeltoft 2001). Furthermore, the Vietnamese revolutionary leadership themselves were often associated with male-centered gender ideology (Luong 1988). Vietnamese socialist institutions often reproduced patriarchal structure and gender hierarchies through, for example, evaluating male labor forces more highly than female labor forces in collectives (Wiegersma 1988).

The revival of the family following the end of the collectives and the distribution system provided women with a new basis for their free agency. However, it also brought about another style of restrictive gendered norms upon women. The Đổi Mới policy was, as Werner and Bélanger argue, a "gendered project" (Werner and Bélanger 2002a, 15). Gender construction in sexuality, marriage, the household, and the workplace was one of the central fields of reform in the Đổi Mới process (21, 23).

First, the family was recognized officially as the unit of production and consumption. Familial ties were reevaluated as crucial for the maintenance of labor forces (Iwai 2012, 413–16). The reevaluation of the family finally brought about the dissolution of agricultural collectives and the complete revival of the family as a social unit. In this process women regained the family as a basis for their autonomy, in which they enjoyed relatively free agency in pursuing personal and family interests.

Second, the family has, at the same time, become a new tool for the state and society to govern the gendered agency of womanhood. As Scornet writes, just as the state withdrew from the economic sphere after the implementation of the Đổi Mới reforms, it strengthened restrictive family policies (2009, 47). Interventions into women's bodies have been justified as the state emphasizing family planning as a way to obtain a happy family (Gammeltoft 1999). Most authors on gender issues in Vietnam see the reform era as detrimental to women, citing an increase in domestic violence and the revival of so-called traditional gender roles among the younger generation (Werner and Bélanger 2002a, 20–21). Bélanger and Khuat (1996) even report young urban women's tendency to become housewives in the emerging industrial socioeconomic conditions. The refeminization of agriculture also occurred in rural areas (Werner 2002, 36–38).

Third, there has been a significant shift of responsibility for health care from the government to the family (Deolalikar 2009). In fact, Vietnamese health care is one of the most "private-sector-dominated health care schemes" in developing Asia, although economic growth in Vietnam dramatically improved family incomes, which offset the decline in access to health services (91). In this situation, "the downsizing of the socialist welfare system and the return of the household as the unit of production and consumption redefined the boundaries between the public and private" (Bélanger and Barbieri 2009a, 2), in which female members of the family often shouldered heavier burdens.

Lastly, the status of daughters changed in the Đổi Mới process (Bélanger and Pendakis 2009, 272–75). The status of daughters in the family has been declining because the preference for having male children was reinforced by the revival of ancestor worship and as well as by the family planning policy. At the same time, daughters' responsibility in the family was reinforced, first as laborers who make money outside the family and, second, as caregivers in the family. The bilateral character of premodern Vietnamese family has been revitalized, which brings about double burdens for young women. The proportion of parents living with a daughter (and not with a son) is about 20 to 30 percent, certainly higher than what Confucian values would have led us to expect (Barbieri 2009, 147).

Thus, for women in Vietnam, the revival of the family has both positive and negative effects. While many studies indicate the ongoing liberation of young women (e.g., Bélanger and Khuat 1996), scholars on gender studies also suggest that Vietnamese women have to struggle with the revival of conventional gender roles under the strong influence of familialism; women were the first category of people excluded from official institutions since the public sector diminished in the Đổi Mới reforms (Werner 2002, 34–35; Tran Thi Minh Thi 2012). In this respect, as Luong's chapter shows, women's status in contemporary Vietnam is still much lower than that of men, and the visibility of women in the public arena, such as political institutions, is not yet sufficient.

In this situation, Vietnamese women's attempts to exercise their agency against conventional gender norms and the existing family framework often result in failure. Gammeltoft (2002) analyzes the complicity between the ideology of virginity, which forces contemporary Vietnamese young women to choose abortion so as not to have a child before marriage, and the idea of fate, which these women use to explain their miserable situations. Young women often devote themselves to their boyfriends as a testimony to their enduring love, while knowing that premarital sexual intercourse is immoral according to traditional values and public opinion. When the marriage fails, all the woman can do is regret her fate (115). Gammeltoft writes that even though moral meanings are, in general, constantly interpreted and negotiated, there are "limits to cultural contingency" (128). Especially, she continues, "to young women in Vietnam, this means that exercising their agency in the sexual sphere can become a highly hazardous and self-defeating enterprise" (128).

However, as Bélanger and Pendakis insist, Vietnamese women's attempts to exercise their agency against conventional norms may also create many "moments of empowerment" (2009, 268, 293). They discuss "factory daughters" (young, unmarried female factory workers) who enjoy the sense of freedom and independence of leaving home and express a desire to go beyond the environment of their family, kinship, and village and earn money for their family members. Like the young Bedouin women Abu-Lughod describes, these factory daughters are caught up in norms and regulations in factories and expectations for daughters to support their natal families even when they are to be freed from the family. Bélanger and Pendakis, however, draw a much more optimistic picture. Along with "an increased capacity to make choices, a sense of having agency or control over one's life and increased power of negotiation within significant relationships," they argue, "women's agency and sense of empowerment permeate the accounts collected and indicate that migration and work do alter daughters' status within their natal families, at least for the period they are working" (268). Though it is not clear whether the accumulation of these moments of empowerment will result in further structural changes, these small attempts shake out the existing social reality of the gendered matrix and create a more comfortable living space for women.

The Agency of Women outside the Family

Besides exercising agency from within the family, it is also possible for women in Vietnam to rely on other institutions outside the family to empower themselves. Working in factories, in the case study by Bélanger and Pendakis, and going to university, in the case study by Ito Miho (in this volume), are two of the possibilities. Participating in mass organizations and religious activities can also become such alternatives.

Before the Đổi Mới policy was launched in 1986, the family, village communities, and religious activities were targets of dissolution or reform. The state only approved these social units as long as they were useful to support the war and the socialist regime. Though familial ties were not totally denied in the socialist reform era and the state even used them to mobilize people for the war, homestead property was restricted to the minimum and the household lost its status as an independent unit of production and consumption under collectivization. Villagers' solidarity was approved as long as it was useful in the war and the administration of collectives. The centralized administrative system of people's committees replaced the former semiautonomous village administrative organizations. Village festivals were abolished. Religious organizations were also strictly restricted. "Superstitious" activities (*mê tín dị đoan*) such as spirit possession and fortunetelling were totally prohibited.

These reforms, on the one hand, released women form the male-centered village order and the bondage of religious dogma and, as a result, promoted their liberation and advancement in society. On the other hand, women's autonomous realms for social networking were subsumed by the state. Women were encouraged to play mostly supportive roles as wives and mothers in the domestic realm to support the war or to work as laborers and administrators in collectives and factories. Women's social realms before the Đổi Mới were mostly under state control, though it was possible for women at that time to appropriate those realms of the household, agricultural collectives, military units, and mass organizations to create their own social spaces, or even create their own social networking through schools and kinship relations.

The revival of autonomous secondary groups in the Đổi Mới period means the pluralizing of women's places of belonging. Though the state has kept utilizing these secondary groups—rural communities and religious organizations—as channels for governance, they also function as a basis for women to interweave their own lives with alternative norms and values which cannot be reduced to the existing state ideology or the family ideology, enabling women to negotiate with the dominant state and social norms that force them to become "good" citizens in the family, community, and the state.

Village community has been recognized and reinforced during the Đổi Mới process. The revival of local community has contradictory effects on women in Vietnam. Women's status in village life has declined because of the revival of male-centered village political and cultural structures (Kleinen 1999), while women have obtained opportunities to represent their own opinions through the Women's Union, which has become one of the most important development agencies in rural areas (Salemink 2006).

Religious organizations were also recognized officially after the Đổi Mới policy was launched. Spirit possession and fortunetelling, once restricted as "superstitions," are now recognized officially as "cultural beliefs" (*tín ngưỡng*). The revival of religious activities means the restoration of places for women. Religious organizations, in many cases, function as public asylums for women to cope with family difficulties. The literature on religious activities in Vietnam has explored how religious activities help women to overcome difficulties in their family lives and integrate them into peer communities as well as into society at large (Pham Quynh Phuong 2009; Endres 2011). While the revival of ancestor worship and village festivals has strengthened male-centered ideology at the local level, Buddhist temples have provided women with their own places of belonging. Luong reports a case study in a village in Northern Vietnam where elderly women organize mutual support activities based on the Buddhist association at the village level (Luong 2010, 231–33). However, there are still few empirical case studies about relationships among women in these religious organizations.

The Structure of this Volume

The chapters in this volume are organized as follows. Chapter 1, by Hy V. Luong, gives an overview of current work on gender changes in the kinship system and in the public sphere. It reveals that the dichotomy of public and private in Vietnamese society overlaps with the gendered division of the masculine and feminine domains, though the line is not drawn simply between inside and outside the family. For instance, while men are responsible for "big issues" (*việc lớn*) such as official dialogues on political issues, weddings, funerals, ancestral worship, and the construction of houses, women are expected to take care of "small issues" (*việc nhỏ*) such as going to the market, cooking, farming, caring for family members, and running small businesses. Chapter 1 analyzes the negative and positive aspects of the gendered division of social domains.

The next three chapters deal with the agency of women in the male-centered family structure. Chapter 2, by Miyazawa Chihiro, describes how Vietnamese women's agency was practiced within male-centered family ideology in the premodern Vietnamese society. Responding to Nhung Tuyet Tran's argument about the "myth" of the high status of women in the premodern Vietnamese family, Miyazawa analyzes testaments in premodern rural society in Northern Vietnam and carefully argues, based on comparison with women's status in the premodern Chinese kinship system, that in Vietnam women's rights to family property not only existed as a norm but were actually practiced in many cases. Vietnamese women in the premodern family clearly had rights and obligations to worship their ancestors and received land on behalf of their branch in the patrilineal kinship group. It should also be noted that women's property rights did not mean they had free agency. Rather, they were expected to act as agents on behalf of the male members of their branch in the kinship group. More importantly in the context of this volume, these rights and obligations were not performed informally by family members but often recognized and authorized by village authorities.

Chapter 3, by Tran Thi Minh Thi, analyzes divorce records in local courts. She discusses the increase in cases of divorce due to "lifestyle differences." The increase means, on the one hand, that individualism is spreading among Vietnamese people in the process of modernization. At the same time, however, through interviews with divorced couples, the author finds that there are many kinds of hidden, often conservative, reasons behind "lifestyle differences," such as domestic violence, adultery, and not having a son. It can be said that these couples express their reasons as "lifestyle differences" in the public domain of the court rather than uttering their actual, private reasons for divorcing. In this respect, the public/private divide helps women to exercise their agency. However, it can be also said that the public/private divide functions as a wall to hide unjust situations, suppressing women in familial life. In this respect, Tran's chapter reveals the positive and negative effects of the modern ideology of the public/private divide on women's agency in contemporary Vietnam.

Chapter 4, by Ito Miho, analyzes young Vietnamese women's narratives on university, career choice, and marriage. Her chapter reveals that most young women who go to university choose to study the humanities, social sciences, and fine arts. The chapter also indicates that most expect to return to their hometown after graduation, find a stable job in the public sector, get married, and continue to support their natal family after marriage. Industrialization and the freedom to select a school and job in the Đổi Mới era have enabled young women to escape from their homes to the wider society and have facilitated their "moments of empowerment." However, they have also revitalized ideology regarding the role of daughters in the family as well as the norms of career choice, produced during the age of total mobilization under the socialist educational and job allocation systems, which have channeled young women toward certain life courses. Ito Miho's case study reveals one aspect of the Đổi Mới as a gendered project, or the process of reproduction of socialistic, "public" gender norms regarding schooling and job selection, framing young women's personal desires and choices under the new regime of liberalization and revealing a unique connection between the public and private in a socialist state.

Successive chapters deal with the agency of women outside the family. Secondary groups such as local communities and religious organizations are, by definition, the locus of conflict between public norms and internal conventions. The identification of these secondary groups as public or private is always under negotiation, subject to appropriation and reinterpretation. Chapter 5, by Kato Atsufumi, analyzes a conflict among members of the Women's Union over whether they should help a troubled village woman based on the village women's mutual love and affection (tương thân, tương ái) or should not help her as the collective (tập thể) action of a state-affiliated mass organization, because her household is defined by the state as "un-cultured." In this case study, the identification of the Women's Union as public or private (or something communal or social) is under negotiation and reinterpretation. Leaders of the village organization insist that the Women's Union, as an official mass organization, is a "collective" of good citizens who adhere to state norms and that it cannot support any woman who does not meet state criteria for good citizenship. Meanwhile, many village women perceive the Women's Union as a group of peer women who "share" (chia sẻ) their difficult circumstances. They try to insert practices of sharing and mutuality between the dichotomy of public, "collective" activities and private, voluntary activities to create an alternative realm for women. This case is not only an example of the confrontation between the state ideology and the communal morality, but a case study of women's struggle to reframe their own relationships to create an alternative sphere.

In the same vein, Chapter 6, by Ito Mariko, on a Caodaist temple as a women's community of practice shows that there are constant conflicts among women in a certain religious organization about the way to organize their place of belonging and relationships. She argues that while there is a female priest, the leader of the temple, who tried to construct a "family" and requested that lay women regularly participate in rituals based on the doctrines of their sect (họ đạo), many female members preferred to construct very flexible, egalitarian, and thân mật (intimate) relationships among themselves to share their private matters, which they call the practice of their "own morality" (đạo mình).

In addition, religious representations of womanhood may empower those who transgress traditional gender norms and function as a symbol of national and ethnic reunification. This volume includes case studies in which religious activities empower gendered agents and enable them to become nodes to reconnect people to society as well as to the nation, specifically Chapter 7, by Kirsten W. Endres, and Chapter 8, by Thien-Huong Ninh. Endres' chapter discusses women and gender-transgressive men who ritually embody female deities. A woman described in this chapter opens a private temple (phủ) in her home to practice spirit rituals to cope with her own fate; then, as followers increase, she voluntarily starts raising funds to conduct memorial services for the war dead. Honoring these heroes and heroines publicly, she empowers herself by becoming somebody in society. Ninh's chapter describes Vietnamese Catholics in the United States who Vietnamize statues of Virgin Mary by dressing them in áo dài, a Vietnamese ethnic costume, as well as the re-importation of the icon of Vietnamese Maria from the United States to Vietnam as a symbol of Vietnamese Catholics' international unity during the reconstruction of diplomatic relationships between the two countries at the end of the 1990s. These activities were not simply caused by the Vatican's directives, changes in the bilateral relationship between the two governments, or the Vietnamese government's promotion of nationalism, but rather by the autonomous activities of ordinary people to reconstruct their identities. Her chapter reveals how the symbolic representation of Maria in the "private" realm of religious activity connects diasporic Vietnamese people to the transnational identity politics of Vietnamese Catholics. Through these case studies we recognize that the representation of womanhood plays an important role in reconstructing the personal and group identities of contemporary Vietnamese people.

References

Abu-Lughod, Lila. 1990. "The Romance of Resistance: Tracing Transformations of Power through Bedouin Women." *American Ethnologist* 17(1): 41–55.

———. ed. 1998. *Remaking Women: Feminism and Modernity in the Middle East.* Princeton, NJ: Princeton University Press.

Barbieri, Magali. 2009. "Đổi Mới and Older Adults: Intergenerational Support under the Constraints of Reform," In *Reconfiguring Families in Contemporary Vietnam*, edited by Magali Barbieri and Danièle Bélanger, 133–65. Stanford, CA: Stanford University Press.

Bélanger, Danièle. 2000. "Regional Differences in Household Composition and Family Formation Patterns in Vietnam." *Journal of Comparative Family Studies* 31 (2): 171–89.

Bélanger, Danièle, and Khuat Thu Hong. 1996. "Marriage and the Family in North Urban Vietnam, 1960–1993." *Journal of Population* 2(1): 83–112.

———. 2002. "Too Late to Marry: Failure, Fate or Fortune? Female Singlehood in Rural North Vietnam." In *Gender, Household, State: Đổi Mới in Viet Nam*, edited by Jayne Werner and Danièle Bélanger, 89–110. Ithaca: Cornell Southeast Asia Program.

Bélanger, Danièle, and Magali Barbieri. 2009a. "Introduction: State, Families, and the Making of Transitions in Vietnam." In *Reconfiguring Families in Contemporary Vietnam*, edited by Magali Barbieri and Danièle Bélanger, 1–46. Stanford, CA: Stanford University Press.

———. eds. 2009b. *Reconfiguring Families in Contemporary Vietnam*. Stanford, CA: Stanford University Press.

Bélanger, Danièle, and Katherine L. Pendakis. 2009. "Daughters, Work, and Families in Globalizing Vietnam." In *Reconfiguring Families in Contemporary Vietnam*, edited by Magali Barbieri and Danièle Bélanger, 265–97. Stanford, CA: Stanford University Press.

Bergstedt, Cecilia. 2012. "The Lie of the Land—Gender, Farm Work, and Land in a Rural Vietnamese Village." Doctoral dissertation, Social Anthropology, School of Global Studies, University of Gothenburg, Sweden.

Burawoy, Michael, and Katherine Verdery, eds. 1999. *Uncertain Transition: Ethnographies of Change in the Postsocialist World*. Lanham, MD: Rowman & Littlefield.

Chakrabarty, Dipesh. [2000] 2008. *Provincializing Europe: Postcolonial Thought and Historical Difference*. Princeton, NJ: Princeton University Press.

Chang, Kyung-Sup. 1999. "Compressed Modernity and Its Discontent: South Korean Society in Transition." *Economy and Society* 28(1): 30–5.

Deolalikar, Anil. 2009. "Health Care and the Family in Vietnam." In *Reconfiguring Families in Contemporary Vietnam*, edited by Magali Barbieri and Danièle Bélanger, 75–96. Stanford, CA: Stanford University Press.

Endres, Kirsten W. 2011. *Performing the Divine: Mediums, Markets and Modernity in Urban Vietnam*. Copenhagen, Denmark: Nordic Institute of Asian Studies Press.

Gammeltoft, Tine. 1999. *Women's Bodies, Women's Worries: Health and Family Planning in a Vietnamese Rural Community*. Richmond, VA: Curzon Press.

———. 2001. "Faithful, Heroic, Resourceful: Changing Images of Women in Vietnam." In *Vietnamese Society in Transition: The Daily Politics of Reform and Change*, edited by John Kleinen, 265–80. Amsterdam, Netherlands: Het Spinhuis.

———. 2002. "The Irony of Sexual Agency: Premarital Sex in Urban Northern Vietnam." In *Gender, Household, State: Đổi Mới in Viet Nam*, edited by Jayne Werner and Danièle Bélanger, 111–28. Ithaca, NY: Cornell Southeast Asia Program Publications.

Geertz, Clifford. 1983. *Local Knowledge: Further Essays in Interpretive Anthropology.* New York: Basic Books.

Hayami, Yoko. 2012. "Introduction: The Family in Flux in Southeast Asia." In *The Family in Flux in Southeast Asia: Instruction, Ideology, Practice*, edited by Yoko Hayami, Junko Koizumi, and Chalidaporn Songsamphan, 1–26. Kyoto, Japan: Kyoto University Press.

Hobsbawm, Eric. 1994. *The Age of Extremes: The Short Twentieth Century, 1914–1991.* New York: Vintage Books.

Iwai, Misaki. 2012. "Vietnamese Families beyond Culture: The Process of Establishing a New Homeland in the Mekong Delta." In *The Family in Flux in Southeast Asia: Instruction, Ideology, Practice*, edited by Yoko Hayami, Junko Koizumi, and Chalidaporn Songsamphan, 411–37. Kyoto, Japan: Kyoto University Press.

Kleinen, John. 1999. *Facing the Future, Reviving the Past: A Study of Social Change in a Northern Vietnamese Village.* Singapore: Institute of Southeast Asian Studies.

Koh, David Wee Hock. 2005. *Wards of Hanoi.* Singapore: Institute of Southeast Asian Studies.

Luong, Hy V. 1988. "Discursive Practices and Power Structure: Person-Referring Forms and Sociopolitical Struggles in Colonial Vietnam." *American Ethnologist* 15(2): 239–53.

———. 2010. *Tradition, Revolution, and Market Economy in a North Vietnamese Village, 1925–2006.* Honolulu: University of Hawai'i Press.

Marr, David. 1981. *Vietnamese Tradition on Trial, 1920–45.* Berkeley: University of California Press.

Ngô Tất Tố. [1937] 2007. *Tắt Đèn (When the Light is Out).* Hanoi, Vietnam: Foreign Languages Publishing House.

Ochiai, Emiko. 2009. "Care Diamonds and Welfare Regimes in East and Southeast Asian Societies: Bridging Family and Welfare Sociology." *International Journal of Japanese Sociology* 18: 60–78.

———. 2010. "Reconstruction of Intimate and Public Spheres in Asian Modernity: Familialism and Beyond." *Journal of Intimate and Public Spheres*, Pilot Issue: 2–22.

———. 2011. "Unsustainable Societies: The Failure of Familialism in East Asia's Compressed Modernity." *Historical Social Research* 36(2): 219–45.

———. 2013. "Reconstruction of the Intimate and Public in Asian Modernity: Compressed Modernity and Familialism." In *Reconstruction of the Intimate and Public: A Perspective from Asian Modernity*, edited by Emiko Ochiai, 1–38. Kyoto, Japan: Kyoto University Press.

Pelzer, C. 1993. "Socio-cultural Dimensions of Renovation in Vietnam: Đổi Mới as Dialogue and Transformation in Gender Relations." In *Reinventing Vietnamese Socialism: Đổi Mới in Comparative Perspective*, edited by W.S. Turley and M. Selden, 309–36. Boulder, CO: Westview Press.

Pham Quynh Phuong. 2009. *Hero and Deity: Tran Hung Dao and the Resurgence of Popular Religion in Vietnam*. Chiang Mai, Thailand: Mekong Press.

Pham Van Bich. 1999. *The Vietnamese Family in Change: The Case of the Red River Delta*. New York: Curzon.

Rydström, Helle. 2003. *Embodying Morality: Growing Up in Rural Northern Vietnam*. Honolulu: University of Hawai'i Press.

Salemink, Oskar. 2006. "Translating, Interpreting, and Practicing Civil Society in Vietnam." In *Development Brokers and Translators: The Ethnography of Aid and Agencies*, edited by David Lewis and David Mosse, 101–26. Bloomfield, CT: Kumarian Press.

Scornet, Catherine. 2009. "State and the Family: Reproductive Politics and Practices." In *Reconfiguring Families in Contemporary Vietnam*, edited by Magali Barbieri and Danièle Bélanger, 47–74. Stanford, CA: Stanford University Press.

Sechiyama, Kaku. 2013. *Patriarchy in East Asia*. Leiden, Netherlands: Brill.

Taylor, Keith W. 1983. *The Birth of Vietnam*. Berkeley: University of California Press.

Tran, Nhung Tuyet. 2006. "Beyond the Myth of Equality: Daughters' Inheritance Rights in the Lê Code." In *Việt Nam: Borderless Histories*, edited by Nhung Tuyet Tran and Anthony J.S. Reid, 121–44. Madison: University of Wisconsin Press.

Tran Thi Minh Thi. 2012. "Social and Family Roles of Working Women in Transitional Vietnam." In *Alternative Intimate Spheres for Women in Vietnam*, GCOE Working Papers (Next Generation Research) 71, edited by Kato Atsufumi, 87–103. Kyoto, Japan: Kyoto University Global COE for Reconstruction of the Intimate and Public Spheres in 21st Century Asia.

Werner, Jayne. 2002. "Gender, Household, and State: Renovation (Đổi Mới) as Social Process in Viet Nam." In *Gender, Household and State: Đổi Mới in Viet Nam*, edited by Jayne Werner and Danièle Bélanger, 29–47. Ithaca, NY: Cornell Southeast Asia Program Publications.

Werner, Jayne, and Danièle Bélanger. 2002a. "Introduction." In *Gender, Household and State: Đổi Mới in Viet Nam*, edited by Jayne Werner and Danièle Bélanger, 13–28. Ithaca, NY: Cornell Southeast Asia Program Publications.

———, eds. 2002b. *Gender, Household, State: Đổi Mới in Viet Nam*. Ithaca, NY: Cornell Southeast Asia Program Publications.

Wiegersma, N. 1988. *Vietnam: Peasant Land, Peasant Revolution*. New York: St. Martin's Press.

Yu, Insun. 1990. *Law and Society in Seventeenth and Eighteenth Century Vietnam*. Seoul: Asiatic Research Centre, Korea University.

PART 1

Gendered Structure and Reframing It from within

∴

CHAPTER 1

Gender Relations in Vietnam: Ideologies, Kinship Practices, and Political Economy*

Hy V. Luong

In the era of economic reforms and globalization during the past quarter of a century, gender relations in Vietnam were at the intersection of major crosscurrents. Within the kinship domain, in the village of Hoài Thị in the northern province of Bắc Ninh, for example, patrilocal residence was practiced *de rigueur*. Throughout Northern and North Central Vietnam, patrilineages were strongly revitalized. Kinship relations became more male-oriented in many aspects. Yet, at least in the village of Hoài Thị, daughters enjoyed a good share of family inheritance, probably more than at any point in contemporary history. Beyond the kinship domain, female bodies were commodified with the resurgence of prostitution throughout the country in the past quarter of a century (see Hoang 2011). For a long time, they were also victimized in police crackdowns as, until recently, it was generally the prostitutes and not their male clients who had to undergo reeducation.[1] Clients might be asked to pay only small administrative fines.[2] On the other hand, the post-1975 decline in women's political representation was reversed in the 1990s: women played a more important role in political leadership toward the end of this decade than they had in the preceding fifteen years. A full understanding of these and other contradictory currents requires a historically grounded analysis of gender relations within larger political, economic, and ideological frameworks.

In this chapter, I focus on how gender relations among ethnic Vietnamese, both within the domestic sphere (*trong gia đình*) and in the public arena (*ngoài xã hội*), were shaped by the interplay of ideologies and political economy in

---

* This contribution is an updated version of a previously published chapter that appeared in *Postwar Vietnam: Dynamics of a Transforming Society*, edited by H. V. Luong (Rowman and Littlefield, 2003).

1   On June 20, 2012, the Vietnamese National Assembly abolished the detention or reeducation of prostitutes. The new law was implemented in 2013 (*Tuổi Trẻ* online, June 20, 2012, http://tuoitre.vn/Chinh-tri-Xa-hoi/497869/Khong-buoc-nguoi-ban-dam-vao-co-so-chua-benh.html).

2   Effective in 2014, clients of prostitutes have to pay stiffer fines than prostitutes do (Articles 22 and 23, Decree 167/2013/NĐ-CP).

the past quarter of a century. I draw heavily on findings about the Vietnamese ethnic majority, since there is considerably less systematic research on gender relations among other ethnic groups in Vietnam.

Vietnamese Kinship and Gender Roles: Historical Perspectives

Vietnamese women have historically maintained a high visibility beyond the domestic domain through their fundamental role in the Vietnamese economy and in generating household incomes through commerce, handicraft production, and agriculture. As early as 1688, a Chinese traveler to Hanoi remarked: "Trade was the domain of women. Even the wives of high-ranking mandarins were not concerned about losing face" [through their trading activities] (Thành Thế Vỹ 1961, 91; see also Dampier 1906, 608).

Barrow, who visited the trading port of Faifo in Central Vietnam at the end of the eighteenth century, similarly observed:

> In Cochinchina it would appear...to be the fate of the weaker sex to be doomed to those occupations which require, if not the greatest exertions of bodily strength, at least the most persevering industry. We observed them day after day, and from morning till night, standing in the midst of pools of water, up to the knees, occupied in the transplanting of rice. In fact, all the labours of tillage, and the various employments connected with agriculture, seem to fall to the share of the female peasantry; while those in Turon, to the management of domestic concerns, add the superintendence of all the details of commerce. They even assist in constructing and keeping in repair their mud-built cottages; they conduct the manufacture of coarse earthen ware vessels; they manage the boats on rivers and in harbours; they bear the articles of produce to market; they draw the cotton wool from the pod, free it from the seeds, spin it into thread, weave it into cloth, dye it of its proper colour, and make it up into dresses for themselves and their families.
> BARROW [1806] 1975, 303–04; SEE ALSO CRAWFURD [1823] 1970, 270

The findings on nineteenth- and early-twentieth-century Vietnam support Barrow's observation on the active roles of Vietnamese women, not only in commerce, but also in agriculture (including land ownership) and manufacturing. In the nineteenth century, female landowners made up 22 percent and 17.5 percent of landowners, respectively, in the northern provinces of Hà Đông and Thái Bình (Phan Huy Lê et al. 1995, 26; 1997, 465), and 6 to 34 percent of those in a sample of six hamlets in the six southern provinces (Nguyễn Đình Đầu 1994, 159–60). In manufacturing, for example, women owned two of the three largest ceramics kilns in the famous northern pottery center of Bát Tràng at the turn of the twentieth century (Luong 1998).

Despite women's major roles in the economy and their wealth accumulation through mercantile and other activities, both Vietnamese public life and the kinship and household system were strongly male-centered. In the public arena, until the French colonial period, education and bureaucratic positions were strictly male domains. Despite the legendary prominence of some women as troop commanders or literary figures in Vietnamese history, women neither had access to formal Confucian education nor to positions in the national mandarinate or in local village administrations before the twentieth century.[3] They had no official roles in village communal houses, which served as the seats of local power and local tutelary deity worship. Their worship fora were mainly restricted to local Buddhist pagodas and various shrines.

Women's lack of public authority had its parallel in a male-centered kinship system familiar to students of East Asian kinship. It was a hierarchical model in which descent was traced mainly through men; postmarital residence was predominantly patrilocal (a newlywed couple residing with the husband's parents after marriage); inheritance was heavily in favor of sons, who were responsible for ancestor worship and patriline continuity; authority, both domestic and public, rested with men (see Luong 2010a, 72–77). In the internal logic of this model, the marriage of a man to many wives in a polygynous relation was to ensure the birth of sons and the male-centered continuity of the patriline. When a first wife was late in or incapable of bearing sons, she might take the initiative in arranging for her husband to take another wife, and she held special maternal responsibilities toward the latter's sons (74–75, 114–15). Although the Vietnamese family and kinship system was also underlaid by an alternative bilateral model that stressed children's additional linkages to their mothers, this model did not operate strongly in the northern and central parts of Vietnam or among the Confucian-educated elite (77–78). The male-oriented kinship model was reinforced by the Confucian ideology that emphasized women's threefold subordination to their fathers, husbands, and

---

3   The prominent figures include the Ladies Trưng in an anti-Chinese campaign in the first century; Lady Triệu in a similar anti-Chinese uprising in the third century; Madame Bùi Thị Xuân, a troop commander in the eighteenth century; and literary figures such as Hồ Xuân Hương and Bà Huyện Thanh Quan in the eighteenth and nineteenth century (see Lê thị Nhâm Tuyết 1975).

sons. Women's visible roles in the economy were intended not to replace their domestic duties, but to increase the financial resources of the households for which they were responsible (see Luong 1989). In the ceramic-manufacturing center of Bát Tràng, for example, it was in many cases women's entrepreneurship that sustained their households' livelihoods and enabled men to concentrate on studying in pursuit of bureaucratic careers (see Luong 1998). While a woman's important role in household management was acknowledged with her appellation as *nội tướng* (domestic general), this acknowledgment and her significant financial contributions did not necessarily lead to any increase in authority.

The French colonial period witnessed the opening of education and low-level public service positions (such as school teachers and nurses) to women. The ratio of female to male students in primary education increased from virtually no female students in 1880, to 1 to 12.5 in 1930 (Indochine 1931, 19–20). However, neither male domination in the public domain nor the dominant male-centered model of kinship and household relations was fundamentally transformed in the French colonial era (see Marr 1981, chap. 5).

The Post-independence Era

After independence from France in 1954, in both the US-allied South and the socialist North, Western ideologies of both non-Marxist and Marxist varieties underlay the significantly improved access of women to educational opportunities (including in higher education), their inroads into the political arena, and the legal prohibition of polygyny. These changes enlarged the space for women in the public arena, as well as involving the state's use of law to intervene in the domestic domain, both in the South and the North. However, it was in the North that the state launched a more frontal attack on the material and ideological foundations of the male-oriented kinship and family system by collectivizing most land, undermining patrilineages, specifying the equal inheritance rights of both sons and daughters in the 1959 family and marriage law, and encouraging the replacement of sacred ancestral worship with commemoration of parents and grandparents among Communist Party members and beyond (Nguyễn Đức Truyến 1997, 51; Phạm Văn Bích 1999). However, the male-oriented kinship model remained powerful in shaping gender relations, even in the socialist North. Postmarital residence remained overwhelmingly patrilocal and household division of labor heavily male-centered. The male-oriented kinship model continued providing an influential conceptual framework that undermined, to some extent, the state's attempts to restructure gender relations in the public and domestic arenas.[4]

By 1989, the gender gap in Vietnam had virtually been eliminated in primary education and significantly reduced at higher levels. As seen in Table 1.1, there was no longer much difference in the school attendance rates of boys and girls below the age of ten. In the next age group, 81.7 percent of boys and 73.2 percent of girls attended schools at the time of the 1989 census, revealing a gap of 8.5 percent. Among teenagers from the age of fifteen to nineteen, 27.9 percent of boys and 19.3 percent of girls still attended schools at that time, showing a similar gap of 8.6 percent. This gap continued in postsecondary education, as 61 percent of the postsecondary-degree holders in 1989 were male and only

TABLE 1.1   *Gender and education in Vietnam in 1989 and 2009 in percentages*

Age group	Male			Female		
	Currently attending school	Stopped attending school	Never attended school	Currently attending school	Stopped attending school	Never attended school
1989 Census						
5–9	60.5	0.8	36.2	59.8	0.9	39.2
10–14	81.7	13.4	7.4	73.2	18.4	8.3
15–19	27.9	64.8	7.2	19.3	73.1	7.6
2009 Census						
5–6	83.5	0.5	16.1	83.7	0.5	15.9
7–11	96.4	1.5	2.1	96.3	1.5	2.2
12–15	87.2	11.2	1.6	88.6	9.5	1.9
16–18	60.4	37.9	1.7	65.8	32.1	2.0

SOURCES: VIETNAM, NATIONAL CENSUS STEERING COMMITTEE 1991, III, 12–13; VIETNAM, POPULATION AND HOUSING CENSUS STEERING COMMITTEE 2010, 313.

---

4   In this chapter, I use the phrase "domestic arena" instead of "intimate sphere." Ochiai (2010) has suggested the use of the latter phrase in order to analyze what she calls the second modernity, an era with a major fertility decline (below the population replacement level) and in which the traditional family with a married couple has become a less dominant foundation of society. According to Ochiai, intimate relations can take place either within a family or beyond (5). However, in Vietnam, fertility has not declined to below the population replacement level, and the family still constitutes a major societal building block.

39 percent were female (Vietnam National Census Steering Committee 1991, 359).[5] However, from a historical perspective, the gender gap in education in the post-independence era had been considerably narrowed from that in the French colonial period.

The narrowing gap in education went hand in hand with the wider participation of women in public life, both through a wider variety of occupations and through a more visible participation in the political arena.

The percentage of women in the state bureaucracy of unified Vietnam reached 51.4 percent in 1989, although they were still overwhelmingly concentrated in certain domains like education, health care, and accounting or finances, which accounted for 70.1 percent of the bureaucratic workforce.[6] In the political domain, the percentage of woman deputies in the pre-Đổi Mới and largely symbolic National Assembly steadily increased, from 2.5 percent in the first election in 1946 to 32.3 percent in 1976 (Table 1.2). Women's greater access to public power was partly facilitated by the historical context of the Vietnam War, during which millions of men were mobilized into armed services. In the North, the state exhorted women to shoulder three main responsibilities (*ba đảm đang*): production and work, the family, and national defense (Lê Thị Nhâm Tuyết 1975, 291–319).

After the end of the Vietnam War in 1975, women's participation in the public domain suffered a precipitous decline. The percentage of female deputies in the National Assembly dropped steadily, from 32.3 percent in 1975–1976 to 17.7 percent in 1987–1992. Those in People's Councils dropped from 28.6 percent in

TABLE 1.2 *Percentages of women in the Vietnamese National Assembly*

Period	1946–60	1960–64	1964–71	1971–75	1975–76	1976–81	1981–87	1987–92	1992–97	1997–02	2002–07	2007–11	2011–16
Percentage women	2.5	11.6	18	29.7	32.3	26.8	21.8	17.7	18.5	26.2	27.3	25.8	24.4

SOURCES: TRẦN THỊ VÂN ANH AND LÊ NGỌC HÙNG 1996; VIETNAM GENERAL STATISTICAL OFFICE 2000A, 102; VIETNAM GENERAL STATISTICAL OFFICE 2012, 18.

---

5 Data are not available for a *regional* breakdown on male and female access to education in 1989.

6 Unfortunately, figures are not available on the changes in the percentages of women in the bureaucratic system from 1954 to 1989 or from 1989 to date.

1985–1989 to 12 percent in 1989–1994 at the provincial level, from 19.4 percent to 12 percent at the district level, and from 19.7 percent to 13 percent at the commune and ward level for the same period (see Figure 1.1; cf. Trần Thị Vân Anh and Lê Ngọc Hùng 1996, 202).[7] The percentages of women in top leadership and executive positions were even lower. In 1991, women made up only 1.4 percent and 2 percent, respectively, of the chairs of the district and provincial people's committees (heads of district and provincial governments); 2.2 percent and 2.4 percent of district and provincial party secretaries (heads of Communist Party organizations at the district and provincial levels), 8.2 percent of the membership of the Central Committee of the Communist Party, and 0 percent in the supreme Politburo of the party (Vietnam General Statistical Office 2000a, 100–01, 109–13).

On one level, the decline in the percentage of woman deputies in the National Assembly, and probably in other public domains, reflects the return of male war veterans, many highly decorated and inducted into the Communist Party during the Vietnam War. They displaced many women who had filled managerial and leadership positions during the war years.

On a deeper level, the aforementioned decline reflects the socialist state's partial ideological concession to the male-centered model in the kinship and domestic domains and the fairly popular support for this model in people's daily lives. For example, a major policy address on women by the late first secretary of the Communist Party, Lê Duẩn, elaborated at length on the significance of the family and the unique domestic role of women in the child-rearing

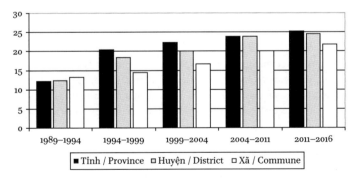

FIGURE 1.1 *Percentages of Women in People's Councils, 1989–2011.*
SOURCE: VIETNAM-GENERAL STATISTICAL OFFICE 2012: 19; VIETNAM NATIONAL COMMITTEE FOR WOMEN'S PROGRESS 2005.

---

7   Local people's councils officially exercise a supervisory role over local administrations. They meet once every few months to review local budgets and other major local issues.

process (Lê Duẩn 1974, 57–69; see also Werner 1981, 187–88).[8] At the local level in the commune of Hải Vân in the northern province of Hà Nam Ninh, the father in a family shared an average of 20 percent of the domestic chores with his wife and children, even when heavy chores such as well-water transportation were included (Houtart and Lemercinier 1981, 175–76; cf. Ngô Thị Chính 1977, 69–70). When male soldiers and cadres returned to this commune from the war in 1975 and 1976, the number of women in the active local workforce decreased by 251 (14.8 percent) in a two-year period, at least partly because many women found the double burden of both domestic work and paid labor participation to be heavy. The ratio of women to men in the local agricultural and industrial workforce dropped dramatically from 1.45 in 1974 (1,695 women and 1,167 men) to 0.92 in 1978 (1,355 women and 1,473 men) (Houtart and Lemercinier 1981, 37).

In the northern ceramic production center of Bát Tràng, the highest-ranked female manager since 1954 and president of a ceramics cooperative from 1985 to 1988 elaborated on some of the difficulties of being a female manager:

> The job of the president of Hợp Thành cooperative…was a demanding job, requiring frequent travel and extensive contact throughout the district and in Hanoi City. Although other people could represent me, or normally accompanied me whenever it was necessary to travel to other provinces, I still had to show up on the more important occasions. Upon returning home, I had to take a rest.
>
> …The time was also irregular. At times, I was still at work at ten at night. At two o'clock in the morning, if a cooperative member came back with raw materials, I had to mobilize members to work to move them to

---

8   Lisa Drummond suggests that state mobilization campaigns in Vietnam shifted their emphasis from women's productive roles to reproductive ones within a "traditional" family: "Women in the family are cast as 'traditional' nurturers, educators, regulators of harmony; there is in public discussion little emphasis on women as producers, only as reproducers" (2005, 167). This took place as the state cut back, starting in the late 1980s, its provision of free social and medical services and shifted the burden to families. The emphasis on women's duties to take care of their families inadvertently and indirectly led to their stigmatization in many cases in the collective era. In the village of Đồng Vàng in the northern province of Hà Tây, many women continued female villagers' tradition of rice trading in order to feed their children and other family members better during the collective era. They were stigmatized by the male-dominated commune government for pursuing private business, in the same way that mercantile activities had been stigmatized in the Confucian ideology in the pre-independence period (Trương Huyền Chi 2001). The stigma on private commerce was reduced with the economic reforms of the late 1980s.

the right areas in the cooperative. On occasion, I was so sick that I could not eat much, but I still had to go. Nobody demanded it, but without me, without orders from above, cooperative members would be reluctant to proceed with tasks.

[How did you handle domestic chores during your terms as the cooperative president?] I was not good at all in domestic work. A cooperative president had no time left for domestic chores. I relied on my husband. [Did your husband take care of domestic chores?] My children did. My daughter was already sixteen in 1985. She did well in her school and attended a school close to our home. She could therefore help with the work at home. But at times, the entire family lost sleep because at midnight, I was called by a cooperative guard.

Even in this case of the female president of the Hợp Thành cooperative in Bát Tràng, her supportive husband contributed little to domestic chores. She could assume the position thanks to the help of a teenage daughter at home and through the informal contacts that she had developed over the years, despite her gender, in order to obtain credit and other forms of assistance. Female managers with younger children or older sons would have encountered the problem of domestic chore arrangements, both for regular daily work outside the home and for extensive travel. This was not a problem faced by active male participants in the public domain.

The persistence of the male-oriented model for kinship and family relations extended well beyond the domestic division of labor. In a survey of 300 agricultural cooperative presidents (mostly male) in Northern Vietnam, 71 percent of the respondents who had only daughters were determined to continue the procreative process until a son was born (Đỗ Long 1985, 33). Many men still justified having multiple wives on the basis of the need for sons to continue the patriline. In a village in Tam Đảo district of Vĩnh Phú province, forty-four cases of polygyny were identified in the period from 1977 to 1982, including a case of a man with four wives and three cases of men with three wives each (Dương Thị Thanh Mai 1985, 67). Research also reveals that a number of community leaders had mistresses or second wives in order to beget sons in the 1960s, 1970s, and 1980s (Bélanger and Magali 2009, 16). In another village of Hà Bắc province, the three daughters of a family having no son reportedly had to yield their ancestral home to their father's patrilineal nephew, although he already owned a house in the neighborhood, because the nephew could worship the father after the father's death (Trịnh Thị Quang 1984, 48). A large number of women in all three regions of Vietnam also shared this male-centered need for sons to continue patrilines. In a 1990 regional comparative study of Northern,

Central, and Southern communes, 41 percent of female respondents without sons in the northern commune of Văn Nhân said that they would like to stop having children, while 80 percent of those with one son and 90 percent of those with two sons said they would like to stop reproductive processes. In the Central Vietnamese commune of Diên Hồng, the corresponding figures were respectively 39 percent, 56 percent, and 86 percent, while in the Southern commune of Thần Cửu Nghĩa, they were 31 percent, 62 percent, and 95 percent (Nguyễn Thị Vân Anh 1993, 39).

Postmarital residence remained overwhelmingly patrilocal. In a systematic and longitudinal analysis of demographic patterns in 1,300 households throughout thirteen communes and towns in Nam Định, Ninh Bình, and Hà Nam (in the lower Red River delta), Hirschman and Nguyễn Hữu Minh have found that 79 to 80 percent of men and women married in the period from 1956 to 1985 lived with the husband's parents upon marriage. The majority of remaining couples (about 15 percent in the aggregate) established separate households (Nguyễn Hữu Minh 1998, 223). A couple normally lived with the husband's parents for a period, then moved off to form their own household, leaving one of the husband's brothers and his wife staying with the parents on a long-term basis.[9] This accounts for the fact that about 75 percent of the households in the Red River delta were nuclear in 1989, while patrilocal postmarital residence was still the norm.[10] Similarly, my comparative data from five

---

9 However, the percentage of couples who reported living patrilocally for more than three years dropped from 68 percent for couples married in 1956–1960 to 60 to 61 percent for those married in 1961–1975 and 46 percent for those tying the knot in the 1976–1985 period (Nguyễn Hữu Minh 1998, 176–235; Nguyễn Hữu Minh and Hirschman 2000, 41–54; see also Mai Huy Bích 2000). A major change in the kinship and family domain involved the married couple's greater input into their spousal selection. Nguyễn Hữu Minh's analysis of data in thirteen Hà Nam Ninh communes and towns indicates that the percentage of nonarranged marriages increased from 32 percent for males and 37 percent for females in the 1956–1960 period, to 72 percent and 74 percent respectively in the 1960–1975 period, to 82 percent and 79 percent for the following decade, and to 86 percent and 85 percent in 1986–1995 (Nguyễn Hữu Minh 1998, 118). The dominant forms of nonarranged marriages involved the couple's decision with their parents' approval and parents' decision with children's approval (see also Phạm Văn Bích 1999).

10 The percentages of extended and joint households in the Red River delta and in the Northern Central panhandle were the lowest in Vietnam in 1989 (standing respectively at 17.7 percent and 21 percent). This percentage reached 25.6 percent in the Northern highlands, 27.4 percent in the central highlands, 28.5–29.4 percent in the Central Coast, the Southeast (around Hồ Chí Minh City), and the Mekong delta (Bélanger 1997, 98). The relatively low percentages of extended and joint households in the Red River delta and the Northern Central panhandle may reflect the division of a number of households in

rural communities in Northern, Central, and Southern Vietnam in 2000 show that about two-thirds of the couples lived with the husband's parents after marriage, while about two-thirds of the households in these communities were nuclear (Luong 2009, 398–99). In general, the majority of newlywed Vietnamese couples still lived with the husband's parents at least for a number of years before establishing their own households. This pattern of postmarital residence added considerable psychosocial pressures on women. They had to take care of not only their nuclear families, but also their husbands' parents and even the latter's nonadult siblings. They had to adapt to daily patterns and food preferences in their husbands' families (further elaborated below). Parents-in-law, and mothers-in-law in particular, seldom allowed their sons to alleviate the daughters-in-law's domestic burdens, since domestic chores were considered the primary responsibility of women. I would suggest that the continuing strength of patrilocal residence contributed to the persistence of domestic labor division and to the emphasis on women's economic contributions simply as a part of their domestic duties, which in turn exerted a major adverse impact on women's abilities to participate on an equal footing with men in the political arena (cf. Werner 2002).

Kinship and Gender Relations in the Era of Economic Reforms and Globalization

Sociocultural and political economic cross-currents on gender relations intensified in Vietnam during the 1990s, when the country became more integrated into the regional and global economies. The male-oriented kinship system continued its resurgence at the same time that women were generally gaining more economic opportunities as well as greater visibility in the political arena under the Vietnamese state's affirmative-action program.

In May 1994, the Central Committee of the Vietnamese Communist Party issued Decree 37, an affirmative-action plan to increase the number of women in governmental and economic management positions. In 2006, the law on gender equality was also passed, with the objective of guaranteeing women equal rights. The national gender strategy was adopted in 2010 to bring about greater gender equality (see also Trần Thị Minh Thi 2012, 87–88). As a result of Decree 37, the percentage of female deputies in the Vietnamese

---

the aftermath of the 1988 land division, when, in a number of communities, each household could buy a certain amount of residential land at relatively low prices (see also Mai Văn Hai and Nguyễn Phan Lâm 2001).

National Assembly increased sharply from 18.5 percent in the 1992 election to 27.3 percent in the 2002–2007 period, although it has gradually dropped since then (Table 1.2). The percentages of women in People's Councils at the provincial, district, and commune levels also increased from 12 to 13 percent in 1989 to over 20 percent in the 2011–2016 period (Figure 1.1). In the more powerful executive branch of the Vietnamese government, the number of female ministers increased from one at the end of the 1990s (the minister of labor) to two by 2012 (labor and health). Women have also filled the deputy-minister ranks in some influential ministries, like finance.[11] The percentages of female chairs of People's Committees (heads of local administrations) fluctuated in the 1.6 to 3.3 percent range in the past two decades at the provincial level, and increased from 1.4 percent in 1991 to at least 3 percent in the 2000s at the district level. Within the Communist Party, a woman was elected for the first time to the Politburo in 1996. The percentage of female Central Committee members also increased from 8.2 percent in 1991 to 10.6 percent in 1996, although it dropped back to 8 percent since 2001 (Table 1.3). More important for the long run is the increase in the percentage of women among the members of the Communist Party, from 21 percent in 2005 to 33 percent in 2010 (Vietnam General Statistical Office 2012, 107), in the context that membership in the Communist Party was a virtual prerequisite for the positions of provincial or ministry department directors (*giám đốc sở, vụ trưởng, cục trưởng*), district chiefs (*chủ tịch ủy ban nhân dân huyện/quận*), or equivalent ones such as institute directors (*viện trưởng*) or university rectors (*hiệu trưởng*) in the contemporary bureaucratic system.[12]

Beyond the political domain and in the public arena, women also participated more actively in the market-oriented economy as white-collar workers,

---

11   In 1976, Mme. Nguyễn Thị Bình, who had been a minister of foreign affairs in the Provisional Revolutionary Government of South Vietnam and highly visible at the Paris peace negotiations, became the first female minister in socialist Vietnam. She was later moved from the Ministry of Education to the ceremonial role of vice president. Over the years, a number of other women were appointed to minister-equivalent positions (president of the National Committee to Protect Mothers and Children, president of the Women's Union), but not to full cabinet positions. The second female cabinet member in socialist Vietnam since 1954 was appointed to the Ministry of Labor in 1998, which has been headed by a woman since then.

12   There have been occasional exceptions to this rule. For example, although not members of the Communist Party, Professor Nguyễn Văn Huyên served as Minister of Education from 1946 to 1975; Professor Hà Văn Tấn was Director of the Institute of Archaeology from 1988 to 2004; and Professor Tôn Thất Bách served as Rector of the Hanoi University of Medicine from 1993 to 2003.

TABLE 1.3 *Percentages of women in leadership positions in the Vietnamese Communist Party and local governments*

	1991–96	1996–2001	2001–06	2006–11	2011–16
Communist Party—National Level					
Politburo	0	5.3	0	0	12.0
Central committee	8.2	10.6	8.0	8.0	8.0
Local Government—Provincial, District, and Commune Levels					
Provincial					
Chief of administration	2.0	1.6	1.6	3.1	1.6
Head of people's council	1.9	7.6	1.6	1.6	4.8
District					
Chief of administration	1.4	1.8	5.3	3.0	n/a
Head of people's council	3.0	3.6	5.5	3.9	n/a
Commune/ward					
Chief of administration	n/a	2.5	3.7	3.4	n/a
Head of people's council	n/a	2.3	3.5	4.1	n/a

SOURCES: TRẦN THỊ VÂN ANH AND LÊ NGỌC HÙNG 1996, 202; VIETNAM GENERAL STATISTICAL OFFICE 2000A, 100, 101, 105, 109–13; INSTITUTE OF FAMILY AND GENDER STUDIES 2010, 59; BÁO NÔNG THÔN NGÀY NAY, APRIL 23, 2004; BÁO LAO ĐỘNG XÃ HỘI, APRIL 18, 2004.

entrepreneurs and company heads, industrial workers, domestic workers, and sexual commodities. Data from the Vietnam Living Standard Survey reveal that women's earnings increased from 71 percent of men's earnings in 1992–1993 to 82 percent in 1997–1998 (Vietnam General Statistical Office 2000b, 188). A similar survey of household living standards suggests that women's wage earnings had increased further by 2006, to 87 percent of men's in urban areas and 88 percent in rural ones (World Bank 2008, 28; cf. World Bank 2011, 52). The growth of private mercantile activities, light industrial jobs in garment and footwear firms, and prostitution, all of which were dominated by women, might have helped to narrow the earning gap between men and women, although further empirical research needs to be conducted on this issue. This narrowing income gap was facilitated by the fact that the gender gap in education has been reduced in the past two decades.[13]

---

13   Trần Thị Minh Thi (in this volume) has attributed the increasing divorce rate from 2000 to 2009 in Vietnam to women's greater economic independence, smaller family size, and the ideological emphasis on self-fulfillment in relationships. This explanation remains a

Among children aged fifteen or below, the gender gap in school attendance was eliminated. Of the postsecondary-degree holders, the gender gap had narrowed from 21 percent (61 percent male versus 39 percent female) in 1989 to 10 percent (55 percent male versus 45 percent female) in 2009 (Vietnam Population and Housing Census Steering Committee 2010, 593; see also World Bank 2011, 29). However, the greater visibility of women in the political arena and the narrowing wage gap between men and women did not result in a fundamental restructuring of gender relations within and beyond the domestic domain. In the labor market, paid maternity leave for women was reduced from six to four months in the early 1990s (Wong 1994, 14), but was restored to six months as of 2013. Women still had to retire at the age of fifty-five, in comparison to the retirement age of sixty for men. Debates in the Vietnamese National Assembly have recurred since 2000, but have been inconclusive, around the solution that the law should give women the option of retiring at the age of fifty-five but the right to work until the age of sixty.

More pernicious within the context of a market economy and growing class differentiation was the commodification of women's bodies through the significant growth of the sex industry and mistress arrangements. In 2001 government sources reported 40,000 female prostitutes in Vietnam, but this figure did not include the considerably larger number of hostesses in dancing clubs, karaoke and beer bars, and some coffee shops, whose earnings came primarily from their sexual services (cf. Kolko 1997, 108).[14] The growth of domestic prostitution in Vietnam since the onset of economic reforms is the result of the double standard of sexual mores in the Vietnamese sociocultural system, the growing wealth and inequality under economic reforms, as well as a gender bias in government clamp-downs on prostitution. Longstanding Vietnamese sexual mores considered men's pre- and extramarital sex, while not ideal, less unacceptable than women's engagement in similar practices. While premarital sex among dating young couples was on the rise in urban contexts, many husbands still expected their wives to be virgins at the time of marriage (Gammeltoft 2002, 120ff.; Khuất Thu Hồng et al. 2009, chap. 2). This moral double standard

---

hypothesis to be tested, as her detailed analysis focuses on divorce in Hanoi and Hà Nam provinces, where there was no clear trend of an increase in divorce between 2000 and 2009.

14 In May 2001, the Vietnamese government launched a nationwide crackdown on prostitution, drug use, and crime, leading to the considerable slowdown in the business of dancing clubs, karaoke and beer bars, and "[hostess] caressing" coffee shops (*cà phê ôm*). However, the impact of this campaign was short-lived. The Coalition Against Trafficking in Women estimates the number of prostitutes in Vietnam at 60,000 to 200,000 (CATW 2012).

also extended to extramarital sex. Emerging with the growing class differentiation, young women's greater concern with their own virginity, and the commodification process in society at large were men with financial resources who were less constrained by social mores than their female counterparts (see Phinney 2008; Khuất Thu Hồng et al. 2009, chap. 4). Even if caught in police crackdowns on prostitution, until 2013 it was generally the female prostitutes and not their male customers who had to undergo reeducation. Besides small administrative fines, the strongest measure undertaken by the police on male white-collar customers of prostitution was to report the behavior to their work units, and not to their families, out of concern about the impact of the report on family harmony.

In the context of growing wealth differentiation, a number of poor young women were also trafficked to Cambodia and other parts of East and Southeast Asia as sex workers (Lê Bạch Dương, Bélanger, and Khuất Thu Hồng 2007; Zhou and Duong Bich Hanh 2011). Through professional matchmaking agents, many poor women, especially in the Mekong delta of Southern Vietnam, married Taiwanese and South Korean men in the hope of escaping poverty, which in many cases was brought about by illnesses in their families and resulting indebtedness within the context of marketized health care in the era of economic reforms.[15] It is estimated that, by 2008, about 130,000 Vietnamese women had married Taiwanese and South Korean men and migrated to Taiwan and South Korea (Bélanger and Trần Giang Linh 2011).

Even if the market economy in Vietnam had not accentuated the commodification of women's bodies, in Vietnamese society under economic reforms, the wider economic and political opportunities for women in the public domain were countered by the strong resurgence of a male-oriented kinship system. This resurgence resulted from state policies, on the one hand, and household strategies and the gender socialization process, on the other (cf. Pettus 2003; see also Luong 2006, 387).

In the 1990s, the Vietnamese state redefined and contracted its role in the economic arena with the shift from a centrally planned to a market-oriented

---

15 By 2012, about 66 percent of the population in Vietnam had been covered under different health insurance schemes. This included compulsory insurance for formal sector employees and retirees; free health insurance for the poor, children under six, ethnic minorities in the highlands, and people of merit; partly subsidized insurance for the near-poor and students; and voluntary health insurance. Health insurance was started in 1992. However, insurance policy holders still had to co-pay for many health services (*Vietnamplus* online, July 23, 2013, http://www.vietnamplus.vn/tang-muc-chi-vien-phi-cho-nguoi-co-bao-hiem-y-te/212532.vnp).

economy. It also restructured its role in the provision of social, medical, and educational services (see Luong 2003), as well as relaxing control of noneconomic and nonsecurity domains. In the relationship between the household and the socialist state, the household has become stronger in the past quarter-century than in the preceding three and a half decades, serving as the locus of economic, social, and cultural reproduction and transformation. This shift took place as households shouldered greater shares of medical and educational costs on top of care for the young and the elderly, while they were protected less from consequences of the shocks of life-cycle-related mishaps (such as serious illness) and became more vulnerable to market-induced economic shocks (e.g., dramatic changes in the prices of agricultural commodities, see Luong 2003).

Throughout the country in the past quarter-century, life-cycle ceremonies (weddings and funerals) became considerably more elaborate, due to households' need to maintain their informal networks of reciprocity, which could be mobilized in times of need (see Luong 1994, 2010b; Malarney 2003). In the Northern Vietnamese communities of Sơn Dương and Hoài Thị, where I did research over the years, the average size of wedding banquets basically doubled from the 1976–1985 period to the 1996–2004 period (Luong 2010a, 237; Luong 2010b, 405). In the southern commune of Khánh Hậu, it increased more modestly, by only 25 percent for the same period. The intensification of rituals and household social networks was not restricted to the three communities where I have done in-depth research over the years. It took place throughout the country (see also Luong 1994; Lương Hồng Quang 1997, 169; Kleinen 1999 chap. 8; Malarney 2003). This mutual assistance on the occasions of life-cycle ceremonies both reflected the strength of social relations and reinforced them in the context of the state's partial disengagement from the public sphere. In the northern part of Vietnam, many people also actively established formal organizations to strengthen their own social networks and to fill the public-space vacuum left by the state. Many of the male-centered organizations, such as patrilineages and the male-exclusive same-age associations, had been reinvented throughout Northern Vietnam by the end of the 1990s (see Kleinen 1999; Lương Hồng Quang and Phạm Nam Thanh 2000, 156–61; Phan Đại Doãn 2001, 185–91; Luong 2010a, chap. 7; Lương Hồng Quang, Nguyễn Thị Thanh Hoa, and Bùi Thị Kim Phương 2011). In its selective emphasis on tradition as an integral part of Vietnamese identity in an age of globalization, the state also became more tolerant of the nonpolitical reinvention and proliferation of traditional organizational forms.

In parallel to the resurgence of many male-centered organizations, in the thirteen Northern communities studied by Hirschman and his colleagues in the 1986–1995 period, the percentage of men and women living patrilocally after marriage increased to 85 percent and 83 percent respectively, from 79 and 80 percent in 1956–1985 (Nguyễn Hữu Minh 1998, 176–235). My analysis of postmarital residence in five communes throughout Northern, Central Coastal, and Southern Vietnam suggests that patrilocal residence was stronger or as strong in the 1996–2000 period as in 1966–1975, 1976–1985, and 1986–1995 (Luong 2009, 400–01). Nguyễn Hữu Minh and Hirschman's regression analysis of data from Northern Vietnam suggests that the younger the husband and wife were at the time of marriage and the more they engaged in agricultural work, the more likely they would live patrilocally (Nguyễn Hữu Minh and Hirschman 2000, 47).[16] Patrilineages continued to be strengthened, and patrilocal residence remained strong in rural Vietnam in the era of the market economy and globalization.

It is not surprising, in the aforementioned context, that the domestic division of labor to the disadvantage of women has persisted in the past two decades. A study conducted by the Center for Women's and Family Studies in Hanoi in the early 1990s revealed that this division of labor pattern was fairly uniform across the Vietnamese lowlands. More specifically, in the communes of Thái Hoà in the northern province of Thái Nguyên, Hoà Phú in the central province of Quảng Nam, and Khánh Hậu in the southern province of Long An, women exclusively handled childcare and cooking as well as other meal-related tasks in at least 63 percent of the surveyed households (Table 1.4). While parent-teacher meetings were attended by both men and women to almost the same degree, men participated more frequently in the more important public meetings of the hamlet and commune. The Vietnam Living Standard Survey indicates that in 1992–1993, women spent an average of 15.52 hours a week on unpaid housework, while men spent only 10.91 hours. In 1997–1998, the gap remained, although the number of hours had been reduced to 12.75 for women and 8.31 for men. The decrease was possibly due

---

16 However, the percentage of men and women who lived with husbands' families for more than three years declined slightly to 42–43 percent in the 1986–1995 period. Nguyễn Hữu Minh and Hirshman attribute the reduction in the length of patrilocal residence over time to later marriage ages, the declining mortality rate, and the consequent increase in the number of siblings (2000, 51) in the context of a more crowded household and the need for only one couple to stay and take care of elderly parents (Nguyễn Hữu Minh 1998, 209, 214–15). If the couple married earlier, if the husband's parents were older than fifty-four, if the husband was the eldest son, and if the husband had fewer siblings, all these factors would increase the likelihood that patrilocal residence would last for more than three years. However, the more educated the couple was, the more likely they would stay longer with the husband's parents. Nguyễn Hữu Minh suggests that this might relate to the more educated people's stronger expression of filial piety in conformity with social norms and governmental encouragement.

TABLE 1.4 *Division of domestic labor in percentages*

	Thái Hòa (North)			Hoà Phú (Central)			Khánh Hậu (South)		
	Husband	Wife	Husband and Wife	Husband	Wife	Husband and Wife	Husband	Wife	Husband and Wife
a. Cooking and other meal-related tasks	2.4	84.9	5.6	3.0	90	2.0	3.2	82.6	2.1
b. Child care	5.0	63.4	28.7	5.0	63.3	31.1	6.5	71.1	19.4
c. Purchase of consumer durables	60.4	12.6		24.3	29		33.3	33.3	
d. Sale of products	28.7	55.7	8.7	8.2	70.1	18	12.3	49.1	33.3
e. PTA meetings	45.7	54.3		50.0	44.6		38.2	38.9	
f. Hamlet/commune meetings	59	28.8		56.8	26.3		40.3	36.4	

SOURCES: NGUYỄN LINH KHIẾU 2001, 29, 36.[17] (CF. LUONG 2010A, 229–30; LÊ NGỌC VĂN 2011, 407–09).

---

17   Needless to say, there is a certain amount of variation in the division of domestic labor among couples, even after we exclude the cases of urban middle- and upper-class households with domestic help. It has been reported that among young and working migrant couples, husbands are more willing to engage in cooking or some other domestic work when wives are at work during meal or meal preparation time, and when wives work away from home and husbands work closer to home (Lê Ngọc Văn 2011, 406–07, 419–23, cf. Vũ Tuấn Huy and Carr 2004). I would suggest two points. First, this pattern more likely emerges in neolocal households separated from husbands' native communities and old networks, in a context where traditional pressure is reduced. Second, it is unwarranted to imply or to suggest (Lê Ngọc Văn 2011, 423) that there was uniformity in domestic division of labor in the past, that women's active participation in the economy is new, and that the greater engagement of husbands in some households in domestic work in this context is a "revolution."

to the availability of household equipment and domestic helpers among the urban middle class and to lunch-delivery services for office workers (Vietnam General Statistical Office 2000b 197, 199; see also Hà Thị Phương Tiến and Hà Quang Ngọc 2001).

In general, it was still much easier for men than for women to maintain extensive public commitments. Men's and women's career trajectories, their earnings in particular, and their roles in the public sphere in general, were strongly shaped by a socioculturally embedded division of labor at home. The strong expectation that women would be married by their late twenties and take primary responsibility for housework and childcare slowed down their career advancement and even steered them to different career trajectories. This can be seen in the two following cases in Hồ Chí Minh City, one of a working-class family and the other of a white-collar one:

> In 2001, Household 932 was composed of a couple (aged 39 and 35) with two children (aged 6 and 4) and the husband's five children (aged 13 through 22) from a previous marriage. The husband was an ethnic Chinese born in Hồ Chí Minh City and with a grade-3 education. Although born in the Mekong Delta province of Long An, the wife lived for a few years as a child with her paternal grandmother in Hồ Chí Minh City before returning to her native village after 1975. Having completed grade 10, she worked as a seamstress in the village but found her work not financially rewarding due to villagers' limited disposable income. She cited the tendency of some of her customers to pay 10,000 VND (US $0.70) in labor cost in very small installments (1000 VND–2000 VND each time). She decided to go to Hồ Chí Minh City to find work. After two brief job stints, she settled in the third job as a garment worker in a Taiwanese factory and earned 800,000 VND to 1 million VND (US $60–$85) a month. She got married at the age of 28, and gave birth to her first child in 1995 and to the second one in 1997. With her child care duties, she quitted her formal sector job and worked as a seamstress at home, in the informal economy. Her earnings were reduced to 360,000 VND (US $26) a month in 1998 and 450,000 VND (US $30) in 2001. From a financial perspective, her job switch made sense to her because if she had continued working in the garment factory, she would have had to spend 600,000 VND a month to send her two children to a daycare center. In contrast, her husband's career was not influenced much by the birth of their two children in 1995 and 1997. He continued working as a security guard in a state enterprise, earning about 1 million VND (US $68) a month, and enjoyed a full social and medical insurance coverage.

In 1998, household 236 had a couple (aged 43 and 42, both university-educated) and three children (aged 14, 12, and 5). Two years before, they had decided that due to the husband's career demand, the wife should give up her formal sector professional position requiring travelling across the city from home to work, and look for a job closer to home, so that she could pick up their children from school. She could not find a professional job reportedly due to employers' age specification or preference for employees less than 35 years old. At the time of our survey and in-depth interview in 1998, the wife in household 236 was pursuing another university degree and worked as a garment home worker. She earned 20,000 VND (about US $1.50) a day when work was available. Her professional career was interrupted. When we did a re-study in 2001 of households in our 1998 sample, the wife in household 236 had found a job in a state agency and earned 2 million VND a month. In the meantime, her husband's career had moved forward. In 2001, he worked as the Director of a state enterprise specialized in seafood export and earned officially 3 million VND a month.

    LUONG AND GUNEWARDENA 2009

The two cases, among many others, illustrate how careers and earnings in the labor market were shaped not only by human capital but also by the socioculturally embedded processes in the gendered division of labor at home and at work.

The underrepresentation of women in leading positions in various domains was rooted in a similar process. A 2009 report based on interviews with women and men in leadership positions suggests three factors affecting women's career trajectories: laws and regulations, sociocultural norms, and the personal attitudes of agency heads. The first two deserve special attention as nonpersonal factors (Trần Thị Vân Anh 2009). Sociocultural norms specified women's heavier domestic duties and consequently did not provide women with the same opportunities for leadership positions in the public domain. Vietnamese laws and regulations also specify women's normal retirement age as fifty-five and men's as sixty, thus shortening women's time to demonstrate their abilities for leadership or senior management positions by five years. According to Trần Thị Vân Anh, the combination of these two factors led to uneven playing fields for men and women in the bureaucratic system and in the public domain:

> When women are young, they are forced to run at high speed while carrying heavier burdens than men (domestic chores and raising small children).

When they get older and they have balanced the work and family, women are forced to leave earlier than men. The men can participate in the race with a speed they want and without carrying anything. Men also have a longer period of time to present themselves and at the final stage of the race they have almost no female rivals.

TRẦN THỊ VÂN ANH 2009, 19

My study in two rural Vietnamese communities also shows that men were able to maintain a much more active profile in the local public arena through their voluntary association memberships than women could. The number of voluntary association memberships for every one hundred people aged sixteen or above was 112 among men and 70 among women in the northern village of Hoài Thị, and 17 among men and 7.6 among women in Dinh Hamlet of the southern commune of Khánh Hậu (Figure 1.2).[18] Most popular among men in Hoài Thị were same-age associations, the education-promotion association, the same-military-service association, and the communal-house group. Most popular among women were the Buddhist prayer association, same-circumstance (women's) association, and incense-offering team (at pagodas and

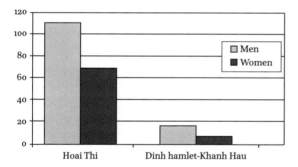

FIGURE 1.2 *Voluntary association membership: number of memberships per 100 residents above the age of 16.*

---

18   Voluntary associations were not sponsored by the state. As a person might join more than one voluntary association, the total number of voluntary association memberships in a population may exceed the number of people. In both Hoài Thị and Khánh Hậu, there were also state-organized associations such as women's associations, peasant associations, elderly associations, youth associations, and a trade union (only in Khánh Hậu). The rate of participation for every one hundred residents above the age of sixteen was: forty-four in Hoài Thị and eleven in Khánh Hậu for the women's association, eighty-four for both men and women in Hoài Thị, and fourteen for men and nine for women in Khánh Hậu for other state-organized associations.

shrines). The first and last of these were mainly for women above the age of fifty, who had fewer domestic obligations, as many women in this age range lived in extended/joint households and had daughters-in-law to take care of domestic work. In the southern commune of Khánh Hậu, the two major voluntary associations were the communal-house association (virtually all male), and the Buddhist prayer association (virtually all female and elderly).

Given the strong and long-existing tradition of community endogamy in Northern Vietnam, many Northern rural women marry within their natal villages and, despite the prevalence of patrilocal residence, can still live in their natal villages after marriage. Major sources of support for a woman marrying within her natal village are her natal family, her own kin, and numerous childhood friends and former classmates.[19] For their Southern counterparts, as the majority of them marry men from other villages and move to their husbands' communities after marriage, support from natal family, kin, and childhood friends is not as readily available. Supplementing the support from natal family and kin are neighborhood ties, coworker relations (for those working outside agriculture), religious communities, and, for a small number of women, associational and political ties. Kato (in this volume) has explored the extent to which women's social sphere may have fostered an alternative ideology. I have examined elsewhere the extent to which women's ties to their natal families, their strong focus on their own children, and the children's matrilineal linkages may have sustained a bilateral model of Vietnamese kinship (Luong 1989, 2010a, 77–78). However, the male-oriented model of kinship and family still plays a dominant role among ethnic Vietnamese, despite the state's ideological adherence to gender equality.

The male-centered domestic labor division and patrilocal residence continued exerting a strong psychosocial pressure on young women as daughters-in-law. The anthropologist Tine Gammeltoft discussed a revealing incident about the local definition of gender relations in the northern commune of Vãi Sơn, near Hanoi, when the mother-in-law of her host family lightly slapped her daughter-in-law, a local schoolteacher, with a stick in public one day. The mother-in-law told the foreign anthropologist:

> You see, this is what I told you. People don't know how to behave anymore, they don't know what is up and what is down [i.e., who is superior and who is inferior], they have no morality. How can I live with a spoilt

---

19   The average rate of community endogamy for the two Northern Vietnamese villages that I have studied over the years is 67 percent, in comparison to 64 percent in the two Central Coastal communes studied in 2000 and 36 percent in the three communes in the Southern Mekong delta.

daughter-in-law like this? She even tells me I cook too salty food. Would *you* ever dare tell *your* mother-in-law her food was too salty?

GAMMELTOFT 1999, 160

Gammeltoft learned from the neighbors that the tension between the mother-in-law and daughter-in-law of her host family was not really over food but over the upbringing of the eldest grandson, who was more unruly than most boys of his age. Although the mother-in-law was known as hot-tempered and difficult, all the neighbors condemned the daughter-in-law. A neighbor explained: "No matter what her mother-in-law tells her, being a daughter-in-law, she should still speak nicely and behave properly" (161).

In the commune of Vãi Sơn, within the domestic domain, as Gammeltoft explained,

> Women's everyday stresses and worries seem to be related to two central facets of their lives: first, the experience of *overwork*, i.e., very hard work every day and responsibility for both working the fields and for all domestic work including the management of the household economy, and second, the experience of *submission*, i.e., having to "please" (*chiều*) one's husband and his family. (162)

Chiều the husband means pleasing him both socially and sexually. In a patrilocal joint family context, pleasing the husband's family also means being especially attentive to the needs and wishes of parents-in-law, as well as being respectful of them.

The psychosocial pressures on young women due to patrilocal residence was not restricted to rural Northern Vietnam. In her study of the relation between daughters-in-law and mothers-in-law in urban Hồ Chí Minh City, Ngô Thị Ngân Bình also suggests:

> This situation [being a daughter-in-law in her husband's family] creates a challenge to the daughter-in-law's performance of roles, which demands tactful skills, endurance, energy, and time. If a working woman in a nuclear family has to perform double duty, balancing between career and family responsibilities, then her counterpart in the extended family has to face triple duty, balancing among work, home and *làm dâu* [being a daughter-in-law] obligations.
>
> NGÔ THỊ NGÂN BÌNH 2001, 149

Those obligations were challenging for an urban daughter, since the mother-in-law seldom adopted a liberal view on the four feminine virtues (work, appearance, discourse, and character). She often emphasized a woman's domestic duties and the primacy of her son's consanguine ties over his marital and affinal relations. In this context, while a mother-in-law in the urban South might not require a new daughter-in-law to make a strict adaptation to her family's lifestyle, the latter might still not be highly prepared for domestic chore demands, since the young woman's own mother might have been relaxed regarding the young woman's domestic performance in order to facilitate the girl's pursuit of education and career.

Studies to date suggest that Vietnamese girls were socialized from an early age in preparation for their gender roles in both the domestic domain and beyond. In both a description and prescription of behavior, local people in Vãi Sơn Commune saw girls as mild, gentle, and enduring hardships, while boys were perceived to have hot and uncontrollable tempers. In a study on gender socialization in the commune of Thịnh Trị in the same province, Hà Tây, H. Rydström similarly reported that local definitions of girls and boys portrayed the former as gentle, responsive, obedient, easy to discipline, emphasizing sentiments (*tình cảm*), adjusting to situations, occupying little space, demanding little attention, and preferring quiet occupations. In contrast, they portrayed boys as mischievous, active, disobedient, difficult to discipline, emphasizing obligations, orchestrating situations, occupying too much space, demanding much attention, and engaging in energetic games (Rydström 1998). While these definitions were stereotypical, they shaped expectations and the sanctioning of children's behavior: a disobedient boy who ignored a request for housework might be forgiven more easily than a disobedient girl, leading to a shift of housework to girls (121–22; see also Rydström 2005).

Beyond childhood and in the larger national arena, the rapidly growing self-help literature, whose readers were mainly members of the middle class, advised women how to preserve happy family lives: by keeping feminine appearances and by providing their husbands with appropriate pleasures (Nguyễn-Võ Thu-Hương 2002, 147–50; see also 2008). This literature plays a role in reinforcing the dominant definition of femininity inculcated in childhood. In the context that the mass media became accessible even in remote parts of Vietnam during the past decade, and as advertising, mainly by multinational corporations, became an increasingly important part of the Vietnamese mass media, Lisa Drummond has suggested that advertising in particular and the mass media in general have emphasized women's men-centered roles as consumers and family members (e.g., beauty products to enhance attractiveness and seductiveness to men, consumption centering on reproductive activities in the domestic domain) (Drummond 2005). A recent analysis of primary-school textbooks in Vietnam also shows systematic biases in gender portrayal, with women overwhelmingly overrepresented in domestic contexts, domestic work, and low-skilled or teacher occupations, and men in public settings and high-skilled or physical work occupations (*VN Express* online February 21, 2012, *Thanh Niên* online, April 2, 2012; see also Vũ Phương Anh 2008).

The definition of women's roles as domestic-centered, even when women worked outside the home, created enormous psychosocial pressures on women. In an illuminating study of the pressures on women in Đồng Vàng village in the northern province of Hà Tây, which in 1999 had about 200 women (aged from the early twenties to the late sixties) working as traders in Hanoi, Trương Huyền Chi reported their mental anguish about leaving their children behind in the village, despite the fact that this village was close to Hanoi:

> As mothers and wives, they [woman traders] struggle with restless feelings of insecurity and loss of chance to fulfill their nurturing and caring responsibilities towards their family members...women are [also] aware of their *major* roles, not simply supporting, but generating cash income for the entire family.
> TRƯƠNG HUYỀN CHI 2001, 141

> On the one hand, a woman's undertaking of the hardship of trading in towns is good because it is driven by her sacrifice for her husband and children. On the other hand, her increasing absence from home should be criticized because it means she does not behave properly (*biết điều*) toward her husband and children.
> TRƯƠNG HUYỀN CHI 2001, 145

While many urban middle-class women could rely on female domestic workers to alleviate their domestic burdens, this did not reduce their guilt about not personally providing better care for their children.

Obviously, Vietnamese women were not simply passive agents in the context of conflicting structural pressures on gender relations in the 1990s. According to Gammeltoft, to deal with psychological distress, a woman in the northern village of Vãi Sơn might first of all confide in other women, who often counseled endurance (1999, 230). Or she could choose foot-dragging, performing work in a sullen manner. However, her children might suffer from her refusal to perform domestic work effectively. Third, she might refrain from eating, drawing other people's attention to her anguish. Fourth would be somatic expressions of illness that might make her husband more caring and her mother-in-law more compassionate toward her (202–37). Ngô Thị Ngân Bình also reports on a major strategy among daughters-in-law to gain more power through the control of their nuclear families' budgets and through an emphasis on their marital ties to their husbands (2001). Although gossip, especially about the source of pressures, has not been systematically studied in Vietnam, I would suggest that this constitutes a major tactic by women in response to their psychosocial pressures. In daily life, Vietnamese women might combine those responses with different degrees of effectiveness. Urban women with some familiarity with a Western language might also marry men from the West to escape altogether the psychosocial pressures from a male-centered family and kinship system.

Beyond family life, Ito Miho (in this volume) has explored how, in the context of their less central role in the dominant kinship system and the state's affirmative action for ethnic minorities in access to higher education, a number of young women have adopted ethnic-minority status as a strategy to gain easier access to universities and colleges. In religion, I would suggest that women's heavy leaning toward Buddhism, with its concepts of karma and the infinite cycle of miseries, was also a reaction to the problems that they faced in the Vietnamese sociocultural and economic system. Women made up a strong majority of people attending Buddhist pagoda ceremonies, both on the first and fifteenth days of lunar months and on major Buddhist or pagoda anniversaries. In rural pagodas, especially in the Northern lowlands, one rarely saw men among the ceremony-attending Buddhist followers. For many women, religion provides both a sense of community, especially in old age, and an explanation for the problems faced in daily life (see Endres's and Ito Mariko's chapters in this volume).

Conclusion

In conclusion, marketization and globalization have increased income-generating opportunities for many women. However, this often means an increase in paid working hours on top of unpaid domestic work. The contraction of the state's role in the public domain and the selective reinvention of tradition outside the government-controlled sphere have also led to the resurgence of the male-oriented kinship model to the disadvantage of women.

On a theoretical level, as pointed out by Goodkind (1995), data on Vietnamese gender relations in the era of economic reforms and globalization do not support the hypothesis, rooted in modernization theory, that gender equality will increase with modernization. Neither do they support a Marxist theoretical framework that sees gender inequality as rooted in the feudal and capitalist modes of production—gender inequality in Vietnam persisted even at the height of socialist reforms. The Vietnamese data on both the economic reform period and in the preceding centuries also challenge a non-Marxist economic-reductionist framework that equates economic power with an increase in status—Vietnamese women's significant roles in the economy do not necessarily lead to a restructuring of gender relations to their advantage (cf. World Bank 2011). While research needs to be conducted in greater depth on the regional, class, and ethnic dimensions of gender relations, as well as on how women took advantage of and reacted to the changing opportunities and constraints, current findings suggest that the socioculturally and historically embedded definition of gender relations may be as powerful as the political-economic framework in reproducing and potentially transforming gender relations in Vietnam (cf. Werner 2002).

References

Barrow, John. [1806] 1975. *A Voyage to Cochinchina*. Oxford: Oxford University Press.

Bélanger, Danièle. 1997. *Rapport intergénerationnel et rapport hommes-femmes dans la transition démographique au Vietnam, de 1930 à 1990*. Ph.D. dissertation, Université de Montréal, Quebec.

Bélanger, Danièle, and Magali Barbieri. 2009. "Introduction: State, Families, and the Making of Transition in Vietnam." In *Reconfiguring Families in Contemporary Vietnam*, edited by Danièle Bélanger and Magali Barbieri, 1–45. Stanford, CA: Stanford University Press.

Bélanger, Danièle, and Trần Giang Linh. 2011. "The Impact of Transnational Migration on Gender and Marriage in Sending Communities in Vietnam." *Current Sociology* 59 (1): 59–77.

CATW (Coalition against Trafficking in Women). 2012. *Trafficking and Prostitution in Asia and the Pacific*. http://catwap.wordpress.com/programs/research-documentation-publications/facts-and-statistics/.

Crawfurd, John. [1823] 1970. "Report on the State of the Annamese Empire." In *The Mandarin Road to Old Hue: Narratives of Anglo-Vietnamese Diplomacy from the 17th Century to the Eve of the French Conquest*, edited by A. Lamb, 225–77. London: Chatto and Windus.

Dampier, William. 1906. *Dampier's Voyages*. Edited by John Masefield. London: E. Grant Richards.

Đỗ Long. 1985. "Tâm lý xã hội truyền thống và kế hoạch dân số ở Việt Nam" [Traditional mentality and demographic planning in Vietnam]. *Xã hội học* 12: 32–33, 41.

Drummond, Lisa. 2005. "The Modern 'Vietnamese Woman': Socialization and Women's Magazines." In *Gender Practices in Contemporary Vietnam*, edited by Lisa Drummond and Helle Rydström, 158–78. Singapore and Copenhagen: National University of Singapore Press and NIAS Press.

Dương Thị Thanh Mai. 1985. "Vấn đề hôn nhân qua khảo sát thực tế ở một số nơi" [The Question of Marriage: Empirical Research in a Number of Localities]. In *Tình yêu, hôn nhân, gia đình trong xã hội ta* [Love, Marriage, and the Family in Our Society], edited by Viện Xã hội học, 64–68. Hanoi: Nhà xuất bản Khoa học Xã hội.

Gammeltoft, Tine. 1999. *Women's Bodies, Women's Worries: Health and Family Planning in a Vietnamese Rural Community*. Richmond, Surrey: Curzon.

———. 2002. "The Irony of Sexual Agency: Pre-marital Sex in Urban Northern Viet Nam." In *Gender, Household, State: Đổi Mới in Viet Nam*, edited by Jayne Werner and Danièle Bélanger, 111–28. Ithaca: Cornell University Southeast Asia Program.

Goodkind, Daniel. 1995. "Rising Gender Inequality in Vietnam since Reunification." *Pacific Affairs* 48(3): 342–59.

Hà Thị Phương Tiến and Hà Quang Ngọc. 2001. *Female Labour Migration*. Hanoi: Women's Publishing House.

Hoang, Kimberly Kay. 2011. "'She's Not a Low Class Dirty Girl': Sex Work in Ho Chi Minh City, Vietnam." *Journal of Contemporary Ethnography* 40(4): 367–96.

Houtart, Francois, and Genevieve Lemercinier. 1981. *La Sociologie d'une Commune Vietnamienne*. Louvain La Neuve, Belgium: Catholic University of Louvain.

Indochine, Gouvernement General de l'. 1931. *Indochine scholaire*. Hanoi: Extreme-Orient.

Institute of Family and Gender Studies. 2010. *Sổ tay hướng dẫn lồng ghép giới* [Manual on How to Incorporate Gender]. Hanoi: Institute of Family and Gender Studies.

Khuất Thu Hồng, Lê Bạch Dương, and Nguyễn Ngọc Hường. 2009. *Sex: Easy to Joke About but Hard to Talk About*. Hanoi: Nhà xuất bản Tri thức & VNN Publications. (Vietnamese version: *Tình dục: Chuyện dễ đùa khó nói*.)

Kleinen, John. 1999. *Facing the Future, Reviving the Past: A Study of Social Change in a Northern Vietnamese Village*. Singapore: Institute of Southeast Asian Studies.

Kolko, Gabriel. 1997. *Vietnam: Anatomy of a Peace*. London: Routledge.

Lê Bạch Dương, Danièle Bélanger, and Khuất Thu Hồng. 2007. "Transnational Migration, Marriage and Trafficking at the Vietnam-China Border." In *Watering the Neighbour's Garden: The Growing Demographic Female Deficit in Asia*, vol. 1, edited by Isabelle Attané and C. Guilmoto. Paris: CICRED.

Lê Duẩn. 1974. "Role and Tasks of the Vietnamese Woman in the New Revolutionary Stage." In *Some Present Tasks*, edited by Lê Duẩn, 48–84. Hanoi: Foreign Language Publishing House.

Lê Ngọc Văn. 2011. *Gia đình và biến đổi gia đình ở Việt Nam* [The Family and Its Transformation in Vietnam]. Hanoi: Nhà xuất bản Khoa học xã hội.

Lê Thị Nhâm Tuyết. 1975. *Phụ nữ Việt Nam qua các thời đại* [Vietnamese Women through Different Eras]. Hanoi: Nhà xuất bản Khoa học Xã hội.

Lương Hồng Quang. 1997. *Văn hoá cộng đồng làng: Vùng Đồng bằng sông Cửu Long thập kỷ 80–90* [Village Community Culture in the Mekong Delta in the 1980–90 Decade]. Hanoi: Nhà xuất bản Văn hoá-Thông tin.

Lương Hồng Quang and Phạm Nam Thanh. 2000. "Sự biến đổi trong văn hoá làng xã" [The Transformation of Village and Commune Cultures]. In *Sự biến đổi của làng xã Việt Nam ngày nay ở đồng bằng sông Hồng* [The Changes in Vietnamese Villages and Communes in the Red River Delta at Present], edited by Tô Duy Hợp, 111–68. Hanoi: Nhà xuất bản Khoa học Xã hội.

Lương Hồng Quang, Nguyễn Thị Thanh Hoa, and Bùi Thị Kim Phương. 2011. *Câu chuyện làng Giang* [The Story of Giang Village]. Hanoi: Nhà xuất bản Đại học quốc gia Hà Nội.

Luong, Hy V. 1989. "Vietnamese Kinship: Structural Principles and the Socialist Transformation in Twentieth-Century Vietnam." *Journal of Asian Studies* 48: 741–56.

———. 1994. "The Marxist State and the Dialogic Restructuration of Culture in Rural Vietnam." In *Indochina: Social and Cultural Change*, by David Elliott H.V. Luong, B. Kiernan, and T. Mahoney, 79–117. Claremont, CA: Claremont-McKenna College.

———. 1998. "Engendered Entrepreneurship: Ideologies and Political Economic Transformation in a Northern Vietnamese Centre of Ceramics Production." In *Market Cultures: Society and Morality in the New Asian Capitalisms*, edited by Robert Hefner, 290–314. Boulder, CO: Westview.

———. 2003. "Postwar Vietnamese Society: An Overview of Transformational Dynamics." In *Postwar Vietnam: Dynamics of a Transforming Society*, edited by Hy V. Luong, 1–26. Lanham, MD: Rowman and Littlefield.

———. 2006. "Structure, Practice, and History: Contemporary Anthropological Research on Vietnam." *Journal of Vietnamese Studies* 1: 371–409.

———. 2009. "Rural-to-Urban Migration in Vietnam: A Tale of Three Regions." In *Post-Transitional Vietnamese Families: The Legacy of Đổi Mới*, edited by Danièle Bélanger and Magali Barbieri, 391–420. Stanford, CA: Stanford University Press.

———. 2010a. *Tradition, Revolution, and Market Economy in a North Vietnamese Village, 1925–2006*. Honolulu: University of Hawai'i Press.

———. 2010b. "Quà và vốn xã hội ở hai cộng đồng nông thôn Việt Nam" [Gifts and Social Capital in Two Rural Vietnamese Communities]. In *Hiện đại và động thái của truyền thống ở Việt Nam* [Modernities and the Dynamics of Tradition in Vietnam], Vol. 1, edited by H.V. Luong et al., 397–424. Ho Chi Minh City: Nhà xuất bản Đại học Quốc gia Thành phố Hồ Chí Minh.

Luong, Hy V., and Dileni Gunewardena. 2009. "Labor Market, Urban Informal Economy, and Earnings during Rapid Economic Growth: The Case of Hồ Chí Minh City." In *Urbanization, Migration, and Poverty in a Vietnamese Metropolis*, edited by Hy V. Luong, 211–56. Singapore: National University of Singapore Press.

Mai Huy Bích. 2000. "Nơi cư trú sau hôn nhân ở đồng bằng sông Hồng" [Post-Marital Residence in the Red River Delta]. *Xã hội học* 4: 33–43.

Mai Văn Hai, and Nguyễn Phan Lâm. 2001. "Luật đất đai và tác động ban đầu tới cơ cấu gia đình ở một làng châu thổ sông Hồng" [The Land Law and Its Initial Impact on Family Structure in a Red River Delta Village]. *Xã hội học* 1: 40–45.

Malarney, Shaun. 2003. "Return to the Past? The Dynamics of Contemporary Religious and Ritual Transformation." In *Postwar Vietnam: Dynamics of a Transforming Society*, edited by Hy V. Luong, 225–56. Lanham, MD: Rowman and Littlefield.

Marr, David. 1981. *Vietnamese Tradition on Trial, 1920–1945*. Berkeley: University of California Press.

Ngô Thị Chính. 1977. "Vài nét về người phụ nữ nông dân trong sản xuất nông nghiệp và trong mối quan hệ hôn nhân gia đình mới" [A Sketch of Woman Cultivators in Agricultural Production and in New Marital Relations]. *Tạp chí Dân tộc học* 3: 61–70.

Ngo Thi Ngan Binh. 2001. "Sociocultural Aspects of the Mother- and Daughter-in-Law Tension in the Southern Vietnamese Family." M.A. thesis, National University of Singapore.

Nguyễn Đình Đầu. 1994. *Tổng kết nghiên cứu địa bạ Nam Kỳ lục tỉnh* [Research on Land Registers in the Six Southern Provinces]. Hồ Chí Minh City: Nhà xuất bản Thành phố Hồ Chí Minh.

Nguyễn Đức Truyến. 1997. "Văn hoá và sự kế thừa văn hoá trong việc chia thừa kế ở đồng bằng sông Hồng hiện nay" [Culture and Cultural Heritage in Inheritance in the Red River Delta at Present]. *Xã hội học* 3: 48–54.

Nguyễn Hữu Minh. 1998. "Tradition and Change in the Vietnamese Marriage Patterns in the Red River Delta." Ph.D. thesis, University of Washington, Seattle.

Nguyễn Hữu Minh, and Charles Hirschman. 2000. "Mô hình sống chung với gia đình chồng sau khi kết hôn ở đồng bằng Bắc Bộ và các nguyên nhân tác động" [Patrilocal Residence Model after Marriage in the Red River Delta and the Factors at Work]. *Xã hội học* 1: 41–54.

Nguyễn Linh Khiếu. 2001. *Gia đình phụ nữ trong biến đổi văn hóa-xã hội nông thôn* [Women's Households in Social and Cultural Changes in Villages]. Hanoi: Nhà xuất bản Khoa học Xã hội.

Nguyễn Thị Vân Anh. 1993. "Sở thích về sinh đẻ ở một số vùng nông thôn Việt Nam" [Reproductive preferences in a few rural areas of Vietnam]. *Xã hội học* 2: 35–47.

Nguyễn-Võ Thu-Hương. 2002. "Governing Sex: Medicine and Governmental Intervention in Prostitution." In *Gender, Household, State: Đổi Mới in Viet Nam*, edited by Jayne Werner and Danièle Bélanger, 129–52. Ithaca, NY: Cornell University Southeast Asia Program.

———. 2008. *The Ironies of Freedom: Sex, Culture, and Neoliberal Governance in Vietnam*. Seattle: University of Washington Press.

Ochiai, Emiko. 2010. "Reconstruction of Intimate and Public Spheres in Asian Modernity: Familism and Beyond." *Journal of Intimate and Public Spheres: Asian and Global Forum* Pilot Issue: 2–22.

Pettus, Ashley. 2003. *Between Sacrifice and Desire: National Identity and the Governing of Femininity in Vietnam.* New York: Routledge.

Phạm Văn Bích. 1999. *The Vietnamese Family in Change: The Case of the Red River Delta.* Richmond, Surrey: Curzon.

Phan Đại Doãn. 2001. *Làng xã Việt Nam: Một số vấn đề kinh tế-văn hoá-xã hội* [Vietnamese Villages and Communes: A Number of Economic, Cultural, and Social Issues]. Hanoi: Nhà xuất bản Chính trị Quốc gia.

Phan Huy Lê, Vũ Minh Giang, Vũ Văn Quân, and Phan Phương Thảo. 1995. *Địa bạ Hà Đông* [Land Registers in Hà Đông]. Hanoi: Nhà xuất bản Thế giới.

Phan Huy Lê, Nguyễn Đức Nghinh, Vũ Minh Giang, Vũ Văn Quân, and Phan Phương Thảo. 1997. *Địa bạ Thái Bình* [Land Registers in Thái Bình]. Hanoi: Nhà xuất bản Thế giới.

Phinney, Harriet. 2008. "'Rice is Essential but Tiresome, You Should Get Some Noodles': *Đổi mới* and the Political Economy of Men's Extramarital Sexual Relations and Marital HIV Risk in Hanoi, Vietnam." *American Journal of Public Health* 98 (4): 650–60.

Rydström, Helle. 1998. *Embodying Morality: Girls' Socialization in a North Vietnamese Commune.* Linkoping, Sweden: Linkoping University.

———. 2005. "Female and Male 'Characters': Images of Identification and Self-Identification for Rural Vietnamese Children and Adolescents." In *Gender Practices in Contemporary Vietnam*, edited by Lisa Drummond and Helle Rydström, 74–95. Singapore and Copenhagen: National University of Singapore Press and NIAS Press.

Thành Thế Vỹ. 1961. *Ngoại thương Việt Nam hồi thế kỷ XVII, XVII và đầu XIX* [The External Trade of Vietnam in the Seventeenth, Eighteenth, and Early Nineteenth Centuries]. Hanoi: Nhà xuất bản Sử học.

Tran Thi Minh Thi. 2012. "Social and Family Roles of Working Women in Transitional Vietnam." In *Alternative Intimate Spheres for Women in Vietnam*, GCOE Working Papers (Next Generation Research) 71, edited by Kato Atsufumi, 87–103. Kyoto, Japan: Kyoto University Global COE for Reconstruction of the Intimate and Public Spheres in 21st Century Asia.

Trần Thị Vân Anh. 2009. "Report on Insights into Women's Leadership in Viet Nam's Public Sector: Obstacles and Solutions." Commissioned report submitted by the Institute of Family and Gender Studies to UNDP-Vietnam.

Trần Thị Vân Anh and Lê Ngọc Hùng. 1996. *Phụ nữ, giới, và phát triển* [Women, Gender, and Development]. Hanoi: Nhà xuất bản Phụ nữ.

Trịnh Thị Quang. 1984. "Mấy vấn đề về quan hệ thân tộc ở nông thôn" [Certain Questions Regarding Kinship Relations in the Countryside]. *Xã hội học* 6: 47–52.

Truong Huyen Chi. 2001. "Changing Processes of Social Reproduction in the Northern Vietnamese Countryside: An Ethnographic Study of Đồng Vàng Village (Hà Tây Province, Vietnam)." Ph.D. dissertation, University of Toronto, Canada.

Vietnam General Statistical Office. 2000a. *Nữ giới và nam giới ở Việt Nam thập kỷ 90* [Female and Male in Vietnam in the 1990s]. Hanoi: Nhà xuất bản Thống kê.

———. 2000b. *Điều tra mức sống dân cư Việt Nam* [Vietnam Living Standards Survey] 1997–1998. Hanoi: Nhà xuất bản Thống kê.

———. 2012. *Số liệu thống kê giới ở Việt Nam—Gender Statistics in Vietnam, 2000–2010*. Hanoi: General Statistical Office—United Nations Vietnam—United Nations Millennium Development Goals Achievement Fund.

Vietnam National Census Steering Committee. 1991. *Kết quả điều tra toàn diện—Completed Census Results*, vol. 2. Hanoi: Central Census Steering Committee.

Vietnam National Committee for Women's Progress. 2005. *Báo cáo đánh giá việc thực hiện và tác động của dự án "Tăng tỷ lệ nữ tham gia hội đồng nhân dân nhiệm kỳ 2004–09"* [Evaluation Report on the Implementation and Effects of the Project "To Increase the Percentage of Women in People's Councils-2004–09 Term"]. Hanoi: National Committee for Women's Progress.

Vietnam Population and Housing Census Steering Committee. 2010. *The 2009 Vietnam Population and Housing Census: Completed Results*. Hanoi: Statistical Publishing House.

Vũ, Phương Anh. 2008. "Gender Stereotypes in Story Textbooks for Primary School Students in Vietnam." University of Oslo, Faculty of Education, Sweden.

Vũ Tuấn Huy, and Deborah Carr. 2004. "Phân công lao động nội trợ trong gia đình [Division of Domestic Labor in the Family]." In *Gia đình trong tấm gương xã hội học*, edited by Mai Quỳnh Nam, 121–40. Hanoi: Nhà xuất bản Khoa học xã hội.

Werner, Jayne. 1981. "Women, Socialism, and the Economy of Wartime Vietnam, 1960–1975." *Studies in Comparative Communism* 14: 165–90.

———. 2002. "Gender, Household, and State: Renovation (*Đổi Mới*) as Social Process in Viet Nam." In *Gender, Household, State: Đổi Mới in Vietnam*, edited by Jayne Werner and Danièle Bélanger. Ithaca, NY: Cornell University Southeast Asia Program.

Wong, Monica. 1994. "Poverty and Ethnic Minorities in Vietnam." Education and Social Policy Discussion Paper. Washington, D.C.: World Bank.

World Bank. 2008. *How Do Women Fare in Education, Employment, and Health? A Gender Analysis of the 2006 Vietnam Household Living Standard Survey*. Hanoi: World Bank Vietnam.

———. 2011. *Vietnam Country Gender Assessment*. Hanoi: World Bank Vietnam.

Zhou, Lei, and Duong Bich Hanh. 2011. "Sex Work in the Sino-Vietnamese Borderlands." *Asian Anthropology* 10: 81–99.

CHAPTER 2

Rethinking Vietnamese Women's Property Rights and the Role of Ancestor Worship in Premodern Society: Beyond the Dichotomies

Miyazawa Chihiro

Introduction

In this chapter, I focus on women's property rights and the role of ancestor worship in premodern Vietnam. Vietnam has traditionally been an agricultural country; thus land has been an important resource, even for women. Women have had property rights, including land rights, since at least the fifteenth century. There is much historical evidence attesting to this, such as inscriptions (Tran 2008, 63; Momoki 2011, 112). Vietnamese women could become landlords (Ngô Kim Chung & Nguyên Đức Nghinh 1987, 197–8), and they donated their lands to pagodas (Trương Hữu Quýnh 1983, 143; Tran 2008, 63–6). Women's property rights and the role of ancestor worship are closely related to state law, local customs, and the family. Women made good of these rights in seeking their own survival in the family, the household, and society. In this respect, it is crucial to investigate women's property rights and the role of ancestor worship in order to examine women's agency in the private and public spheres.

Studies on Vietnamese women's property rights were numerous in the colonial period. The French colonial government carried out research on popular customs in relation to family, succession, and property for ancestor worship in Tonkin (the northern part of Vietnam) at the end of the 1920s to codify civil law. This research was done by conducting interviews with several French juridical specialists, Vietnamese senior officials, and intellectuals, but not by documental or fieldwork research.[1] Although their information is useful, its credibility is limited. Nevertheless, many scholars wrote theses based on this study without conducting their own documental or field surveys in rural areas (see, for example, Lustéguy 1949 [1935]; Pompeï 1951; Lingat 1952). There were studies on Vietnamese women's property rights in the precolonial period based on historical documents (Deloustal 1911; Makino 1980 [1934]; Niida 1954;

---

1 The results of this research were published in 1930 (Protectorat du Tonkin 1930).

Nguyễn & Tạ 1987; Yu 1990; Tran 2006; Tran 2008), but most of them depended on codified laws. Among them, only Nhung Tuyet Tran examines historical documents written by Vietnamese people in the premodern era. However, Tran's study also has its limitations: her study only examines a quantity of land owned by men and women, and discusses the inequality of property rights between them. In this chapter, I will examine instead both women's property rights and the role of ancestor worship in order to gain a better understanding of women's status.

Before beginning my discussion, I explain the long-term changes in social structures that occurred in East Asia from the tenth century onwards, when neo-Confucianism became the ruling principle of the state, society, and family in this region. With the increase in population and the disappearance of non-cultivated land in East Asia (China, Korea, and Japan), agriculture became labor-intensive between the tenth and eighteenth centuries. Throughout this process, an East Asian peasant society was established in which families cultivated small plots of land. To adapt to this change, East Asian countries adopted neo-Confucianism. In China, patrilineal lineage had solidified since the time of the Sung Dynasty (Miyajima 1994a, 92–3). In Korea, the names of daughters disappeared from genealogical accounts; at the same time, eldest sons were given priority over daughters' inheritance (Miyajima 1994b, 147–150, 161).

A similar transformation happened in Vietnam (Momoki 1997). The Lê Dynasty (1428–1789) and the Nguyễn Dynasty (1802–1945) recognized neo-Confucianism as the principle of the state and strengthened it to establish their regimes (Nguyen Tai Thu 2006, 165–9, 223–4). However, in contrast to Korea, daughters' names were not excluded from genealogy; more importantly, equal inheritance rights between men and women were preserved in Vietnam. A bilateral character was also preserved, in that daughters were kept as representatives of the family in ancestral worship as well as in branches of patrilineal lineage after marriage. Although the structural changes in Asian societies occurred simultaneously beyond national borders, these changes differed between societies.[2]

---

2   I would like to thank Mrs. Nguyễn Thị Oanh and Mrs. Hằng (Institute of Hán Nôm, Hà Nội) for helping my work at the institute in 1995 and 2012 go smoothly. I thank Professor Ochiai Emiko, Professor Shimao Minoru, Professor Matsuo Nobuyuki, Professor Okada Masashi, and Dr. Ueda Shinya for sharing their articles and documents. I thank Professor Suenari Michio for commenting on my draft, as well as Professor Kobayashi Yasuko, Professor Ohashi Atsuko, Professor Yoshihara Kazuo, and Dr. Ueda Shinya for commenting on my presentation at a meeting of the Japan Society for Southeast Asian Studies in 2014. I also thank Professor Shimao Minoru for revising my English translations of Chinese texts.

Reexamining the Myth of Equal Property Rights and the Autonomy Thesis

As Bélanger (2009, 10–2) summarizes, many scholars in Vietnam and other countries have pointed out the gap between theory and practice of Vietnamese family in the presocialist period. In theory, the Vietnamese family followed the idealized Confucian model. Principles of hierarchy between genders and generations are central. However, in practice, the Vietnamese family and kinship system seemed much more complex and flexible than the Confucian model. The question about women's property rights is central because, in the Confucian model, only sons can continue the family line and inherit the paternal estate. If daughters can inherit the paternal estate, it is a deviation from the Confucian model. Many scholars have insisted that property rights were equal between women and men in the premodern Vietnamese society (see, for example, Makino [1934] 1980; Niida 1954, 211, 218, 219–34; Tran 1990, 274–83) and have argued that this equality was based on the bilateral character of the premodern Vietnamese family (Taylor 1983, 13, 77, 284; Yu 1999, 215–31). They use state laws and regulations as evidence, asserting that Quốc Triều Hình Luật (QTHL, 国朝刑律, or Lê Code)[3] stipulated equal division of household property between sons and daughters[4] and that, if a father died with no sons, state law permitted the eldest daughter to inherit "fire and incense" (*hương hỏa*, 香火),[5] or property (Taylor 1983, 77; Nguyễn & Tạ 1987, vol. I, 81–84; Yu 1990).[6]

---

3   Quốc Triều Hình Luật (QTHL) was the most important legal document in the Lê dynasty. However, there was considerable controversy over the date and process of codification, promulgation, and revision of this document. Nguyễn and Tạ conclude that the bulk of this code was compiled and promulgated from the time of Emperor Lê Thái Tổ to 1449, the reign of Emperor Lê Nhân Tông, but later emperors, especially Lê Thánh Tông (1460–97), also contributed enormously to the codification process (Nguyễn & Tạ 1987, vol. I, 19–20). QTHL borrowed from the Chinese T'ang Code and the Ming Code. However, it also had many articles that maintained Vietnamese popular customs and practices. Of its 722 articles, 412 had features unique to Vietnamese legal traditions (Nguyễn & Tạ 1987, vol. I, 54–6).

4   QTHL Article 388 is recognized as a stipulation for daughters' equal property rights.

5   This was special property for ancestor worship. The stipulation of QTHL was different from its management in practice. See the next footnote and the discussion in this chapter for further detail on this.

6   QTHL Article 391 stipulates: "The management of the *hương hỏa* property shall be entrusted to the eldest son or, failing that, to the eldest daughter" (Nguyễn & Tạ 1987, vol. I, 204).

However, Nhung Tuyet Tran (2006, 130–31) asserts that this is just a myth. Reexamining the codified laws—QTHL and Hồng Đức Thiện Chính Thư (洪德善政書)[7]—she concludes:

> The law (QTHL) never guaranteed daughters equal rights over household division. Rather, the language of law specifically invested parents with the duty to bequest property equally among their sons, and their male offspring with duty to their parents' will. The logic implicit in these regulations is one of maintaining the male line, while daughters inherit household property subject to the will of the parents and the power dynamics in the family.

There are several reasons behind her conclusions. First, although Article 388 of QTHL forms the basis for the interpretation that daughters enjoyed an equal claim over household property, this was the case only in the absence of a will or testament of the parents. If the parents left such a testament (*chúc thư*, 嘱書) which stipulated unequal division between brothers and sisters, then it shall be followed (Tran 2008, 48–9). Second, even if household property is divided among brothers and sisters, the statute uses the phrase "to divide among" (*tương phần*, 相分), not "to divide equally" (*quân phần*, 匀分)[8] (Tran 2008, 48–9). Third, a reexamination of the Lê Code and legal cases related to succession reveals that the law complied with the principle of succession. If a daughter inherited her father's property, she could only keep it in her lifetime; upon her death, the property and religious duties associated with it were returned to her father's lineage, precluding her from passing the maintenance of those duties to her children, regardless of whether they were male or female (Tran 2008, 59). Fourth, testaments and wills reveal that local customs gave priority to the property rights of sons. Tran introduces examples of testaments and

---

7 Hồng Đức Thiện Chính Thư is a collection of laws, decrees, and summaries of cases pertaining not only to the Hồng Đức period (1470–97) but also to several other reign periods of the Lê dynasty and even the Mạc Dynasty. It was probably compiled in the period of the Mạc Dynasty, after 1543. Thus the title of this collection is misleading (Nguyễn & Tạ 1987, vol. I, 20).
8 However, Shimao Minoru points out that in the beginning of the eighteenth century, the author of *Tiệp Kính Gia Lễ* commented on equal inheritance between men and women. "In our kingdom, land is inherited equally by men and women"(如我南国、係男女其田産等物均分相斉)(Shimao 2008, 224; 2011, 60, 84). Shimao asserts that most Vietnamese people in the premodern era recognized equal inheritance between men and women as their own custom (2008, 227–8).

wills from the eighteenth century, in which parents wanted to give more to sons than daughters or left nothing to their daughters (Tran 2008, 51–5). By referring to recent studies about women's property rights in China and Korea, Tran successfully broadens the perspective on this issue. At the same time, by making use of testaments, she reveals what people really thought and did.

In this chapter, I provide additional insight based on my article on the same topic (Miyazawa 1996) and several new documents I acquired through research in Vietnam and Japan. I argue, first, that some parents requested that all of their children (including daughters) should keep inherited property forever and that all children participated in ancestral worship activities and helped one another when organizing ancestral worship activities. Tran points out that testaments define inheritance practices much better than prescriptive legal sources, and that wills and testaments demonstrate that daughters did not enjoy equal inheritance in practice (Tran 2006, 133–34). However, the examples of testaments that she introduces are limited to several unequal-inheritance cases. According to my research on testaments in the nineteenth century, some parents wanted to divide household property equally between sons and daughters, though this was not completely equal and, as I show below, daughters were sometimes excluded from inheritance of "fire and incense." However, they enjoyed rights to another type of land for ancestor worship. Second, as discussed below, daughters in Vietnam often had the responsibility and duty to worship patrilineal ancestors even though they were not heirs and were married. These responsibility and duty were clearly written in the testaments. In a sense, daughters were representatives of their families, sublineages, and lineages, as well as connected to their communities, the state, and even heaven and the other world where deceased ancestors were living, which means their lives were not restricted to "housekeeping" (*nội trợ*, 內助). This is crucial to our understanding of the public and private spheres for Vietnamese women.

Testaments in the Nineteenth Century

Article 390 of the QTHL stipulates that "a father and a mother should make their testaments when they feel themselves approaching old age." Article 366 explains that

> a testator or a person entering into a contract who does not ask officials or elders of his village to serve as witnesses for his will or contract shall receive eighty strokes from the heavy stick and be fined in proportion to

the importance of the case. Those who are literate may draft documents themselves.

NGUYỄN & TẠ 1987, 196, 204

Signatures or fingerprinting were required of both the person who gave property to descendants and those who received it, even in cases of ordinary women. In Vietnam, mothers and wives could also make wills; daughters used their fingerprints to sign these documents as recipients of their ancestors' legacies. The representatives of the lineage signed their names as witnesses. The testament was copied and given to every person who received property so that everyone had proof of the contract. In this respect, testaments were official public documents.

Case Study 1: A Testament[9]

This case is an example of equal division according to a testament. Lê Khắc Địch (黎克廸) and his wife Đỗ Thị Sâm (杜氏森), who lived in Hà Đông province, issued a testament on the twenty-sixth day of the eighth month in the lunar calendar in the fifteenth year of Emperor Tự Đức (1862). They had one son, five daughters, and one adopted son (dưỡng tử). The testament recorded that the total amount of "fire and incense" was one sào twelve thước thirteen khẩu.[10] Trường Tùng (the only son) was not appointed as heir in the testament, and two daughters (Lê Thị Cưu and Lê Thị Đạn) were chosen to inherit even more than their only brother (see Table 2.1). In addition, there are accounts for both sons' and daughters' responsibility to give offerings to two specific ancestors on a certain day and place and with a certain amount of offerings at the eldest son's house. This means that sons and daughters have rights over the inheritance of their parents' property as well as duties to worship ancestors of their natal family. The implications are that both "fire and incense" and the inheritance of ordinary property came with duties of ancestor worship, which is unique to Vietnam. In premodern China only sons could be heirs. Sons

---

9   Chúc thư. This testament is document number R528 in Digital Collections of the Vietnamese Nôm Preservation Foundation, NLVNPF-0555, http://lib.nomfoundation.org.

10 Generally speaking, in Northern Vietnam, one mẫu is 3,600 square meters, one sào is 360 square meters, and one thước is 24 square meters. One khẩu may be one-tenth or one-fifteenth of one thước. Those measurements were not the same in each village.

TABLE 2.1   *The Testament of Lê Khắc Địch and Đỗ Thị Sâm*

	Rice field	Rice seedling field	Mulberry field	Autumn rice field	Total
Lê Trường Tùng 黎長松 (the eldest son)	1S8T 1S5T 10T	7T5	3T5	0	4S4T
Lê Thị Cừu 黎氏鳩	2S7T5 1S	1S	5T	0	4S12T5
Lê Thị A[a]	2S 1S	10T	3T5	3T	4S1T5
Lê Thị Đạn 黎氏憚	1S8T 1S5T	10T 10T	3T	5T	4S11T
Lê Thị Gỡ 黎氏撑	1S10T 1S	1S	3T5	3T5	4S2T
Lê Thị Trạch 黎氏擇	1S8T 1S5T 1S	0	3T5	4T	4S5T5
Lê Văn Vị 黎文謂 (an adopted son)	1S 1S 1S	0	5T	0	3S5T

[a]   *Chữ nôm* is not clear.

inherited family property and had a duty to fulfill ancestral worship duties (Kawamura 1988, 4–5; Guan 2009, 141–42). Daughters had rights to inherit their father's property by the so-called "half-share law" in the T'ang and Sung Dynasties (Aoki 2012, 138–141).[11] However, daughters rarely had duties to fulfill

---

11   There has been a long and complicated dispute over the half-share law. Recently, Aoki concluded that the existence of the half-share law could not be denied (Aoki 2014, 152–9). As Tran points out, Chinese daughters enjoyed a fair amount of property rights (2008, 47). However, a woman's share was at most one-half of her brothers' share in Chinese law (Aoki 2014, 137).

their natal ancestor worship. A family without a son in China had to appoint an adopted son to continue ancestor worship even if there were unmarried daughters at home.[12] On the other hand, in Vietnam, Hồng Đức Thiện Chính Thư stipulated that "fire and incense" should be entrusted to the eldest daughter in case the family is without an eldest son during her lifetime (Nguyễn & Vũ 1959, 16). As Suenari Michio (1995, 17–20) points out, in premodern Vietnamese society, after several generations passed, the responsibility for worship was not always distributed to the eldest son but to other descendants. There were even some cases where a daughter had the responsibility to worship a particular ancestor, although that ancestor's altar was not in her husband's house. An example of this involved Nguyễn Bá Đa, who lived in Đông Ngạc village near the Hanoi citadel in 1851 and who made a testament that stipulated the duty of each child. The duties were divided up so that the sixth daughter, Nguyễn Thị Ngoạn, would give offerings at the ancestral hall of her natal family on the death anniversaries of her ancestors on the twenty-fifth day in the third month and the third day of the sixth month.[13]

Case Study 2: The Nguyễn Lineage Testament in An Cảnh Village[14]

This case is another example of equal division. This testament was issued on the twenty-fourth day of the twelfth month in the lunar calendar in the twelve years of Emperor Thành Thái (1900). In this case, the mother (Nguyễn Thị Phiến) arranged an almost equal division for each child's main share of inheritance (本分), including the daughters. Similar to the previous example, no sons were appointed as heirs of "fire and incense." This testament is also unique because "fire and incense," which Phiến's two elder brothers (Nguyễn Văn Kỳ and Nguyễn Văn Chấn) and a sister (Nguyễn Thị Miến) owed, was passed on from Phiến to her three sons. This inheritance case does not align with Tran's assertion that even if a daughter could maintain "fire and incense," she could do so only in her lifetime (Tran 2008, 60). It should be also noted, however, that Phiến's daughters were excluded from inheriting a part of this "fire and incense" property.

12　A famous judge in the Sung Dynasty era ordered that a daughter without any brothers was to take over ancestor worship activities after the death of her father and mother (Kawamura 1988, 17, Tkahashi 2006, 296–8). Both Kawamura (1988, 6–7, 17) and Takahashi (2006, 296–9) point out that this was an exceptional or new case.

13　*Đông Ngạc Village Nguyễn Bá Đa Testament* (*Đông Ngạc Xã Nguyễn Bá Đa Chúc Thư*, 東鄂社阮伯多囑書), preserved in Hán Nôm Institute, Hanoi. A. 1771.

14　*Nguyễn Lineage Testament in An Cảnh Village* (*An Cảnh Xã Nguyễn Tộc Chúc Thư* 安境社阮族囑書), preserved in Hán Nôm Institute, Hanoi. A. 1978.

At the end of this testament, the daughters signed with their fingerprints along with their mother and brothers, as well as witnesses from their lineage and relatives through marriage. All representatives were title-holders, including an ex–deputy canton chief, a military-unit chief, an old man, and an ex–village chief. Finally, as official witnesses, the incumbent village chief and deputy canton chief authorized this testament. Daughters swore an oath to keep their mother's testament for their lineage, in-laws, community, and state.

Case Study 3: Phạm Gia An's Testament in Đông Ngạc Village[15]

On the sixth day of the fifth month in the fourth year of Emperor Tự Đức (1851), a testament was made by a wealthy landlord who lived in a village near the center of Hanoi. Using this case as an example, we can observe the bilateral-like character of the premodern Vietnamese family,[16] which Tran denies as just a "myth." The testators had a strong interest in having both sons and daughters continue to commemorate the husband and his late wife's death anniversaries. Thus the husband (Phạm Gia An) gave his children the rights to the land.

> [Original text]
> 懷德府慈廉縣春早総東鄂社、范嘉安、自念行年衰老、凡身後一切家事所當分囑、俾子孫分承、遵爲此立囑書、所有私土壹區、連池壹口、該壹高柒尺五寸五分、在本社民居蕚巷內、居宅壹座柒間、置爲祠堂、幷祭堂壹座五間、使之永世奉祀、並有私田在本社地分肆拾貳畝拾參尺、及本縣(省略)田共貳百柒拾畝陸高拾尺九寸二分、兹將本社田肆拾畝參高貳寸內、參拾畝參尺、置爲忌田、供諸忌臘、拾貳畝(一字不明)寸、置爲祀田、供諸祭用、又別置墓田在小旺所、拾尺柒寸、存貳百參拾畝五高拾貳尺貳寸貳分、均分子女柒分、及賜故嫡孫次嫡孫各欵、另有分書留照、所有合行事宜、逐欵詳計如有左、這遺下土宅田產、係是積年同與故正室潘氏辛苦得之、爾子女各宜敦睦相保世守、以承祭祀、若恣賣忌田廢欠忌臘礼、坐以不孝之罪、其詞分寫七道、交與子孫各執壹道爲照、一、祠堂壹座⋯長支居住、幷祭堂⋯並交長子范光晟世守奉祀、倘有壞漏、是年本祠堂二忌、量随減殺、仍取粟錢柒支、協全修理、俾得永固⋯

---

15 *Phạm Gia An's Testament in Đông Ngạc Village* (Đông Ngạc Xã Phạm Gia An Chúc Thư 東鄂社范嘉安囑書), preserved in Hán Nôm Institute, Hanoi. A. 1739.

16 I do not think that the Vietnamese traditional family was perfectly bilateral. However, as I will discuss below, especially in case study 4, sometimes ancestors' property was passed on to their daughters' children and grandchildren. It means that the property was passed on beyond the borders of the inner lineage (the father's lineage) and outer lineage (the lineages of married-out daughters' husbands).

[Translation]

I, Phạm Gia An, living in Đông Ngạc Village, Xuân Tảo Canton, Từ Liêm District, Hoài Đức Prefecture, having considered my old age and weakness, issue this testament to divide all the property to my descendants after my death. I have one lot of private land about one *sào* seven *thước* five *thốn* three *phần*. In the people's residential area of the village, I have one house to use as an ancestral worship hall (祠堂) and one festival hall (祭堂). I also have land of forty-two *mẫu* thirteen *thước* and have property in other villages in the same district. The total amount is 270 *mẫu* six *sào* ten *thước* nine *thốn* two *phần*. In Đông Ngạc village, I own forty *mẫu* three *sào* [the word is not clear] *thước* two *thốn* of rice fields. Thirty *mẫu* three *thước* of these are designated as anniversary rice fields (*kỵ điền*, 忌田)[17] to organize death anniversaries and festivals. Twelve *mẫu* [the word is not clear] *thốn* are allocated as worship rice fields (*tự điền*, 祀田), and ten *thước* seven *thốn* are allocated as tomb rice fields (*mộ điền*, 墓田) at another place. The rest is 230 *mẫu* five *sào* twelve *thước* two *thốn* two *phần*. I indicated equal division among seven children as well as other points (about this division) related to the principle grandson and other grandsons. I distributed copies of the testament to each as proof. I and my late principal wife from the Phan lineage had bought these houses and lands with great difficulty, so you, every child, must be harmonious in preserving these properties and continuing to worship. If not, you would be punished for not being pious. I have now written a testament and made one copy given to each of you as proof. Total: One ancestral hall, the eldest family branch (*chi*, 支) lives in…a festival hall…would be given to the eldest child [sic] Phạm Quang Thịnh, who must commit to worship. If the ancestral hall is damaged, payments for two death anniversaries of parents at the hall will be diminished depending on the (financial) situations of each *chi*, and seven family branches will sell rice to cover the costs of repair and cooperate to rebuild the hall for eternity (citation from page 1–a to 2–b).

---

17 According to Protectorat du Tonkin, *kỵ điền* were rice fields created in order to celebrate funeral anniversaries for a constituent, or for their family members. These were entrusted to a grand-parent or to a branch of the family. Being different from *hương hỏa*, legally their management belonged not to a single beneficiary but to all members of the family to which it was entrusted in rotation (*luân-phiên*). It could not be given away. However, it could be sold or exchanged if the family to which it was entrusted agreed collectively (Protectorat du Tonkin 1930, 179).

As the testament shows, Phạm Gia An was a very rich landlord. In regard to only real estate used for ancestral worship and festivals, he owned thirty *mẫu* three *thước* of anniversary rice fields, twelve *mẫu* of *tự điền*, ten *thước* seven *thốn* of *mộ điền*, one ancestral worship hall, and one festival hall.

He made a testament that anniversary rice fields in the village were to be divided equally among all of the children, including two daughters and a grandson. The testament says that

[Original text]
一、忌田在本社地分、壹百柒拾捌所、参拾畝参尺、交與子女范氏睿、范光晟、范氏姵、范光酉、范光興、范光亮、及故范光就之子范光彙、以次輪流耕作。每年二支、均爲甲乙弍分、兄娣耕作、弟妹耕作、乙分每分拾五畝零、遞年所得粟、平價每畝拾五貫、共錢弍百拾弍五[18]貫、內除二務租、每畝錢四貫共錢六拾貫、存供忌臘各節

[Translation]
Anniversary rice fields in this village, thirty *mẫu* three *thước* with 178 parcels, shall be given to Phạm Thị Quyến (the eldest daughter), Phạm Quang Thịnh (the eldest son), Phạm Thị Dâu (the second daughter), Phạm Quang Dậu (the second son), Phạm Quang Hưng (the fourth son), Phạm Quang Lượng (the fifth son), and Phạm Quang Vị (the second son of the late third son Phạm Quang Tựu). They cultivate crops in rotation. Every year, two family branches divide anniversary rice fields to the first (*giáp*) part and the second (*ất*) part equally. Brothers and sisters cultivate the second part with fifteen *mẫu*. Every year the harvest of rice is to occur. The ordinary price is fifteen *quán* per *mẫu*. The total is 225 *quán*.[18] Of this, except four *quán* per *mẫu*, or the total of sixty *quán* for biannual tax payments, the rest will be paid for organizing death anniversaries and winter rituals. (citation from page 4–a)

Anniversary rice fields were not to be given to each child and grandson but to seven family branches (*chi*). Each family branch would cultivate anniversary rice fields to pay for death anniversaries and festivals in rotation.

In general, "family branch" means a sublineage of the Confucian patrilineal lineage, *nội tộc* (內族) or *dòng họ*. However, the meaning of "family branch" here is broader. For example, in the testament, An wrote:

---

18   The original document was incorrect about the order of the number. Twenty-five (弍拾五) must be correct.

[Original text]
一、臘日遞年定以拾弐月弐拾日辰牌、柒支各一人會在祠堂、同行省掃、列先墳墓、若某支不就省墓、示罰、如忌日遲緩不同行之咎…

[Translation]
Every year, the winter festival day shall be on the twentieth day of the twelfth lunar month. One person of every seven family branches shall meet at the ancestral hall and visit the tombs of ancestors to clean them. If any family branches chooses not to go, this will be punished similarly to crimes such as delaying performing rituals at death anniversaries. (citation from page 7–b)

Seven children were seen as the initial person of each family branch, so that a family branch includes the lineage members of a daughter's husband who were not seen as members of Phạm Gia An's lineage. If two daughters had already married and could not participate in the ancestral worship activities of their natal family, a member of their husband's family had to participate on their behalf. In addition, An requested the cooperation of seven family branches and asked them to distribute labor and payment for ancestral worship activities. If any family branches had trouble accomplishing this, other family branches had to help. In the testament, he says:

> First, if the new ancestral worship hall is damaged, depending on which family branches pay more or less, then seven family branches operate and sell rice so that it can be restored, preventing it from being stolen and sold (citation from page 8–b).

> Second, after death anniversaries, inner (i.e., patrilineal) lineages (*nội tộc*) and outer (i.e., matrilineal) lineages (*ngoại tộc*) should have friendly meals together. Older and younger people must respect each other. If anyone is drunk and says impolite things so that officials have to punish them, then the seven family branches have to share the costs (citation from page 10–a to 10b).

The first (*giáp*) and the second (*ất*) parts of anniversary rice fields would be divided into seven small parts and each given a number from one to seven. Each of the 180 parcels was recorded in detail. For example, details included the seller's name, the time of An and his wife's purchase, its location in the village in relation to other people's land or homes, the parcel size, and the length of each side, so that we can know the size of each small segment (see Table 2.2).

TABLE 2.2 *Ky Điền of Phạm Gia An in his testament*

	Size	The number of parcels
Giáp One (甲壹分)	2M1S12T2Th	10
Two (甲貳分)	2M0S10T5Th	12
Three (甲參分)	2M2S3T3Th	12
Four (甲肆分)	2M0S3T7Th	10
Five (甲五分)	0M2S9T5Th5P	16
Six (甲陸分)	2M1S1T1Th	13
Seven (甲柒分)	2M0S12T3Th	20
Subtotal	12M9S7T5Th5P[a]	93
Ất One (乙壹分)	2M1S8T6Th5P	10
Two (乙貳分)	2M3S0T9Th	10
Three (乙參分)	2M1S4T6Th	11
Four (乙肆分)	2M0S4T6Th	14
Five (乙五分)	2M1S14T8Th	14
Six (乙陸分)	2M0S7T7Th	14
Seven (乙柒分)	2M1S4T3Th	14
Subtotal	15M0S0T5Th5P[b]	87
Total	27M9S3T2Th0P[c]	180[d]

a This is my calculation. The original text has many mistakes.
b Author calculated because account in the testament is not clear.
c According to the testament, the total amount of *ky điền* is 30M3T. The original text, however, has many mistakes. Thus we cannot know the correct total amount. Nevertheless, we can observe the testator's strong will to divide the property equally among the descendants.
d Phạm Gia An wrote that the total number of parcels was 178. However, I could find only 180 parcels.

With the exception of the fifth part of the first group, each part was of similar size. Every year, each family branch would be allocated one portion from the first part and one from the second part, and in turn, each family branch cultivated them. In addition, they had to pay for ancestral worship activities. Thus, it can be said that the equal rights between sons and daughters in this case included: (1) the equal right of cultivation, but not ownership, and (2) the equal right for the chance of cultivation, but not of parcel size. In this case, the father stipulated that ordinary rice fields should be divided equally among all the children, including daughters. In addition, anniversary rice fields were not distributed to each child, but instead the father arranged for each child to cultivate it in rotation; the daughters and their in-laws (i.e., their husbands' family members) could have access to it.[19]

The most interesting point is that the rights for anniversary rice fields would be inherited by the daughters' children, the "outer grandchildren" (*cháu ngoài*), who belonged to the "outer lineages" of Phạm Gia An. As noted previously, An expected that his descendants would keep his property forever. If this testament was realized, An's family would have a bilateral-like character. By examining other cases of the Phạm lineage, I will describe how the testament was realized in the case studies below.

Case Study 4: The Đông Ngạc Village Phạm Lineage Distribution Agreement

This case illustrates the importance of daughters as beneficiaries of inheritance from their fathers. At the same time, it illustrates that they, as wives or mothers, passed on their fathers' inheritance to their husbands' lineages. The case also shows how descendants (including those who belonged to the outer lineage) tried to realize his testament more than half a century after his death. The original document was not completely preserved; the first page was torn.[20] By reading the genealogy of the Phạm lineage, *Phạm Thị Thế Phả*, we can see that the distribution agreement in this document was written for Phạm Gia Vũ's (范嘉宇) property, which was given to his descendants on the twenty-fourth day of the second lunar month of the eleventh year of Emperor Gia Long (1812). Phạm Gia Vũ was Phạm Gia An's great-grandfather's brother-in-law. Vũ's father, one of the most successful candidates in his lineage, Phạm Quang Trạch (范光宅), took his older brother's second son, Hoàn, as an adopted son (*quá phòng tử*, 過房子)[21] in 1676, when Trạch was twenty-three years old.[22] I suspect that Vũ's property was not initially divided in 1812 because Vũ's

---

19 Phạm Gia An had another category of rice fields called *tự điền* for death anniversaries and festivals in other villages, all of which would be given to the eldest son, Thịnh. As a whole, An's property was not divided equally among sons and daughters, even though he insisted on equality in Đông Ngạc village.
20 *Đông Ngạc Xã Phạm Tộc Giao Thư*, Hán Nôm Institute, Hanoi, A. 1772.
21 In China, *guò feng zi* often means 'heir' (Katakura 1987, 456). However, regardless of whether Hoàn was Trạch's heir or not, accounts in genealogies of the Phạm lineage were ambiguous and this adoption was against the rule of order in Confucianism.
22 *Phạm Thị Thế Phả*, Hán Nôm Institute, Hanoi, A. 1197, 133-b.

signature was not at the end of the document, as is traditional in testaments. Moreover, Vũ died in 1757,[23] when the distribution of his property should have been decided for the first time. However, in 1812, fifty-five years after Vũ's death, his descendants redistributed property to continue worship for him.

The twenty people (all male) who signed the document included one son, eleven grandsons, and eight great-grandsons. The eleven grandsons included Đào Duy Hiền, Đào Duy X (the eldest son and second son of Vũ's second daughter Úc),[24] and Nguyễn Thời Mẫn (the eldest son of Vũ's third daughter Trừu). One of the great-grandsons was Đoàn Văn Tấu (the eldest grandson of Vũ's eldest daughter).

Ten *mẫu* of anniversary rice fields would be given to the sons' family branches. They were responsible for cultivating crops in rotation, paying taxes, and organizing death anniversary rituals and festivals for the harmony of lineage (citation from page 1-ab). "Of two *thước* seven *thốn*, rice would be given to the chief of 'outer lineage' in Phú Diễn Village." On the sixth day of the first lunar month every year, "any family in charge of anniversary fields has to go to the village and visit the tomb of the principal mother, purify it, and offer the ritual" (citation from page 7-b).[25] Another piece of property, five *mẫu* four *sào* four *thước* seven *thốn*, was divided into eleven family branches (eight sons and three daughters) equally.

Each of the eleven family branches would receive between four *sào* twelve *thước* (sixth son's family branch) and five *sào* zero *thước* seven *thốn* (the eldest daughter's branch). In this case, the descendants (both inner and outer lineage) had tried to maintain their grandfather's property for ancestral worship for more than half a century.

---

23 According to genealogies of the Phạm lineage, Vũ was born in 1690 (the year of Canh Ngọ) and died in 1757 (the year of Đinh Sửu) (*Phạm Lineage Genealogy, Phạm Thị Tộc Phả* 范氏族譜, 36ab; *Đông Ngạc Village Phạm Lineage Genealogy, Đông Ngạc Phạm Tộc Phả* 東鄂范族譜, 42ab). These genealogies are available on CD-ROM, *Gia Phả Các Dòng Họ ở Đông Ngạc. Từ Liêm-Hà Nội* (*Genealogies of Lineages in Đông Ngạc Village. Từ Liêm District, Hà Nội*). Dr. Okada Masashi, one of the editors of this CD-ROM, shared the PDF data with me.

24 Chữ Nôm is 㗂. I cannot find it in dictionaries.

25 …共肆高拾弐尺捌寸、內拾弐尺柒寸粟子交與富演社外族長。逓年正月初六日…本族某支監守忌田者伊社場頻処。具嫡母墓行洒省禮。

Case Study 5: The Phạm Lineage Council on Donation Regulation in Đông Ngạc Village[26]

This case illustrates how long descendants (including those of both the inner and outer lineage) continued to commemorate their ancestors, although the memories of people in the outer lineage were weaker than those of people in the inner lineage. On the first month of the first year of Emperor Đồng Khánh (1886), in Đông Ngạc village, the council of the Phạm lineage made regulations about the ancestral worship hall.

[Original text]
同慶元年正月日、懷德府慈廉縣東鄂社、河静督學范□先公祠堂、仝各支等爲会議給錢詞事。緣本祠堂年前已置忌田、以供忌臘、但迩來間有年税粟所入不足以供、且偶有應需亦難取卞。茲竊擬凡繋屬□本祠堂者、應各随情給錢多者拾貫以上、少者壹貫間、或加多此數、或嗣後再加增給者尤好。此会議…其某名氏給錢列計于後、仍寫爲五道、每支執一道、以爲永照者、茲會詞。

[Translation]
[About] the ex-director of the school in Hà Tĩnh province, Duke Phạm's[27] worship hall, all of the family branches organized the council in order to decide on payments. Anniversary rice fields were previously donated to this hall for anniversaries and festivals. However, there have recently been years of poor crops. Thus, it is difficult to satisfy demands…meeting at this worship hall. All the people related to this worship hall, according to his/her situation, those who can pay a lot should pay more than ten *quán*, and those who can pay less should pay one *quán* or add several

---

26 This document is Đông Ngạc Village Phạm Lineage Council about Donation Regulation (*Đông Ngạc Xã Phạm Tộc Hội Nghị Cấp Tiền Từ* 東鄂社范族會議給錢詞), preserved in Hán Nôm Institute, Hà Nội, A.1778.

27 According to the Phạm lineage genealogy, this ex-director of the school in Hà Tĩnh was Phạm Quang Nguyên (范光元). He passed the examination in the sixth year of Emperor Gia Long (1807) and became an official (*The List of Mandarins in Từ Liêm District, Từ Liêm Đăng Khoa Lộc* 慈廉登科録, Digital Collections of the Vietnamese Nôm Preservation Foundation, NLVNPF-1244, R990, 22, http://lib.nomfoundation.org). However, when he worked as an official in Quảng Nam province (next to Đà Nẵng port), "a small Western country" (perhaps France) came there in spite of the closed-door policy. He was involved in this accident and was demoted to the director of a school in Hà Tĩnh (*Phạm Lineage Generations, Phạm Thị Thế Phả* 范氏世譜, 71ab).

quán. If it becomes possible to pay more afterward, it is acceptable. The council…recorded the names of those who donated money and calculated the amount, wrote five copies, and gave one copy to each lineage as proof.

At the end of the written regulations there were fifty-seven names, of which thirty-four were male and twenty-three were female. (See Table 2.3 for the donation amounts, the distinction between "inner" and "outer" lineage, and generational differences.)

TABLE 2.3 *Donations to the worship hall for Phạm Quang Nguyên in 1886 by Phạm lineage*

Generation	Amount of donation (*quán*)	Number of people	Subtotal (*quán*)
Son	30	1	30
Daughter	0	0	0
Grandson	20	3	60
	10	3	30
	1	1	1
Granddaughter	10	2	20
	6	1	6
	5	2	10
Great-grandson	15.5	2	31
	10	6	60
	5.5	1	5.5
	5	3	15
	3	2	6
	1	4	4
	less than 1	1	less than 1
Great-granddaughter	10	5	50
	5	1	5
	2	1	2
	1	3	3
	less than 1	3	less than 3
Great-great-grandson	10	1	10
	1	1	1
Total		47	352.5

TABLE 2.3   *Donations to the worship hall for Phạm Quang Nguyên in 1886 by Phạm lineage* (cont.)

Generation	Amount of donation (*quán*)	Number of people	Subtotal (*quán*)
In-laws (*ngoại tộc*)			
Generation	Amount of Donation (*quán*)	Number of People	Subtotal (*quán*)
Outer Grandson(外孫)	30	1	30
	10	1	10
	5	1	5
	1	1	1
Outer Granddaughter(外女孫)	5	1	5
	1	4	4
Outer Great-grand-son (外曾孫)	1	1	1
Total		10	56

Forty-seven "inner lineage" family members donated money, compared to just ten "outer lineage" members; "inner" lineage members' total donations were more than six times greater, at more than 350 *quán* versus the "outer" lineage's 56 *quán*. The average donation per capita from a person in the "inner lineage" was more than 7 *quán*; from a person in "outer lineage," 5.6 *quán*. This suggests that Phạm Quang Nguyên's descendants' interest in ancestral worship activities was inclined to be patrilineal. However, some people from the daughters' lineages (Nguyên had at least three daughters) did not forget their external great-grandmothers' father and were ready to donate money. Seven of ten individuals were recorded as having "already donated" at the end of regulation, which means that they donated money before organizing the council. Similar to the will of Phạm Gia Nguyên, Phạm Quang Nguyên's descendants, including "outer lineages," tried to maintain the ancestral hall for him. According to one genealogy of the Phạm lineage, Phạm Gia Nguyên died in 1850.[28] So even

---

28   He was born in 1775 and died in 1850 (*Đông Ngạc Phạm Tộc Phả* 東鄂范族譜, 121b–122a).

thirty-six years after his death, his descendants were conscious about worshipping for him beyond the boundaries of "inner" and "outer" lineage, which shows the bilateral-like character of the premodern Vietnamese family.

Conclusion

It can be concluded, first, as Tran asserts, Vietnamese state law and local customs gave priority to sons over daughters with regard to the rights of inheritance of household property. Second, although it was true that women in premodern Vietnam were hesitant to accept some kinds of household property, like "fire and incense," daughters often enjoyed equal inheritance rights with their brothers. Third, in contrast to the Confucian norm, a daughter was responsible for the ancestral worship activities of her natal family in Vietnam. If there was no brother in her natal family, she had to accept the property for ancestral worship ("fire and incense"); this continued beyond her lifetime. "Fire and incense" was inherited by her children, such as in Nguyễn Thị Phiến's case (case study 2). Fourth, even if she was not the heir of her natal family and did not accept the "fire and incense," she often had to fulfill the ritual duties of ancestral worship in exchange for inheriting another kind of property for ancestral worship or receiving the right to use property even after she married. In such cases, her name was recorded with her share of the property or her rights and her duties in the testament of her parents. Fifth, these testaments were witnessed by the representatives of family or lineage as well as the village chief, who all signed the document. In this respect, daughters' duties were public affairs for family, lineage, community, the state, and even for heaven and the other world where her deceased ancestors were living. Finally, some parents wanted their children and descendants to maintain their heritage. Parents wanted the cooperation of all of their children, including their married daughters. If a married daughter observed her parents' will, her own children and grandchildren participated in worship activities for their mother's or grandmother's parents over many decades. In this case, a daughter became the founder of the branch of her natal father's lineage. Her husband and children had duties to participate in worship rites, to clean tombs, and to donate money to repair the ancestral worship halls of her natal family, the same as descendants of her natal brothers, who were seen as members of the patrilineal lineage. The activities of a daughter, her husband, and her children continued for several decades. This reflects the bilateral-like character of the premodern family in Vietnam.

As Hayami points out, there has been a gap in the points of view of historians and anthropologists with regard to gender and family in Southeast

Asia: "Anthropologists' studies primarily examined rural societies. Models created by anthropologists have been attuned to local differences, yet (had an) ahistorical and class-blind nature.... Work by historians, on the other hand, has been largely confined to the lives of elites and courtly notables due to the skewed nature of available documentation" (Hayami 2012, 4–5). In this chapter, I adopt "the bottom-up approach" (5) and investigate local documents that were written by ordinary people, not by elites or notables. Although some male testators were Confucian-educated or were officials, testaments were not issued according to a homogeneous Confucian ideology but by the consent of testators (including wives), beneficiaries (male and female descendants, including the families of women's husbands), and witnesses (including elder lineage members or notables in village communities). Testaments were issued as a result of negotiating multiple principles. In the process of those negotiations, Vietnamese women fulfilled their agencies as wives, mothers, and daughters.

Vietnamese women had property rights and the role of conducting ancestor worship; they acted as media between the inner lineage and the outer lineage. As I discovered, women's natal ancestors' property was passed on to the women's children and grandchildren. According to Momoki, when patrilineal *ie* (イエ, which means the house, the family, or the family system)was established in Japan, the problem was that property given to women was passed on to another *ie* upon the next generation's succession. To avoid losing property, Japanese elites such as *bushi*(武士, the ruling class in the premodern Japan) fulfilled endogamy and succession by the eldest son. In addition, they limited women's property rights to the woman's lifetime. After the woman's death, the property was returned to her natal *ie*. Momoki points out that this was similar to Vietnam in the Trần and Lê Dynasties. In particular, the QTHL stipulated that when a husband or a wife died without children, half of the deceased's property was returned to each of their natal lineages and that the living spouse was permitted rights on the other half of the property, during his or her lifetime only. After the spouse's death, the property was returned to the original owner's lineage (Momoki 2011, 316–17). Perhaps the limitation of the rights of "fire and incense" for the eldest daughter during her lifetime was stipulated on a similar principle.

The Vietnamese patrilineal ideal emphasized the distinction between the father's or husband's side (*nội*, inside) and the mother's or wife's side (*ngoại*, outside). This distinction has been very strong in daily life. However, based on my results from the case studies of women's property rights and the role of ancestors in premodern Vietnam, people did not care if patrilineal property was passed on to daughters' husbands. The patriarchy system in Vietnam had not been fully established because women's rights and individuals' rights were still strong. This was a reason why the Trần Dynasty was forced to establish a patriarchy system through a top-down policy (Momiki 2011, 317). Based on the case studies in this chapter, I suggest that patriarchy was not fully established in Vietnam at least until the end of the nineteenth century.

References

Aoki, Atsushi. 2014. *The World of Civil Law in the Sung Dynasty Era*. Tokyo: Keio Gijyuku Daigaku Shuppankai.(青木敦『宋代民事法の世界』慶應義塾大学出版会).

Bélanger, Danièle and Magali Barbieri. 2009. "Introduction: State, Families, and the Making of Transitions in Vietnam." In *Reconfiguring Families in Contemporary Vietnam*, edited by Magali Barbieri and Danièle Bélanger, 1–46. Stanford, CA: Stanford University Press.

Deloustal, Raymond. 1911. "La Justice dans L'Ancien Annam." *Bulletin de l'Ecole Francaise d'Extrême-Orient* (11): 25–66.

Guan, Wen Na. 2009. "The Historical Examination Regarding Japanese and Chinese Kinship Structure Seen in the Form of Marriage and Adoption." In *The Historical Demography and The Comparative Family History*, edited by Ochiai Emiko, Kojima Hiroshi, and Yagi Toru, 130–66. Tokyo: Waseda Daigaku Shuppannbu. (官文娜「婚姻・養子形態に見る日中親族血縁構造の歴史的考察」落合恵美子・小島宏・八木透編『歴史人口学と比較家族史』早稲田大学出版部、130–66頁).

Hayami, Yoko. 2012. "Introduction: The Family in Flux in Southeast Asia." In *The Family in Flux in Southeast Asia: Institution, Ideology, Practice*, edited by Yoko Hayami, Junko Koizumi, Chalidaporn Songsamphan, and Ratana Tosakul, 1–26. Kyoto: Kyoto University Press.

Katakura, Yuzuru. 1987. *The Basic Examination on Premodern Law in Vietnam*. Tokyo: Kazama Shobo. (片倉穣『ベトナム前近代法の基礎的研究』風間書房).

Kawamura, Yasushi. 1988. "Law of Adoption in Sung China." *Waseda Law Review* 64(1): 1–55. (川村康「宋代における養子法(上)」『早稲田法学』64(1), 1–55頁).

Lingat, Robert. 1952. *Les Régimes Matrimoniaux de Sud-est de L'Asie: Essi de Droit Comparé Indochinois*. Hanoi: Ecole Francaise d' Extrême-Orient.

Lustéguy, Pierre. ca. 1949 [1935]. *La Femme Annamite du Tonkin dans L'Institution Biens Cultuels (Huong-Hoa)*. Doctoral dissertation, Paris: Université de Paris. *Human Relations Area Files*, AM1, 61.

Makino, Tastumi. 1980 [1934]. "The Family Institution Represented in Lê Code in Annam." In *The Study on Chinese Family*, vol. 2, 205–34. Tokyo: Ochanomizu Shobo. (牧野巽「安南の黎朝刑律にあらわれた家族制度」『中国家族制度研究(下)』御茶の水書房、205–234頁).

Miyajima, Hiroshi. 1994a. "Formation of Small Peasant Society in East Asia." In *Long-Term Social Change*, edited by Mizoguchi Yuzo, Hiraishi Naoaki, Hamashita Takeshi, and Miyajima Hiroshi, 67–96. Tokyo: Tokyo Daigaku Shuppankai. (宮嶋博史 「東アジア小農社会の形成」 溝口雄三、平石直昭、浜下武士、宮嶋博史編『長期社会変動』東京大学出版会、67–96頁).

———. 1994b. "Formation of Yangbang Society in Korea." In *State and Society*, edited by Mizoguchi Yuzo, Hiraishi Naoaki, Hamashita Takeshi, and Miyajima Hiroshi, 131–64. Tokyo: Tokyo Daigaku Shuppankai. (宮嶋博史「朝鮮両班社会の形成」溝口雄三他編『社会と国家』東京大学出版会、131–164頁).

Miyazawa, Chihiro. 1996. "Women's Property Rights in the North Part of Vietnam: From the 19th century to the Late 1920s." *Japanese Journal of Ethnology* 60(4): 330–41. (宮沢千尋 「ベトナム北部における女性の財産上の地位:19 世紀から 1920年代末まで」『民族學研究』60(4), 330–341頁).

Momoki, Shiro. 1997. "The Periphery of Ming-Qing History: The Case of Economic History in Vietnam." In *The Basic Question of History in the Ming-Qing Era*, edited by Mori Masao, Noguchi Tetsuro. Hamajima Atsutoshi, Kishimoto Mio, and Satake Yasuhiko, 607–34. Tokyo: Kyuko Shoin. (桃木至朗「周辺の明清時代史:ベトナム経済史の場合」森正夫他編『明清時代史の基本問題』汲古書院、607–634頁).

———. 2011. *The Formation and Transformation of the Medieval State of Đại Việt*. Osaka: Osaka Daigaku Shuppankai. (桃木至朗『中世大越国家の成立と変容』大阪大学出版会).

Ngô Kim Chung, and Nguyễn Đức Nghinh. 1987. *Propriété Privée et Propriété Collective dans L'Ancien Viêtnam*. Paris: L'Harmattan.

Nguyễn Ngọc Huy, and Tạ Văn Tài. 1987. *The Lê Code–Law in Traditional Vietnam: A Comparative Sino-Vietnamese Legal Study with Historical-Juridical Analysis and Annotations*. Athens: Ohio University Press.

Nguyễn Si Giác và Vũ Văn Mẫu. 1959. *Hồng Đức Thiện Chính Thư*. Sài Gòn: Nam Hà Ấn Quán.

Nguyen Tai Thu, Dinh Minh Chi, Ly Kim Hue, Ha Thai Minh, and Ha Van Tan. [2003] 2006. *The History of Buddhism in Vietnam*. Washington, DC: Institute of Philosophy, Vietnamese Academy of Social Sciences, Council for Research in Values and Philosophy.

Niida, Noboru. 1954. "Succession Law of Lê Dynasty in Annam and Chinese Law." *Memoirs of the Institute for Advanced Studies on Asia* 5: 209–28. (仁井田陞「黎氏安南の財産相続法と中国法」東京大学東洋文化研究所『東洋文化研究所紀要』5、209–228頁).

Pompeï Paul. 1951. *Le Droit Familial et Patrimonial au Viet-Nam*. Paris: Librarie du Recueil Sirey.

Protectorat du Tonkin. 1930. *Recueil des Avis du Comité consultatif de Jurisprudence Annamite sur les coutumes des Annamites du Tonkin en matière de famille, de succession et de biens cultuels.* Hanoi: Imprimerie Trung-Bac Tân-Van.

Shimao, Minoru. 2008. "The Basic Examination Regarding Thọ Mai Gia Lễ." *Reports of the Keio Institute of Cultural and Linguistic Studies* 39: 215–31. (嶋尾稔「寿梅家礼に関する基礎的考察(三)」『慶應義塾大学言語文化研究所紀要』39, 215–231頁).

———. 2011. "Confucian Family Ritual and Popular Culture in Vietnam." *Memories of the Research Department of the Toyo Bunko* 69: 57–96.

Suenari, Michio. 1995. "Genealogy in Vietnam." *Toyo Bunka* 127: 1–42. (末成道男「ベトナムの家譜」東京大学東洋文化研究所『東洋文化』127、1–42頁).

Takahashi, Yoshiro. 2006. *Translation and Annotation: Collection of Decisions by Famous Judges to Clarify and Enlighten Tokyo: Sobunsha* (高橋芳郎『訳注「名公書判清明集」戸婚門』創文社).

Taylor, Keith Weller. 1983. *The Birth of Vietnam.* Berkeley: University of California Press.

Tran, My-Van. 1990. "The Position of Women in Traditional Vietnam: Some Aspects." In *Asian Panorama: Essays in Asian History, Past, and Present,* edited by K.M. De Silva and Sirima Kiribamune, 274–83. New Delhi: Vikas.

Tran, Nhung Tuyet. 2006. "Beyond the Myth of Equality: Daughters' Inheritance Rights in the Lê Code." In *Việt Nam: Borderless Histories,* edited by Nhung Tuyet Tran and Anthony J.S. Reid, 121–44. Madison: University of Wisconsin Press.

———. 2008. "Gender, Property, and the 'Autonomy Thesis' in Southeast Asia." *Journal of Asian Studies* 67(1): 43–72.

Trương Hữu Quýnh. 1983. *Chế Độ Ruộng Đất ở Việt Nam Thế Kỷ XI–XVIII.* Tập II, Thế Kỷ XVI–XVIII. Hà Nội: Nhà Xuất Bản Khoa Học Xã Hội. [*Land Institution in Vietnam, Century XI—XVIII*, vol. II, Century XI—XVIII].

Yu, Insun. 1990. *Law and Society in Seventeenth and Eighteenth Century Vietnam.* Seoul: Asiatic Research Center, Korea University.

———. 1999. "Bilateral Social Patterns in Traditional Vietnam." *South East Asia Research* 7(2): 215–31.

Genealogies in Hán Nôm Institute (Viện Nghiên Cứu Hán Nôm), Hà Nội

Đông Ngạc Village Nguyễn Bá Đa Testament (Đông Ngạc Xã Nguyễn Bá Đa Chúc Thư 東鄂社阮伯多嘱書). A. 1771.

Đông Ngạc Village Đông Ngạc Village Phạm Lineage Council about Donation Regulation (Đông Ngạc Xã Phạm Tộc Hội Nghị Cấp Tiền Từ 東鄂社范族會議給錢詞). A.1778.

Đông Ngạc Village Phạm Lineage Distribution Agreement (Đông Ngạc Xã Phạm Tộc Giao Thư 東鄂社范族交書). A. 1772.

Nguyễn Lineage Testament in An Cảnh Village (An Cảnh Xã Nguyễn Tộc Chúc Thư 安境社阮族嘱書). A. 1978.

Phạm Gia An's Testament in Đông Ngạc Village (Đông Ngạc Xã Phạm Gia An Chúc Thư 東鄂社范嘉安嘱書). A. 1739.

Genealogies on CD-ROM

Genealogies of lineages in Đông Ngạc Village, Từ Liêm District, Hà Nội (Gia Phả các Dòng Họ ở Đông Ngạc, Từ Liêm-Hà Nội, edited by Đại Học Quốc Gia Hà Nội Trung Tâm Nghiên Cứu Việt Nam và Giao Lưu Văn Hóa, Chương Trình Ngiên Cứu Gia Phả Việt Nam, 2003).

Đông Ngạc Village Phạm Lineage Genealogy (Đông Ngạc Phạm Tộc Phả『東鄂范族譜』).

Phạm Lineage's Genelations (Phạm Thị Thế Phả『范氏世譜』).

Phạm Lineage Genealogy (Phạm Thị Tộc Phả『范氏族譜』).

Documents in the Digital Collections of the Vietnamese Nôm Preservation Foundation (*http://lib.nomfoundation.org*)

The List of Mandarins in Từ Liêm District (Từ Liêm Đăng Khoa Lộc『慈廉登科録』), VNPF-1244, R990.

Testament (Chúc thư『嘱書』), NLVNPF-0555, R528.

CHAPTER 3

Divorce Prevalence under the Forces of Individualism and Collectivism in "Shortcut" Modernity in Vietnam

Tran Thi Minh Thi

Introduction

In the last several decades, marriage and family in Vietnam have experienced a significant transition from the traditional style to more modern characteristics. "Traditional family" is a common term when discussing Vietnamese society, which refers to family forms prevailing during the presocialist period, mostly prior to the 1950s. The traditional family was organized under the influence of Confucianism and in a hierarchical order according to age and sex that strongly influenced marriage and divorce decisions (Luong 1989; 1992). Since the mid-1950s, traditional norms such as arranged marriage, a dominant male as head of household, strong patriarchy and patrilineal relations, having many children, son preference, filial piety under the Confucian cultural heritage, and the prohibition of premarital sex have significantly declined. At the macro level, changes in the legal system, gender roles in society, and socioeconomic development have also greatly influenced individual perceptions of marriage patterns, including divorce (Tran Dinh Huou 1991; Haughton & Haughton, 1995; Hollander 1996; Goodkind 1997; Haughton 1997; Nguyễn Hữu Minh 2000, 2011; Hirschman & Nguyen Huu Minh 2002; Bélanger 2002; Luong 2003; Barbieri & Bélanger 2009; Tran Thi Minh Thi 2011, 2012; Trinh Duy Luan, et al. 2011; Vu Manh Loi 2011).

Divorce is a major concern of scholars when discussing family issues. Previous studies have identified prevalence and determinants of divorce in different national contexts, which include cultural, demographic, socioeconomic, and life-course factors (Hirschman & Rindfuss 1980; Mauldin & Segal 1998). In Vietnam, recent studies on divorce show that, though divorce has long been culturally discouraged and limited, it has rapidly increased in both number and rate since the Đổi Mới (Renovation) policy was launched in the late 1980s (Tran Thi Minh Thi 2011; 2012).

However, very few studies have been implemented based on statistical analyses of individual divorce data on the prevalence and patterns of divorce in Vietnam. This gap in literature is due primarily to the scarcity of extensive data on divorce in Vietnam until recent years. Using both existing and new data, this chapter attempts to describe the general prevalence of divorce nationwide and the forces of traditional and modern norms involved in divorce in contemporary Vietnam.

Data and Method

This study analyzes every divorce case in the divorce profiles at two district courts in the Red River Delta in the ten-year period from 2000 to 2009. One court is located in the inner city of Hanoi, which represents the urban divorced population, and the other in Hà Nam province, which represents the rural divorced population. In total, 2,033 divorce cases were reviewed, of which 1,534 couples lived in the urban district and 499 in the rural district. For the first time in Vietnam, the entire divorced population over a ten-year period is reviewed, which can provide the comprehensive trends, characteristics, and determinants of divorce in the society.

A divorce-court record is registered in two profiles: the Annual Divorce Entry Registration and the Annual Divorce Court Results. The former provides information about couples who apply for divorce, such as the date of the divorce application registration, information about the initiator and the dependent spouse (name, gender, year of birth, and address), marriage year, divorce year, reported causes of divorce, number of children, and other professional notes recorded by the court. This registration profile can thus provide us with the basic demographics and social variables for the study. However, not all cases in the Annual Divorce Entry Registration result in divorce; some couples may withdraw their divorce applications under the reconciliation process or resolve their marital problems by themselves. The Annual Divorce Court Results included the following information: date of registration entry; date of decision; information about the initiator and the spouse (name, gender, year of birth, address, and so on); number of children; divorce decision about child custody, house, and property arrangements (if required); subsidies after divorce; debt responsibility; and court fees. This analysis is restricted to couples granted divorce under the divorce decision.

In addition, quantitative case studies were conducted to collect detailed information to provide possible explanations and investigate the sociocultural background of divorce. In each case, the respondent was asked to provide his or her life history from childhood up to the time of the interview. The information included narratives about family background; childhood memories; mate selection; wedding experiences; living arrangements after marriage; birth of the first child, if any; sequence of the marital conflict; divorce and reconciliation procedures; actors involved in the divorce decision; their memories about the divorce court; negotiation process of child custody and house/property arrangements; their relationships with their children and ex-spouses; and their current lives, such as remarriage and attitudes toward life. Overall, twenty-one divorced people are successfully and repeatedly interviewed from 2008 to 2011, of which there were twelve wives and nine husbands, residing in Hanoi city (an urban area) and Bình Lục district, Hà Nam province (a rural area).

Marriage and Family in Vietnam

Scholars often mark 1945 as the ending point of the feudal model of family and marriage institutions in Vietnam, though many traditional forms and values of marriage and the family remain. The year 1945 was the turning point, with the establishment of the Democratic Republic of Vietnam. Traditional marriage norms were undermined by the period's dramatic socioeconomic changes and turbulent political events.

Old-fashioned customs of feudal marriage were legally brought to an end. The arranged marriages were abolished in the Law on Marriage and the Family in 1959. Polygamy was declared illegal and monogamy adopted as the official form of Vietnamese marriage. Equality between men and women was to be practiced. The basic rights of women and children, such as freedom from abuse and oppression in the home, were also protected (Mai Thi Tu & Le Thi Nham Tuyet 1978). The updated 1986 Law on Marriage and the Family clarified the legal obligations of married partners, identified parental responsibilities more clearly, and established new procedures for divorce. The 2000 Marriage and Family Law and the most recent update in 2012 address contemporary concerns about rapid modernization and its influence on marriage and the family.

In the 2012 Marriage and Family Law, divorce is defined as a marriage dissolution granted by the family court based on one or both spouses' application. The divorce can be granted as a consensus decision, which means that both parties agree to divorce, or divorce as required of one spouse with particular reasons. Children are consulted about with whom they wish to stay if they are nine or older. The law allows the custodial parent to change in the following years. The law is specific regarding property division: the common property is basically half and half division. If the wife is pregnant or is nursing an infant under twelve months of age, the husband is not entitled to request a divorce. The law is more specific about land and housing arrangements after divorce. Housework is considered as a work for income. The law protects the rights of wives and children who cannot work for income and own no property.

In Vietnam, the nuclear family is now the main social and economic unit, with an average household size of 3.8 (GSO 2011a). A transitional trend from an age pattern of early marriage to one of later marriage has occurred, though marriage is still universal (Nguyễn Hữu Minh 2000; Lê Ngọc Văn 2006). Women tend to marry earlier than men, even though, on a lifetime basis, marriage is more universal among men (GSO 2011a). Patrilocal coresidence is common. The pattern of coresidence not only reflects the traditional expectation that children are obliged to care for elderly parents, but also expresses a desire among parents to help their children before they can afford to establish an independent household. Although patriarchy is strong, women have substantial decision-making power within the family (see Luong's chapter in this volume) and it is perceived that this power has increased. Decision-making in some areas remains men's prerogative, but the most common situation was one in which the husband and wife shared equally in the decisions (Knodel et al. 2004; IFGS 2008). Recent data show that men are still the default head of the family (IFGS 2008). Vu Manh Loi (2011) states that "household head" is a multifaceted category, as it refers to economic power, prestige, decision-making power, and power to represent the family. The household head also reflects the traditional patriarchal culture, which accords more respect to the elderly in the family. Recently, the number of female-headed households has increased, a tendency which may be causing profound changes in marriage and family structures.

Urbanization and modernization have been seen as instigators of fertility decline in many societies (Coale 1973; Caldwell 1976; Easterlin 1983), including Vietnam. As levels of schooling, quality of health care, urbanization, and exposure to modern forms of mass communication have increased, fertility has dropped rapidly. The state's population policies add other important dimensions to marriage and family patterns. In Vietnam, each couple is required to have two or fewer children, regardless of the sex of the child. The total fertility rate has declined steadily, falling from 5.6 children per woman in 1979 to 3.9 by

1989 (Haughton 1997) and, in 2009, to 2.14 children per woman in rural areas and 1.80 children per woman in urban areas. Sex ratios at birth are attracting serious concern because they are increasing quickly, which shows a son preference among the population recently (GSO 2011b).

Theoretical Approaches

Modernization and "Shortcut" Modernity

The changes in marriage, the family, and divorce relate closely to the modernization process. Previous literature argues that modernization presents two opposing forces with regard to divorce. On the one hand, socioeconomic development, together with modernization and urbanization, may reduce the divorce rate. Social changes associated with modernization can account for the decline in divorce, including the rise of conjugal family systems, an increase in the autonomy of youngsters, and increased freedom from extended family control—all of which serve to increase the marriage age and expand education, greater freedom in mate selection, and improvements in women's status (Goode 1963; 1971; 1993; Lee 1982; Hirschman & Teerawichitchainan 2003; Johns 2003). On the other hand, at later stages of modernization, socioeconomic development increases the incidence of divorce. Most theorists suggest that, in the long run, the trend toward egalitarianism and the replacement of patriarchies increase the incidence of divorce. Goode treats modernization as the root of the elevated divorce rate and emphasizes the destabilizing force of female empowerment (Goode 1963; 1993). Improvements in women's status create a sociocultural environment that makes divorce more easily attainable. Women's increasing economic independence, smaller families, and ideological emphasis on self-fulfillment in relationships and on individual choices may shift the tide toward less stable marital relationships.

Asian scholars have recently developed the concept of "compressed modernity" (Chang 2010) to express the contemporary Asian situation, which is marked by the simultaneous progression through "first modernity" and "second modernity" in a state of "catching-up" in terms of modernizing over a short time (Ochiai 2010). Transforming directly from feudalism to socialism in the historical events of wars from the 1950s to 1970s, the Đổi Mới in 1986, and the following decades of market-economy-oriented socialism with a "shortened" strategy of modernization and industrialization—which can be called the Vietnamese version of "shortcut" modernity—the government of Vietnam has had an important role in the formulation of marriage patterns through its introduction of legal documents and other socioeconomic development policies.

The resulting "shortcut modernity" has led to a social situation in which the dynamic coexistence of traditional and modern elements leads to the maintenance of traditional values and the perception of new values and knowledge. The unique feature of "shortcut modernity" in contemporary Vietnam is that it comprises the features of first modernity (i.e., an ideology of full employment connected to the achievement principle in work; nuclear families; and a collective solidarity) and second modernity (i.e., industrialization, a market economy, and cultural globalization) (Beck 1992), or "hyper-compressed modernity" in terms of the coexistence of transitional and modern values that new institutions have not perfected while old institutions still exist.

At the same time, the Vietnamese government carries out many activities in the areas of employment and economic status, education and training, health care, leadership, and decision-making for women. The gender equality campaign has dramatically improved women's rights and status in the family and in the entire society. Rapid socioeconomic development since the Renovation has significantly changed people's attitudes toward divorce and has largely relaxed the restrictive legal and administrative procedures of divorce (Tran Thi Minh Thi 2011; 2012).

Shortcut Modernity, Gender Equality, and Divorce

Empirical research strongly supports a positive relationship between women's status and divorce in Asian societies. Increases in economic opportunities for women provide the requisite independence for dissolving unhappy marriages. For many women, divorce was not an option a few decades ago, as it was associated with social stigma or considered a betrayal of the husband's families. Scholars have shown that many Asian women are heavily burdened by the dual pressure of housework and childcare duties (Inoue & Ehara 1999; Lee 2006). However, with increasing educational attainment and economic opportunities for women and more tolerant attitudes toward delayed marriage and maternal employment, the conventional gender roles in marriage have changed gradually. Many Asian women now prefer the social and economic independence that they have gained from gender equity in education and the labor market (Choe 1998; Atoh 2001; Tsuya et al. 2004).

Some Asian countries share a heritage of Confucianism, the values of which center on male domination, filial piety, and collectivist goals over individualistic fulfillment (Diener & Lucas 2000; Xu & Lai 2002). There is no gender equality in this cultural milieu, though several studies also emphasized the high status of women in practice (see Luong and Miyazawa's chapters in this volume). Under a patriarchal familial system with androcentric values, young women are often viewed as temporary residents of their natal homes (Yang & Yen 2010). Vietnam has been strongly influenced by Confucian ideology, but gender equality and women's status have been promoted significantly over the years. It is expected that there would be gender and generational differentiations in divorce prevalence and patterns, as well as reasons for divorce in contemporary Vietnam.

Intimate Relationships and Divorce
Research by feminist scholars suggests that differences between women and men in the number and types of marriage problems are rooted in gendered expectations about intimate relationships. Compared with men, women take on greater responsibility for and spend more time responding to the emotional and psychological needs of their spouses and children, as well as monitoring the status of intimate relationships. Women tend to become aware of relationship problems sooner than their partners and are more likely to initiate discussions of relationship problems (Thompson & Walker 1991). Perhaps for these reasons, wives are more likely than husbands to initiate divorce. With respect to perceived causes of divorce, women appear to be more likely than men to refer to relational or emotional issues, such as basic unhappiness and incompatibility. In contrast, men, more often than women, blame the divorce on external factors, such as work or problems with in-laws (Kitson 1992; Amato & Previti 2003). Women emphasize the personality characteristics and behaviors of their spouses more than men do. In particular, women often cite the husband's use of authority, cruelty, drinking habits, immaturity, infidelity, poor money management, values, or lifestyle as cause for divorce. Husbands often cite the wife's infidelity, work commitments, or drinking (Hochschild 1989; Amato & Rogers 1997).

Familialism, Collectivism, and Individualism
The family is the fundamental unit of Vietnamese society and is at the center of individuals' relations with the community and the state. As stated, Vietnamese families can be divided into two basic forms: "traditional" and "modern." Familialism places priority on well-being and prosperity of the family over individual freedom and autonomy. There was strong familialism in the presocialist period, which compelled family members to engage in activities for the common interest of the family. Close ties between extended families and communities have had a major influence on individual behavior. Familialism organized the collectivist culture of Vietnam, which is strongly

oriented toward the family and community. As the feudal system collapsed, familialism gradually degraded, leading to the reification of a couple-centered structure and a gender-equal, small-family system, as seen in the capitalist system.

It is also important to understand the notions of collectivism (*tính tập thể, tính cộng đồng*) and individualism (*tính cá nhân*) in relation to familialism as they manifest in the interpretation of disparate marriage and family behaviors in contemporary Vietnam. A recent study on collectivism and individualism in Vietnam (Do Long & Phan Thi Mai Huong 2002) showed that collectivism prevailed over individualism among Vietnamese as compared with other nationalities, such as Americans, Japanese, and Koreans, in the early 2000s. However, the dimensions of collectivism and individualism varied according to gender and subcultures of geographical regions. Generally, Vietnamese women were more collectivist than men, but these two variables are complicated when it comes to different subcultures of the North and South, rural and urban areas, and the Kinh (the main ethnic group in Vietnam) and minorities.

In the realm of marriage, family, and kinship, the transitional process of shortcut modernity comprises the maintenance of traditional values and the appearance of new values. In Vietnamese society, nuclear and stem families are increasing, while extended family patterns have never disappeared completely. Through the processes of contestation, adaptation, resistance, and negotiation, these renovations vividly illustrate how families have propelled and made possible the transition while living in continuity with the past (Barbieri & Bélanger 2009). In other words, with the influences of modernization, legal changes, and comprehensive international integration, old and new values, as competing forces, are operating in the realm of marriage and family in Vietnam.

Divorce Procedures

Understanding the procedure of divorce can show how society perceives this family event. It is obvious that divorce procedure is constituted differently among different social groups and settings. As mentioned above, previous studies have stated that Vietnamese women are more collectivist than men, though this varies among different subcultures of the North and the South and rural and urban areas. Moreover, collectivism and individualism in the Vietnamese value system differ substantially from behaviors in actual situations (Do Long & Phan Thi Mai Huong 2002). For instance, prenatal diagnosis is often not only a matter of husband and wife but also of their parents and siblings (Gammeltoft 2007), while mate selection is decided mostly by the couples, with parents' opinions consulted (Nguyen Huu Minh 2009).

In a rural village, marital dissolution is not a single event but rather a quite complicated process. Divorce decision in rural areas is influenced significantly by collective participation involving the direct interventions of family, relatives, and mass organizations. The parental family and relatives constitute a significant support source for the individuals during divorce procedures. Some form of family meeting or even a lineage meeting is held when an individual wants a divorce. The chair is a male head of the lineage. They assess the situation of the marriage, its current problems, and the possibility of reconciliation. The family meeting also determines issues of childcare and family members' responsibilities for supporting the couple after divorce.

Married women identify themselves with their in-laws but also maintain close relationships with their biological families (Nguyen Huu Minh 2009; 2011). Crucial decisions regarding getting married, bearing and rearing children, the marital relationship, and even divorce are regarded as collective decisions made by the women's biological families. Especially when women experience problems in their marriage, such as economic hardship, domestic violence, spousal adultery, or conflicts with in-laws, they seek advice, encouragement, and help from their biological parents and siblings. Thus, the divorce decision often results from a common agreement with their biological family (Tran Thi Minh Thi 2011).

Reconciliation is the first formal step of intervention attempted by local governments and social organizations to avoid a divorce. At the village level, village authorities, including representatives of the village Women's Union, village leaders, and the village judiciary visit the couple in their home to encourage them to reconsider the need to divorce. This counseling service leads to surprisingly effective results in several cases, such as husbands refraining from beating their wives or wives withdrawing their divorce applications. When village reconciliation is unsuccessful—that is, it is not possible to meet with the couple or the couple insists on a divorce—the divorce application is sent to the Commune People's Committee to process a standard administrative procedure, beginning with commune reconciliation. The purpose of government conciliators is to consult with the couple to determine if they can withdraw their divorce request, reconcile with each other, and live together happily regardless of faults (Tran Thi Minh Thi 2011). There are several steps at this level of reconciliation. The reconciliation commission involves one leader of the Commune People's Committee and the commune judicial official. The commission meeting meets with the plaintiff and defendant separately to listen to their opinions and expectations. After these two private meetings, a general meeting is held with the couple, the People's Committee representatives, the Women's Union leader, the judicial official, and representatives of other relevant mass organizations

(Tran Thi Minh Thi 2011). There are high expectations for women to sacrifice their own happiness for the sake of their family, which prevents many divorces (Rydström 2010).

Couples have two possible options after participating in these meetings. First, the couple can withdraw their divorce request. The divorce application will then be suspended at the commune level. Second, one or both parties may have no desire to reunite and insist on a divorce. In this case, the commune government will produce an explanatory report and send the divorce profiles, including the divorce application, minutes of the meeting, and the case report to the District People's Court, which is the deciding authority. The time taken for this process, from when the divorce application is received until the reconciliation process occurs and the divorce is reported to the district court, ranges from two to six months, depending on how complicated the case is.

A divorce judgment includes several procedures: a divorce application receipt, reconciliation, judgment, and the divorce decision. The case will be suspended if the plaintiff withdraws the application. The divorce court is open for seven days after the two parties sign the divorce agreement. After the judge

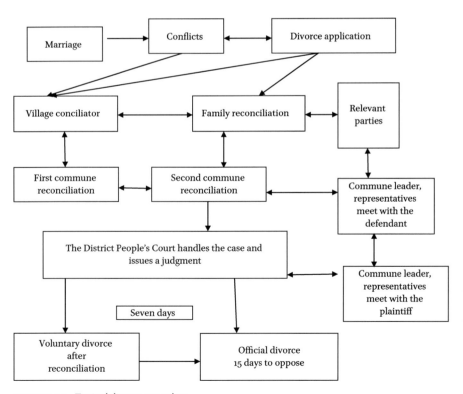

FIGURE 3.1 *Typical divorce procedure*

issues the divorce decision, which clearly states the arrangements regarding childcare, housing and property, subsidies, and so on, the couple is given fifteen days to reconsider or oppose the decision in terms of childcare, subsidies, and property division. After that period, the divorce takes effect and the marriage is officially dissolved (Figure 3.1).

Key Findings

Finding 1: Increase in Divorce Incidence
The number of divorces is gradually rising in Vietnam and the incidence is much stronger in urban areas than in rural areas, as can be seen in Figure 3.2. The number of divorces shows little change in the 1960s and 1970s: around 15,000 cases per year. Divorce increased slightly in the following two decades, the 1980s and 1990s, and has risen fast since the 2000s. In 2000, there were 51,361 divorces in the entire country. This number nearly doubled, to nearly 100,000, in 2010. Other Southeast Asian countries, such as Indonesia, Malaysia, and the Philippines, share this divorce trend (Tran Thi Minh Thi 2011; 2012).

Divorce rates are rising slightly across Vietnam, which is also similar to other Asian countries, such as China and Singapore (Ochiai 2011). In 2000, the crude divorce rate (CDR) was 0.66; it increased to 1.05 in 2009 (Table 3.1). The general divorce rate (GDR) rose from 0.97 in 2000 to 1.49 in 2010.

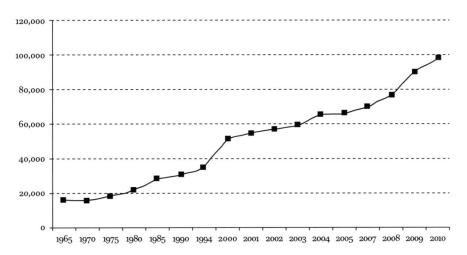

FIGURE 3.2 *Number of divorces in Vietnam, 1965–2010*
SOURCE: SUPREME COURT OF VIETNAM STATISTICS.

TABLE 3.1   *Crude divorce rate and general divorce rate in Vietnam, 2000–2010*

Year	Divorces[a]	Population[b]	CDR	Population 15+[c]	GDR
2000	51,361	77,630,900	0.66	53,148,971	0.97
2001	54,226	78,685,000	0.69	53,872,252	1.01
2002	56,487	79,727,000	0.71	55,405,348	1.02
2003	58,708	80,902,000	0.73	56,935,391	1.03
2004	65,336	82,031,000	0.80	58,613,453	1.11
2005	65,929	82,393,500	0.80	60,065,667	1.10
2006	67,058	83,313,000	0.80	61,279,802	1.09
2007	69,646	84,221,100	0.83	62,618,033	1.11
2008	76,490	85,122,300	0.90	63,702,050	1.20
2009	90,092	86,025,000	1.05	64,948,875	1.39
2010	97,627	86,932,500	1.12	65,311,641	1.49

[a] *Supreme Court of Vietnam: Annual Statistics.*
[b] GSO: *Statistical Yearbook of Vietnam 2000–2010.*
[c] GSO and UNFPA *Data Warehouse on Annual Population Change and Family Planning Survey.*

Divorce rates in East Asia are also rising notably. For instance, after the late 1960s, when the divorce rate in Europe started rising, an increasing trend was also seen in Japan, where the CDR spiked during the 1980s to 1.50 and in 2002 reached an all-time high of 2.30. In Taiwan and Korea, divorce rates began rising in the 1980s. By the start of the 1990s they were closing in on those of Japan, passing it during the Asian financial crisis, with Korea's 2003 record level of 3.50 almost the same as the United States' 3.60 (Ochiai 2011). In Indonesia, the rising participation of women in the labor force, rising educational levels, increasing self-choice of spouse, and therefore greater commitment to the chosen partners (Jones 1997; 2007). China experienced rapid increases in divorce rates between 1980 and 1995, which could be attributed to changes in the legal system making it easy to get divorce and changes in the attitudes of the people such that it is no longer a stigma to be divorced especially for a woman (Yi & Deqing 2000).

Divorce prevalence in Vietnam in the 1960s and 1970s was influenced by the constitution and the first Law on Marriage and the Family in 1959, which introduced modern marriage based on love and intimacy, promoted gender equality, protected women's basic rights of property ownership, and enabled divorce. However, the Vietnam War may have limited the communication of the law and its effectiveness regarding marriage and family. Individuals served in the country's fight for independence and unification, and marriage and the family came second to these collective priorities. In short, divorce was a taboo before the Đổi Mới.

After the Đổi Mới, divorce increased constantly. During this time, the level of modernization and urbanization and economic development increased, as did the average age at first marriage, education, freedom to choose marriage partners, and individualized intimacy, which may account for the increase in the incidence of divorce. The rapid socioeconomic development since the Đổi Mới has significantly changed people's attitudes toward divorce and largely relaxed the restrictive legal and administrative procedures (Tran Thi Minh Thi 2012). Women generally gained higher status, giving them more autonomy in marital decisions; divorce was relatively easy to obtain (Hirschman & Teerawichitchainan 2003). Globalization has also led to changing attitudes toward less traditional forms of gender and family relationships, as individuals become more liberal in their marital decisions and social opinion on divorce becomes more open.

On the other hand, it should be noted that divorce in Vietnam, while it is rising, remains relatively low compared to developed countries. The low prevalence of divorce can be linked to increasing age at marriage, educational expansion, and greater freedom to choose marriage partners, as shown in explanations of decline in divorce in other Southeast Asian countries, such as Indonesia (Jones 1994; 1997; 2007; Heaton et al. 2001; Hirschman & Teerawichitchainan 2003).

Finding 2: Significant Differences in Divorce Procedures of Rural and Urban Areas

Divorce is a long procedure that involves many negotiated steps, especially in rural settings, and spouses have time to reconsider and change their minds. They have more than one opportunity to examine their feelings, assess the situation, and consult with government officials throughout the different levels of marriage reconciliation and counseling.

However, sometimes attempts at reconciliation are in vain, as is shown in Ms. Hồng's case. In August 2004, Ms. Hồng, a farmer born in 1981, applied for divorce. In her own words, "I gave him a divorce application to sign at least five times, but he avoided signing it." After receiving Hồng's divorce application, the District People's Court informed her it would handle her case in the divorce court. The court convened for her husband several times, but he was always absent without reason. Thus, the court gave the announcement letter to his mother. The court also posted notice of the case at the Commune People's Committee. His mother confirmed that she had forwarded the court notice to her son, but he had said, "That is Hồng's business with the court," and then pretended that he had not received the court's announcement. The court officials were unable, therefore, to hear his version and continued their reconciliation efforts. Finally, the court issued a divorce without the husband's consent on the grounds that the conflict was considered "severe and marital cohabitation had ended a long time ago."

On the contrary, in an urban setting, family relations are not as tightly knit, which may lead to more individualism in divorce decisions and less complicated divorce procedures. The couple may not undergo the entire process of meetings, reconciliation, and so on when applying for a divorce, but may still seek advice from family members and intimate friends on relevant issues such as child arrangements and property settlement, and adjustment after the marital dissolution.

> Divorce is never easier than now, especially if you do not have a property conflict. Unless you have to divide property at court due to not being able to compromise, divorce is so simple. Reconciliation is a kind of required procedure. In my case, I feel it was simple, and so was the case of my friend. (Ms. Trang, born in 1982, university educational level, counselling staff, Hanoi)

> It's very quick. They called to reconcile two times, preparing the meeting minutes of reconciliation, and then granted the divorce decision after one week. The divorce decision is just a paper, but, you know, the marriage registration paper is very nice, but the divorce one is... It's torture. (Ms. Thủy, nurse, born in 1958, one daughter, Hanoi)

Finding 3: Divorced Couples with Longer Marriages Live in Urban Areas, while Divorced Couples with Shorter Marriages Live in Rural Areas

With respect to duration of marriage, divorces occur more often in the early rather than the later years of marriage (White 1990). Becker (1991) argues that people generally have imperfect information about their partners during courtship but learn substantially more about their spouses after marriage. Consequently, early divorces are disproportionately due to the discovery of basic incompatibility, conflict in values, and personality clashes. Indeed, studies have shown that marital duration is associated with long-term declines in marital happiness (Johnson et al. 1992). Goode's (1956) research reveals that

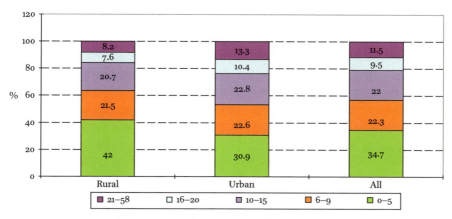

FIGURE 3.3 *Marriage duration in years by rural/urban differential, 2000–2009*
SOURCE: TRAN THI MINH THI 2011 (STUDY ON DIVORCE RECORD PROFILES AT THE DISTRICT PEOPLE'S COURTS IN HANOI AND HÀ NAM PROVINCES, 2000–2009, N = 2033).

complaints of infidelity, drinking, and the general quality of home life increased with duration of marriage, whereas complaints about personality and value conflicts decreased. Bloom et al. (1985) finds a positive correlation between length of marriage and infidelity.

Figure 3.3 shows that 34.7 percent of couples dissolve their marriage within the first five years; 22.3 percent divorce within six to nine years; and 22 percent after sixteen to twenty years of marriage. In other words, three-fifths of marriages end during the first ten years, and the highest percentage of dissolution occurs within the first five years.

It is interesting to look at the differences in marriage duration between rural and urban couples. More rural couples divorce within the first five years of marriage than urban couples (42 percent versus 30.9 percent). In all the marriage-duration categories, after the first six years, a higher proportion of divorces occurred among couples from urban areas than those in rural areas.

Table 3.2 presents the mean marriage duration by social determinants of the divorced population from 2000 to 2009. The mean marriage duration of all divorced couples in the last ten years is 10.3 years, of which the marriage duration of urban couples is longer than that of rural couples (11 years versus 9.1 years). The trend of longer marriage duration among urban couples can be seen across the entire ten-year period, with 2008 being the only exception. Urban couples are typically more highly educated and may have more opportunities to access mass media and information; hence, they may be more skillful at maintaining marital stability than rural couples.

TABLE 3.2   *Mean of marriage duration by year by rural/urban differential, 2000–2009*

Year	Rural	N	Urban	N	Total	N
2000	10.2	49	11.5	87	11.0	136
2001	10.3	48	11.9	88	11.3	136
2002	7.2	50	11.0	92	9.7	142
2003	10.6	50	11.2	100	11.0	150
2004	7.8	55	12.5	125	11.0	180
2005	8.0	40	9.2	146	8.9	186
2006	9.3	49	10.6	160	10.3	209
2007	7.3	49	10.5	123	9.6	172
2008	10.9	58	9.4	22	10.5	80
2009	9.1	50	14.5	24	10.8	74
Total	9.1	498	11.0	967	10.3	1465

SOURCE: TRAN THI MINH THI 2011 (STUDY ON DIVORCE RECORD PROFILES AT THE DISTRICT PEOPLE'S COURTS IN HANOI AND HÀ NAM PROVINCES IN 2000–2009, N = 2033).

Finding 4: The Dominant Trend of Women's Initiation in Divorce

Though the proportion of women and men who are divorced has been gradually increasing in last two decades from 1989, the levels of increase among women are stronger than among men at all ages. As seen in Figure 3.4, more women than men initiated divorces (52.9 percent and 38.1 percent respectively). Reports in both rural and urban areas show higher percentages of women initiating divorces than their husbands, with the percentage being higher in rural districts. In addition, the proportion of joint initiation is higher in urban areas than in rural areas. The result of higher divorce initiation among women supports the results of a previous study by IFGS (2008), which showed that the proportion of wives initiating divorce is twice as high as that of their husbands (47 percent compared to 28.1 percent). The percentage of divorces initiated by wives increased yearly from 2000 to 2009. As shown in Figure 3.5, the percentage of divorces initiated jointly by the husband and wife was much higher in 2000 than it was from 2006 to 2009, while in the latter period almost all divorces were initiated by one party. One possible reason is that divorces were more difficult to obtain in the past; thus, couples were encouraged to apply for divorce together to make the procedure less complicated.

Another reason why divorce initiation is increasing among women is that women have more control in their marriage life than before, because of

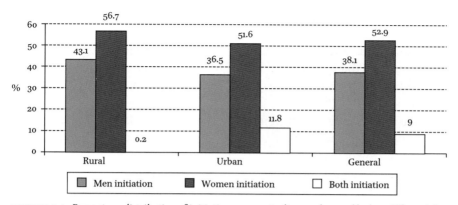

FIGURE 3.4 *Percentage distribution of initiating spouses in divorces by rural/urban differential, 2000–2009*
SOURCE: TRAN THI MINH THI 2011 (STUDY ON DIVORCE RECORD PROFILES AT THE DISTRICT PEOPLE'S COURTS IN HANOI AND HÀ NAM PROVINCES, 2000–2009, N = 2033).

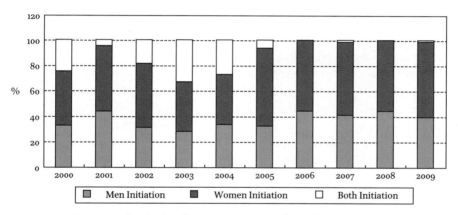

FIGURE 3.5 *Percentage distribution of initiating spouses in divorce by year, 2000–2009*
SOURCE: TRAN THI MINH THI 2011 (STUDY ON DIVORCE RECORD PROFILES AT THE DISTRICT PEOPLE'S COURTS IN HANOI AND HÀ NAM PROVINCES, 2000–2009, N = 2033).

increasing gender equality in Vietnam. Empirical research strongly supports a positive relationship between women's status and divorce (Mason & Jensen 1995). For many Asian women, divorce was not an option a few decades ago, as it was associated with social stigma or betrayal to the husband's family. It is expected that there would be gender differentiations in divorce prevalence and patterns, as well as the reasons for divorce, toward increasing the proactive role of women, especially young women.

Finding 5: A Trend Toward Higher Individualism in Divorce

It is obvious that, in Vietnam, marriage is universal and familialism remains significant. At the same time, however, individual freedom has increased, in the context of the informal control of families and kinship over individuals weakening due to the pressure of social and residential mobility (Trinh Duy Luan et al. 2011).

In this study, an increasing number of couples ended their marriages due to individualistic reasons such as lifestyle disputes. Lifestyle differences have become the major reason for divorce in Vietnam, accouning for 73.6 percent of divorces (see Figure 3.6). The proportion of urban couples citing this reason was higher than it was among rural couples (80 percent versus 60 percent, respectively). This may be a sincere reason for divorce, which implies the Vietnamese are becoming more individualistic, or it may just be an excuse to carry out divorce procedures in a setting where obtaining a divorce has become easier.

The pattern of divorce due to lifestyle differences tends to increase by year. As Figure 3.7 shows, divorce due to lifestyle conflicts gradually increased in the ten-year period under study. In 2000, only 63.7 percent of couples asked for a divorce because of lifestyle conflicts. In 2006, the percentage increased to 78.8 percent, and it peaked at 85.4 percent in 2009. There was a sharp increase in the percentage of divorces resulting from lifestyle conflicts in rural areas. In 2000, only 45.8 percent of couples reported lifestyle conflicts as the cause of divorce. By 2008 and 2009, the percentage had nearly doubled. Meanwhile, the number of divorces in urban areas due to lifestyle conflicts was high in 2000 (73.6 percent). The percentage increased slightly in the following years, rising to 86 percent in 2009 (Figure 3.8). Divorce due to lifestyle differences is most

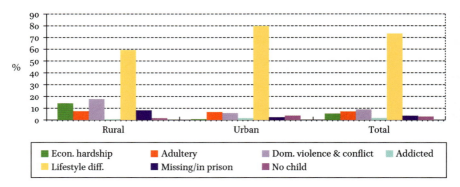

FIGURE 3.6 *Reported reasons for divorce, 2000–2009*
SOURCE: TRAN THI MINH THI 2011 (STUDY ON DIVORCE RECORD PROFILES AT THE DISTRICT PEOPLE'S COURTS IN HANOI AND HÀ NAM PROVINCES, 2000–2009, N = 2033).

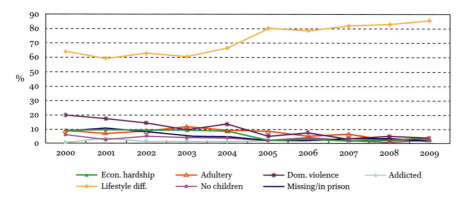

FIGURE 3.7 *Divorce reasons by year, 2000–2009*
SOURCE: TRAN THI MINH THI 2011 (STUDY ON DIVORCE RECORD PROFILES AT THE DISTRICT PEOPLE'S COURTS IN HANOI AND HÀ NAM PROVINCES, 2000–2009, N = 2033).

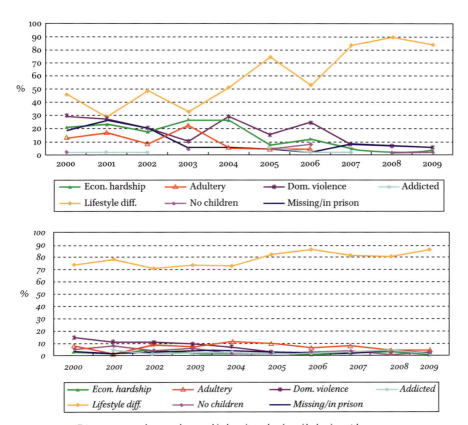

FIGURE 3.8 *Divorce causes by year by rural (above) and urban (below) residence, 2000–2009*
SOURCE: TRAN THI MINH THI 2011 (STUDY ON DIVORCE RECORD PROFILES AT THE DISTRICT PEOPLE'S COURTS IN HANOI AND HÀ NAM PROVINCES, 2000–2009, N = 2033).

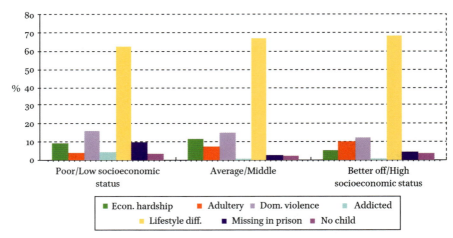

FIGURE 3.9 *Divorce reasons by wealth, 2000–2009*
SOURCE: TRAN THI MINH THI 2011 (STUDY ON DIVORCE RECORD PROFILES AT THE DISTRICT PEOPLE'S COURTS IN HANOI AND HÀ NAM PROVINCES, 2000–2009, N = 2033).

common among those with a high socioeconomic status and least common among those with a low socioeconomic status (Figure 3.9).

> I did not like her habits and she, too, [did not like mine]. She liked dancing, but for me it's wasting time and boring. I liked reading, and she said reading was so useless and had nothing to do with business. She fell asleep after reading no more than three pages of any book.... I am more open, but she likes living in her inner world. That's the main point. I like meeting with friends and [going to] parties, but she prefers staying at home, taking care of kids. She complained when I invited my friends home. One more thing: I often stayed up very late at night reading books or watching television and got up late. She was totally reversed, going to bed early and waking up early. (Mr. Công, born in 1962, university educational level, businessman, one son, Hanoi)

However, case studies of divorced people also reveal that "lifestyle differences" sometimes hide other reasons, such as family conflicts.

> After about three months of marriage, I knew we did not share the same lifestyle. My wife was so disorderly and clumsy. She did not know how to do the housework nicely. She is irresponsible. For example, we lived with my parents, but she did not obey them.... She asked my parents if she could visit her parents, about two kilometers away from my house, but

> she stayed overnight regardless of having a hungry baby at home. She also placed a two-month-old baby in an iron vessel on a very cold winter day. We share the same background, but we are so different in terms of living style and family traditions. (Mr. Hưng, born in 1963, rural Hà Nam)

Women seemed to resign themselves to tolerating their husbands' behavior; few ask for a divorce when they experience conflicts with different lifestyles. Divorce is the final solution when they see no potential for happiness or affection from their husbands. Following is the story of Ms. Trang, who divorced because of lifestyle disputes and economic conflicts:

> He is very arbitrary and patriarchal, with so many abnormal thoughts. He said he loved me, but he always showed that he was more valuable and belonged to a higher class. He looked down on me and dismissed my values by saying such things as if I had not married him I would be a prostitute. Or I was so lucky to marry him, so I must behave well. (Ms. Trang, born in 1982, university educational level, counselling staff, Hanoi)

As mentioned above, "lifestyle difference" could be cited as an excuse to carry out divorce procedures in a "modern" setting in which divorce has become easier. Even so, there are shadows of individualism—part of the process of modernization and more likely to be characteristic of people in a "modern" setting, such as an urban area, high socioeconomic status, or those who were older at marriage.

> We are from the countryside near Hanoi. After graduating from university, we found jobs in Hanoi and wanted to settle down here. We had to worry about everything, including rent, childcare expenses, living expenses, working to achieve permanent positions to stabilize our life, and so on. My wife started to think about buying a house in Hanoi, which I thought was out of reach since we could not afford it. But she thought differently. She went to everywhere in Hanoi to find a place and obtained the money, borrowing from both sides of the family. How could my family help when my parents did not have lots of money, and my heritance land in my hometown was cheap?.... One day, I came home from work and found the house totally empty. I was nervous since I thought we had been robbed. But I could not see my wife and child, either. Finally, I found a note saying that my wife could not live with me any longer and that she had rented a new place to live with our child. (Mr. Tư, editor of a TV program, born 1978, Hanoi)

Adultery is more likely a "modern" reason for divorce. Rindfuss and Morgan stated in 1983 that a quiet but profound sexual revolution was taking place in Asia. It is reasonable to suggest that the Vietnam family is also experiencing such a quiet sexual revolution, which in turn may have a strong influence on traditional ideas about faithfulness in marriage. Individuals may be more and more open-minded about sexuality, love, and happiness. They can seek an extramarital relationship and be ready to dissolve their marriage.

Figure 3.5 indicates that adultery ranks third among the causes of divorce (7.2 percent). There is no significant difference between rural and urban couples in this regard. The percentage of divorcing couples who cited adultery as the reason was highest from 2000 to 2005; the percentage dropped remarkably in the following years. It is interesting to note that divorce resulting from adultery was extremely high in rural areas at the beginning of the 2000s and also relatively high in urban areas. Several case studies validate the quantitative findings, as in the following examples:

> After my maternity leave, I was back to work and recognized strange signals. He was a driver, and he left from 6 a.m. until midnight. All the housework was left to me. He did not stay at home even on the weekends. The time I lived with my parents-in-law was longer than living with my husband. I heard he met with a woman with two daughters in cafés. I asked him where he was going. He said he went to work, but I came to the cafés and met him there. He then promised to solve the relationship completely. He changed his cell number and stopped visiting those cafés. I accepted this, but the situation was pending for several years. I was so tired and decided to separate. After a long time dating that woman, he was tired, too, and wanted to come back again. I forgave him and returned home, living with him again. After one week, that woman dared to call my home phone and asked frankly to meet my husband. They talked almost two hours, and then, the next morning, he left. I understood it was over completely. (Ms. Thơ, born in 1960, worker, Hanoi)

> At the beginning of the marriage, we were in a very hard situation because our daughter was small, and he had to write his dissertation. After five years, our economic condition became better. We decided to have a second child but failed. Among the students coming to my home, he fell in love with a girl from the countryside and rented a house in Hanoi for her to study. When the story came out, my neighborhood was shocked and so were my parents-in-law. The girl's parents also prohibited this relationship because it was immoral. My husband

then decided to stop, but the girl did not. She was pregnant. My husband moved out to live with her. He told me that he could not leave the baby inside her, and he was a responsible man, without thinking that he was abandoning his elder daughter and was not being responsible with me. That girl insisted on keeping the baby even though her mother asked her to have an abortion. The reason was that keeping that baby was the only solution in which she could have everything. I was so depressed and left home for several days. I was crazy with the thought of why I was being treated in such a nasty way. As I reached the maximum level of pain, everything was over. (Ms. Thủy, nurse, born in 1958, one daughter, Hanoi)

Results from the qualitative study show that adultery is related to migration to earn a living. Husbands are more likely to engage in an extramarital relationship than wives. This study shows that men's extramarital relationships are more furtive. Most men are not ready to break up with their spouses, nor do they desire to end the new relationship. They want their wife and girlfriend to compromise with each other and sacrifice to share the husband.

Ms. Nhung was born in 1980 and married in 2002 at the age of twenty-two. The story of her marriage and divorce is one of migration, adultery, and separation:

We migrated to Hồ Chí Minh City to work after our marriage. In 2003, I came back to give birth alone and then returned to Hồ Chí Minh City to stay with my husband. When my child was two years old in 2005, I discovered that my husband had had an extramarital affair with a girl in Ninh Bình province. That girl was born in 1986 and was younger than me.... In 2006, my husband returned home to apologize to me. I forgave him and we decided to live together again. However, half a month later, his girlfriend phoned him and said that she was pregnant. My husband convinced me to let her stay with us to give birth, promising that he would end the relationship definitively after she had given birth. I agreed because I believed him. I went to Hanoi to work. I left my baby with my parents. I left the house for the girlfriend. Several months later, my husband's girlfriend gave birth and, after one month, she left my house. It was in December 2006. My husband went to Hanoi to bring me home again. We had been living together for several months when my father-in-law became sick and was hospitalized in Hanoi in March 2007. My husband went to Hanoi to take care of his father and has lived with that woman since then. I was extremely hurt because he had lied to me many times, regardless of the fact that I was ready to forgive him. I want a divorce to liberate a credulous woman like me and to take the initiative to take care of my destiny. (Ms. Nhung, born in 1980, Hà Nam)

Ms. Đào, another woman from a local community, told her divorce story:

In 2001, due to economic difficulties, we went to Vũng Tàu city to earn a living. I worked at a shop, and my husband worked at a café. After one year, my father-in-law became sick, and then my husband asked me to come back home to take care of him and our kids. Since I came back home, my husband had never phoned me, even though our kids were small then. I felt strange then. I phoned my friends who worked with my husband. They said my husband was living with his new wife, Dung, and had a baby. I was shocked since I was also his wife.... I got the phone number of Dung's parents and talked to them. I was told that, after I returned home, they had started the relationship and lived with each other. They had even invited friends to come to greet them officially and celebrate their happiness. I then called my husband and said I knew the truth. He was so surprised.... Several months later, my husband returned to our hometown and wanted me to accept the new situation. However, I did not want to and did not see any possibility of living with my husband again, after trying several times unsuccessfully to convince him to come back. (Ms. Đào, born in 1973, farmer, Hà Nam)

These individualistic reasons for divorce in Vietnam are similar to those in many other societies. For instance, in the 1990s, Japan saw the return of divorce in society. Grounds for divorce there include retaining adultery, malicious desertion, unknown whereabouts, and the no-fault provision. In the late 1990s, the image of divorce as a positive step of liberation for women was especially promoted in print media as "divorce with a smile" or "happy divorce" (Geertz 1961; Fuess 2004).

Finding 6: Traditional Divorce Remains
If we carefully consider the real reasons for divorce and consider these interviews, it becomes clear that domestic disputes based on traditional family ideology still exist. It has become easier for Vietnamese people to obtain divorces in the process of modernization. However, it also means that people can get

divorced more casually for traditional reasons. The most profound evidence of the influence of traditional reasons for divorce is the number of divorces due to domestic violence, which ranks second (9.2 percent) among all reasons given for divorce.

Over ten years, the percentage of divorces ending because of domestic violence was significant but decreased sharply, especially after 2005. In 2000, approximately 20 percent of couples who divorced did so because of domestic violence. As the Law on Domestic Violence Prevention and Control comes into effect, the situation is gradually changing. Until 2009, only 4.2 percent of divorces resulted from domestic violence, which still ranked second among the reasons but had significantly declined (Figures 3.6, 3.7 and 3.8). The trend, however, does not simply mean that domestic violence in Vietnam is declining. In some cases, husbands do not want to register domestic violence as an official reason for their divorces because it is disadvantageous to them to do so, as it is now clearly defined by the state law as illegal. Although gender equality and freedom from violence are guaranteed under the law, inequality and violence persist in most communities and in institutions entrusted with overseeing and implementing the law (Vu Manh Loi et al. 1999; Nguyễn Hữu Minh & Trần Thị Vân Anh 2008).

The stories of divorced women validate this study's data. Ms. Hồng is a young woman who was born in 1981. She stayed at home to help with agricultural work after high school. Similar to other women in the village, she married at age nineteen. Her marriage was characterized by economic hardship, domestic violence, conflicts with her mother-in-law, adultery, separation, and a complicated divorce. Hồng said that she and her husband had a happy courtship. Their parents organized a traditional wedding for them. They had been happy for two years after the wedding. However, her husband, according to Hồng, was lazy, gambled, and drank. Hồng suspected him of having an extramarital affair, and the conflicts began. She told us:

> After that, my husband migrated to Hanoi to earn a living. I stayed at home with my in-laws. My mother-in-law and I had conflicts. I could not stand her insults and maltreatment. At the worst time, she came to my room to throw away my belongings; my clothes were piled in a corner of the garden to be burned. I found it so rude. When my husband came back home, he listened to her side of the story and then beat me. He had no way and will to solve the problem and left home again. I brought my daughter back to my parents' home. At that time, we broke up; no emotions, no relations,

nothing. My husband sometimes came back home to visit his mother, but he never showed up to visit our daughter. He never came to my parents' house to bring me and his child back. He never stopped by the kindergarten to see his daughter. After that, he brought a new girl home, and they lived as husband and wife. (Ms. Hồng, born in 1981, farmer, Hà Nam Province)

Domestic violence usually implies husbands beating wives. Women generally do not request a divorce the first time they are beaten by their husbands. According to this study, divorce occurs when the violence is severe, systematic, and unchangeable. There are many reasons for domestic violence. Women accept the violence to try to keep the family peace, for the sake of the children, or out of the shame they would feel if others learned about it. Therefore, many husbands give themselves the "right" to control their wives by using violence if their wives do not obey or satisfy them.

Divorce due to economic hardship is another dimension of the traditional style of divorce. Among the divorces in this study, 5.4 percent of couples divorce due to economic hardship (Figure 3.6). There is a huge difference between rural and urban areas in terms of divorce due to economic hardship. A very small number of urban couples divorce for this reason, but the percentage is significantly higher in rural areas. Figure 3.7 indicates that the percentage of divorces caused by economic hardship changed slightly in the ten-year period studied. At the beginning of the 2000s, economic hardship accounted for the highest percentage of divorces, whereas it accounted for the lowest percentage of divorces by the late 2000s. Since 2005, economic hardship as a cause of divorce has dramatically decreased. The percentage of divorces reported as being caused by economic hardship has dropped to only 1.8 percent, 2.5 percent, and 2.1 percent in 2007, 2008, and 2009. This seems to correspond well with the recent economic growth in Vietnam.

This study implies that in rural areas, economic hardship is a crucial factor influencing marriage happiness and stability and is often the factor that triggers separation and other changes. This is seen in the following example. Ms. Thuyết, born in 1971, married in 1990 and gave birth to a son in 1991. In 1993, the couple left for Bình Dương province. Her marriage is a story of economic hardship, migration, drinking, adultery, domestic violence, and family conflicts. Thuyết's husband told us the following story:

> When we got married and had a baby, we had no property except for two paddy fields the government assigned to citizens. In addition, we

repeatedly lost our harvest because of bad weather and pestilent insects. Thus, we decided to migrate to the South with the expectation that we would be better off. But the new life in the new land was also very difficult. We were not able to overcome it and often quarreled. This made me extremely sad. In 2007, I decided to separate from my wife. I wanted a divorce soon to start a new life.

This is an example of how economic stress can become the source of marital problems. Most divorced families in rural areas are poor, with a low, unstable income and little agricultural land. Farmers with less than a high-school education usually make a living from two rice harvests and some livestock. After marriage, most of them are happy for the first few years. After the first child is born, their economic condition becomes more difficult because they are on a fixed income and have increased expenditures. Couples struggle together to raise themselves above the poverty level, but they are trapped by their destiny. Some men leave home and go to cities to find jobs (becoming free migrants, seasonal migrants, or rural-urban migrants). They take almost any job to send remittances home. This can be seen as a positive aspect of migration. However, the negative aspects of migration include new problems, such as gambling, drinking, and adultery.

Difficulties and constraints in life lead to a couple's inhibition and dissatisfaction. Wives may reproach their husbands for lacking the capacity to earn money and compare them with other husbands who have better jobs. They have to take care of farming, housework, and children in the condition of economic shortage and have little decision-making power in the family.

Divorce due to economic hardship is a characteristic of couples with a rural residence, low socioeconomic status, more than three children, and, as mentioned above, domestic violence. Couples living on their own are more likely to divorce due to economic hardship than couples living with parents (Tran Thi Minh Thi 2012). The case studies used for this chapter show that economic hardship might be the root of a great deal of marital dissolution. Such problems even relate to men's use of and addiction to alcohol, drugs, and gambling. Economic hardship is also related to domestic violence, a major cause of divorce in rural areas. Migration and its link to extramarital sexual relations are also put forward as a cause for divorce. There are also more traditional factors involved in divorce decisions, such as tensions in the relationship between a mother-in-law and her daughter-in-law, and the tradition of polygyny.

Another traditional style of divorce is divorce that results from childlessness, which is related to the high value children have among Vietnamese people (Houghton and Houghton 1995). They are believed to bind couples together and help the family overcome conflicts, because sacrificing for children is valued. Childlessness was cited as a reason for 3.4 percent of divorces during the period studied. More couples in urban areas divorce because they have no children than do rural couples (3.8 percent and 2.2 percent, respectively), but the difference is not very significant (Figure 3.7), which means there is no difference in how children are valued in these settings. Data show that divorces due to childlessness seem to be gradually decreasing in urban areas yearly. This trend is not clear among rural couples (Figures 3.6, 3.7 and 3.8). In the early 2000s, a significant percentage of divorces resulted from childlessness; for example, about 6 percent of divorces were due to childlessness in 2000. Recently, the number of couples who divorced because of childlessness has slightly decreased, which may show a more modern attitude toward the value of children in Vietnamese families.

Living with parents-in-law is a contributing factor to many divorces. According to qualitative results, it is a reason for marital conflicts caused by generational conflicts and limited intimacy between the couple. On the one hand, living with parents increases the level of communication between daughter-in-law and mother-in-law. Conflicts may appear if living values, personal characteristics, and benefits are different. Conflicts arise mainly when a mother-in-law imposes traditional points of view and a traditional lifestyle on her daughter-in-law. She may also impose economic activities or interject her views about the couple's intimate life. In other words, extended family arrangements may cause generational conflicts, which may lead to divorce (Werner 2009). Ms. Hiền recalls:

> After marriage, we lived with my parents-in-law. I did not suit my mother-in-law, since she was very frightening and had conflicts with all the neighbors. When my husband and I were dating, she permitted it. However, after marriage and living with her, we had conflicts. She often drove me out of the house. After two years of married life, we lived separately, but she still controlled everything, even whether my husband should be at home with my children and me for the Lunar New Year holiday. I tried to endure the bad treatment. When I was pregnant with my youngest child, my husband and mother-in-law beat me and drove me out. My husband knew I was pregnant then, but he

still drove me out because he listened to his mother. I went to my mother's place, but she told me to go back to my husband. That night, I followed my mother's advice to come back to my husband's house to ask for forgiveness, but they kept on driving me away. My husband then applied for divorce. I felt that he did not want to divorce me, but his mother asked him to do so. (Ms Hiền, born in 1963, divorced in 1999, farmer, Hà Nam)

Conclusion

Divorce in Vietnam is increasing in both number and rate. The upturn is much stronger in urban areas than in rural areas. The trend is similar to that in other Southeast Asian countries, but remains low compared to developed countries. At the same time, modernization, accompanied by the infiltration of egalitarianism, the improvement of women's socioeconomic status, and the expansion of individualism, explains the increasing number of divorces in Vietnam. State policies and strategies on marriage, family, population, and gender equality; socioeconomic development; the international integration of socio-culture; and mass-media institutional settings are significant factors influencing this trend toward divorce. Social changes associated with modernization have eroded traditional norms. Women's increased economic independence, smaller family sizes, and an ideological emphasis on self-fulfillment in relationships, as well as individual choice, may be shifting the tide toward less stable relationships.

Modernization has brought about autonomous ways of life among the Vietnamese. Since the 1950s, the position of Vietnamese women has significantly improved in many aspects. Gender equality and increased independence for women in marriage and family have resulted in the dominant trend of women initiating divorce. The socioeconomic miracle that followed the country's opening to the outside world and the post-1986 Rrenovation have dramatically changed social mores, and divorce no longer carries the social stigma it once did. Vietnam's transition to a market economy also began to reshape lifestyles and values, including those regarding marriage and divorce. Socio-structural and legal changes under the increasing modernization process have caused individuals to adopt more liberal values toward marriage, family, and divorce than before. Collectivism is weakening, while individualism, which used to be weak in traditional society, has become one of the most influential factors in the rising divorce rate. With material comforts vastly improved, people are no longer satisfied with marriages that merely fulfill the need to carry on the family line and require women to obey and sacrifice.

It has become easier for Vietnamese people to get divorced due to the process of modernization. However, this also means that people can get divorced much more easily for traditional family reasons.

In rural areas, divorce procedures are more complicated, and collective decision-making occurs with the direct intervention of those who possess relevant power, such as family members, extended families, and mass organizations, revealing stronger social ties and collectivism in rural areas. Of these, local governments and social organizations play significant roles in individual divorce decisions through their intervention efforts to achieve reconciliation and through receiving and preparing divorce profiles at the commune level. In other words, divorce is a long and complicated process, with attempts at reconciliation, counseling, and the intervention of the family, lineage, village, and commune authorities. Other factors involved in divorces are cohabitation arrangements, tensions in the relationship between a mother-in-law and her daughter-in-law, vestiges of polygyny, and parents' influence in mate selection.

There is a competing force between modern and traditional influences on the reasons for divorce. The most profound evidence of the influence of traditional reasons for divorce is the second-place ranking of domestic violence among all the reasons for divorce. Divorce due to economic hardship is another dimension of traditional divorce. Economic hardship is a significant reason leading to marital dissolution in rural areas, and it influences marital quality, explosive tempers, and irritable behavior, as well as promotes interactional difficulties. Another traditional style of divorce is divorce due to childlessness, which shows the value for children among Vietnamese people.

It is worth noting that couples in urban settings are more likely to divorce for lifestyle differences and adultery, which constitute a more open-minded viewpoint on marriage and happiness. More couples are ending their marriages for "modern" reasons, resulting from greater individualism. The majority of people who divorced for individualistic reasons (i.e., lifestyle differences) are couples who live in an urban area, have a high socioeconomic status, and marry at an older age. This tendency may arise owing to the conflict between the greater social pressure to maintain the traditional values of family and this increasingly open viewpoint.

Divorces in Vietnam are reported for both traditional and modern styles, and some are transitioning between the two processes. The disparate coexistence of various levels of traditional, transitional, and modern values in a context that new institutions have not perfected and the continuing existence of old institutions is the general model of divorce in contemporary Vietnam.

References

Amato, Paul, and S.J. Rogers. 1997. "A Longitudinal Study of Marital Problems and Subsequent Divorce." *Journal of Marriage and the Family* 59: 612–24.
Amato, Paul, and Denise Previti. 2003. "People's Reasons for Divorcing: Gender, Social Class, the Life Course, and Adjustment." *Journal of Family Issues* 24(5): 602–26.
Atoh, M. 2001. "Very Low Fertility in Japan and Value Change Hypothesis." *Review of Population and Social Policy* 10: 1–21.
Barbieri, Magali, and Danièle Bélanger, eds. 2009. *Reconfiguring Families in Contemporary Vietnam.* Stanford, CA: Stanford University Press.
Beck, Ulrich. 1992. *Risk Society: Towards a New Modernity.* London: Sage.
Becker, G.S. 1991. *A Treatise on the Family*, enlarged ed. Cambridge, MA: Harvard University Press.
Bélanger, Danièle. 2002. "Son Preference in a Rural Village in North Vietnam." *Studies in Family Planning* 33: 321–34.
Bloom, B.L., R.L. Niles, and A.M. Tatcher. 1985. "Sources of Marital Dissatisfaction among Newly Separated Persons." *Journal of Family Issues* 6: 359–73.
Caldwell, J. 1976. "Toward a Restatement of Demographic Transition Theory." *Population and Development Review* 23(4): 321–66.
Chang, Kyung-Sup. 2010. "Individualization without Individualism: Compressed Modernity and Obfuscated Family Crisis in East Asia." *Journal of Intimate and Public Spheres* Pilot Issue: 23–39.
Choe, M.K. 1998. "Changing Marriage Patterns in South Korea, Manson." In *The Changing Family in Comparative Perspective: Asia and the United States*, edited by Karen Oppenheim Mason et al., 43–46. Honolulu: East Center.
Coale, A.J. 1973. "The Demographic Transition." *Congrès International de la Population*, Vol. I, 53–71. Liège.
Diener, E., and, R.E. Lucas 2000. "Explaining Differences in Societal Levels of Happiness: Relative Standards, Need Fulfillment, Culture, and Evaluation Theory." *Journal of Happiness Studies* 1: 41–78.
Do, Long, and Phan Thi Mai Huong, eds. 2002. *Collectivism, Individualism and "the Self" of the Vietnamese Today.* Hanoi: Chinh Tri Quoc Gia Publisher.
Easterlin, R.A. 1983. "Modernization and Fertility: A Critical Essay." In *Determinants of Fertility in Developing Countries*, Vol. II, edited by R.A. Bulatao and R.D. Lee, 562–86. New York: Academic Press.

Fuess, Harald. 2004. *Divorce in Japan: Family, Gender, and the State 1600–2000*. Stanford, CA: Stanford University Press.

Gammeltoft, T. 2007. "Prenatal Diagnosis in Postwar Vietnam: Power, Subjectivity and Citizenship." *American Anthropologist* 109(1): 153–63.

Geertz, H. 1961. *The Javanese Family: A Study of Kinship and Socialization*. New York: Free Press.

General Statistics Office. 2011a. *Central Population and Housing Census. The 2009 Vietnam Population and Housing Census: Major Findings*. Hanoi: Statistics Publishing House.

———. 2011b. *Age-Sex Structure and Marital Status of Population in Vietnam*. Hanoi: Statistics Publishing House.

Goode, William J. 1956. *Women in Divorce*. New York: Free Press.

———. 1963. *World Revolution and Family Patterns*. New York: Free Press.

———. 1971. "Family Disorganization." In *Contemporary Social Problems*, 3rd ed., edited by Robert K. Merton and Robert Nisbet, 467–544. New York: Harcourt Brace Jovanovich.

———. 1993. *World Changes in Divorce Patterns*. New Haven: Yale University Press.

Goodkind, Daniel. 1997. "The Vietnamese Double Marriage Squeeze." *International Migration Review* 31(1): 108–27.

Haughton, Jonathan. 1997. "Falling Fertility in Vietnam." *Population Studies* 512: 203–11.

Haughton, Jonathan, and Dominique Haughton. 1995. "Son Preference in Vietnam." *Studies in Family Planning* 26: 325–37.

Heaton, T.B., M. Cammack, and L. Young. 2001. "Why Is the Divorce Rate Declining in Indonesia?" *Journal of Marriage and Family* 63: 480–90.

Hirschman, Charles, and Nguyen Huu Minh. 2002. "Tradition and Change in Vietnamese Family Strucure in the Red River Delta." *Journal of Marriage and Family* 64(2): 1063–79.

Hirschman, Charles, and Bussarawan Teerawichitchainan. 2003. "Cultural and Socioeconomic Influences on Divorce during Modernization: Southeast Asia: 1940s to 1960s." *Population and Development Review* 29(2): 215–53.

Hirschman, Charles, and R. Rindfuss. 1980. "Social, Cultural, and Economic Determinants of Age at Birth of First Child in Peninsular Malaysia." *Population Studies* 34: 507–18.

Hochschild, Arlie. 1989. *The Second Shift: Working Parents and the Revolution at Home*. New York: Viking Adult.

Hollander, D. 1996. "Son Preference Remains Strong among Vietnamese Women, but Has Only a Modest Effect on Fertility." *International Family Planning Perspective* 22: 84–85.

Inoue, T., and Y. Ehara, eds. 1999. *Women's Data Book, 3rd Edition*. Tokyo: Yuhikaku.

Institute for Family and Gender Studies (IFGS). 2008. *Survey on Vietnam Families 2006*. General Report. Hanoi: IFGS.

Johnson, D., T. Amoloza, and A. Booth. 1992. "Stability and Developmental Change in Marital Quality: A Three-Wave Panel Analysis." *Journal of Marriage and the Family* 54: 582–94.

Jones, G.W. 1994. *Marriage and Divorce in Islamic Southeast Asia*. Oxford: Oxford University Press.

———. 1997. "Modernization and Divorce: Contrasting Trends in Islamic Southeast Asia and the West." *Population and Development Review* 23(1): 95–114.

———. 2007. "Delayed Marriage and Very Low Fertility in Pacific Asia." *Population and Development Review* 33(3): 453–78.

Kitson, G.C. 1992. *Portrait of Divorce: Adjustment to Marital Breakdown*. New York: Guilford.

Knodel, John, et al. 2004. *Gender Roles in the Family: Change and Stability*. Population Studies Center Research Report No. 04–559. Ann Arbor: University of Michigan.

Lê Ngọc Văn. 2006. "Về quan hệ hôn nhân hiện nay" [Today's Marriage Relations]. *Tạp chí Nghiên cứu Gia đình và Giới* [*Journal of Family and Gender Studies*] 16(2): 3–15.

Lee, Gary. 1982. *Family Structure and Interaction: A Comparative Analysis*, 2nd edition. Minneapolis: University of Minnesota Press.

Lee, Yean-Ju. 2006. "Risk Factors in the Rapidly Rising Incidence of Divorce in Korea." *Asian Population Studies* 222: 113–31.

Luong, Hy V. 1989. "Vietnamese Kinship: Structural Principles and the Socialist Transformation in Twentieth-Century Northern Vietnam." *Journal of Asian Studies* 48(3): 741–56.

———. 1992. *Revolution in the Village: Tradition and Transformation in North Vietnam: 1925–1988*. Honolulu: University of Hawaii Press.

———. 2003. "Gender Relations: Ideologies, Kinship Practices, and Political Economy." In *Post-war Vietnam: Dynamics of a Transforming Society*, edited by Hy V. Luong, 201–24. Boulder, CO: Rowman-Littlefield.

Mai Thi Tu and Le Thi Nham Tuyet. 1978. *Women in Vietnam*. Hanoi: Foreign Language Publishing House.

Mason, K.O., and A.M. Jensen. 1995. *Gender and Family Change in Industrialized Countries*. Oxford: Oxford University Press.

Mauldin, P., and S. Segal. 1998. "Prevalence of Contraceptive Use: Trends and Issues." *Studies in Family Planning* 19: 335–53.

Nguyễn, Hữu Minh. 2000. "Các yếu tố tác động đến khuôn mẫu tưởi kết hôn của dân cư đồng bằng sông Hồng" [Factors that Affect the Marriage Age of Population in the Red River Delta]. *Tạp chí Xã hội học* [*Sociology*] 72: 21–32.

———. 2009. *Vietnamese Marriage Patterns in the Red River Delta: Tradition and Changes*. Hanoi: Social Sciences Publishing House.

———. 2011. "Post-Marital Living Arrangements in Rural Vietnam". In *Rural Families in Doimoi Vietnam*, edited by Trinh Duy Luan, Helle Rydström and Wil Burhoorn, 58–89. Hanoi: Social Sciences Publishing House.

Nguyễn Hữu Minh and Trần Thị Vân Anh. 2008. *Bạo lực gia đình trên cơ sở giới ở Việt nam: Thực trạng, diễn tiến và nguyên nhân* [*Evolving Processes of Domestic*

Violence: Detection from Qualitative Research]. Hanoi: Social Sciences Publishing House.

Ochiai, Emiko. 2010. "Reconstruction of Intimate and Public Sphere in Asia Modernity: Familialism and Beyond." *Journal of Intimate and Public Spheres* Pilot Issue: 2–22.

———. 2011. "Unsustainable Societies: The Failure of Familialism in East Asia's Compressed Modernity." *Historical Social Research* 136(36): 219–46.

Rindfuss, R., and Philip Morgan. 1983. "Marriage, Sex and the First Birth Interval: The Quiet Revolution in Asia." *Population and Development Review* 9: 259–78.

Rydström, Helle. 2010. "Introduction: Gendered Inequalities in Asia." In *Gendered Inequalities: Configuring, Contesting, and Recognizing Women and Men*, edited by Helle Rydström, 1–21. Copenhagen: NIAS Press.

Thompson, L., and A.J. Walker. 1991. "Gender in Families: Women and Men in Marriage, Work, and Parenthood." In *Contemporary Families: Looking Forward, Looking Back*, edited by A. Booth, 76–102. Minneapolis, MN: National Council on Family Relations.

Tran Dinh Huou. 1991. "Traditional Families in Vietnam and the Influence of Confucianism." In *Sociological Studies on the Vietnamese Families*, edited by Rita Liljestrom and Tuong Lai, 25–47. Hanoi: Social Sciences Publishing House.

Tran, Thi Minh Thi. 2011. "Divorce in the Rural Red River Delta: A Case Study of Individual Choices and the Forces of Tradition." In *Rural Families in Đổi Mới Vietnam*, edited by Trịnh Duy Luân, Helle Rydström and Wil Burghoorn, 128–52. Hanoi: Social Sciences Publishing House.

———. 2012. "Prevalence and Patterns of Divorce in Vietnam, 2000–2009." *Vietnam Journal of Family and Gender Studies* 7(1): 55–79.

Trinh Duy Luan, Helle Rydström, and Wil Burghoorn, eds. 2011. *Rural Families in Đổi Mới Vietnam*. Hanoi: Social Sciences Publishing House.

Tsuya, N.O., et al. 2004. "Views of Marriage among Never-Married Young Adults." In *Work and Family Life in Comparative Perspective: Japan, South Korea and the United States*, edited by N.O. Tsuya and L.L. Bumpass, 39–53. Honolulu: University of Hawaii Press.

Vu Manh Loi. 2011. "Who Are the Household Heads in Rural Vietnamese Families?" In *Rural Families in Đổi Mới Vietnam*, edited by Trịnh Duy Luân, Helle Rydström and Wil Burghoorn, 38–58. Hanoi: Social Sciences Publishing House.

Vu Manh Loi, et al. 1999. *Domestic Violence from Gender Aspects*. World Bank.

Werner, Jayne. 2009. *Gender, Household, and State in Post-Revolutionary Vietnam*. London and New York: Routledge.

White, Lynn K. 1990. "Determinants of Divorce: A Review of Research in the Eighties." *Journal of Marriage and Family* 52(4): 904–12.

Xu, X., and S. Lai. 2002. "Resources, Gender Ideologies, and Marital Power: The Case of Taiwan." *Journal of Family Issues* 23: 209–45.

Yang, Wen-Shan, and Pei Chih Yen. 2010. "A Comparative Study of Marital Dissolution in East Asia: Gender Attitudes and Social Expectations towards Marriage in Taiwan, Korea and Japan." *Asian Journal of Social Science* 39(6): 751–75.

Yi, Zeng, and Wu Deqing. 2000. "Regional Analysis of Divorce in China since 1980." *Demography* 37(2): 215–19.

CHAPTER 4

Negotiating with Multilayered Public Norms: Female University Students' Struggle to Survive the Đổi Mới Period

Ito Miho

Introduction

> You know, students who are studying in the humanities will have a hard time finding jobs after graduation. Very hard. However, we can find good husbands more easily than female students who study in other majors. This is the fate of female students in the humanities!
> INTERVIEW WITH THE AUTHOR, 2012

These are the words of a female student in the history department at one of the top universities in Hanoi. Her pessimistic outlook is partially true: university graduates in the humanities have faced difficulties in finding good work opportunities in Vietnam. According to the Ministry of Education and Training (MOET), about 63 percent of university graduates were unable to find employment immediately after graduation (*Báo Giáo dục Việt Nam*, September 9, 2012). Although the methodology of the study and the actual time of the research were unclear, this significant percentage of the "unemployment of university graduates" reveals that the Vietnamese labor market, which contains young people who have obtained high academic skills, has serious problems. The interview quoted here perhaps reflects this hardship. Nonetheless, why did the interviewee demonstrate the recognition that "we"—that is, female graduate students in the humanities—"find good husbands more easily than other female students in other majors"? Finding good job opportunities in the marketplace and getting married to a good man essentially belong to different dimensions, particularly for people who attain high academic backgrounds; thus, why did she carry the self-directive that she should find a good husband if she failed to find employment after graduation?

As Bélanger and Pendakis (2009, 265) have pointed out, young, single women who migrate from rural to industrial areas to work for wages struggle against and continually negotiate with the social norms of gender in

Vietnam. One of the main purposes of the literature relating to this topic is to clarify whether women's experiences in work outside their natal villages may empower them, and if so, to what extent, with regard to their role change not only in relation to their families and kinship but also in society. Specifically, "factory girls" in many rapidly industrializing countries in Asia, including Vietnam, have focused on their experiences in moving away from their families in rural areas and finding new social relationships in cities or rural industrialized zones (Nguyen-Vo 2006). The literature on such "factory girls" shows that their wage work has served to achieve measurable outcomes, such as education or better health, as well as contributing to those which cannot be measured as easily, such as empowerment (Bélanger & Pendakis 2009, 268). Although these young women experienced many "moments of empowerment" through their work in factories (268), they also were conflicted, struggling against changes in their identity and family status that resulted from their becoming too urbanized. By physically separating from parents, even tentatively, single female workers become disconnected from the normative notions of femininity ascribed to daughters unrelated to sexuality, which is considered a somewhat dangerous and immoral force that needs to be controlled, even to the point of being excluded as a "social evil" (Rydström 2006, 284).

Another way exists, however, for young, single women to leave their rural villages for a while: they can "migrate" to large urban centers by attending university. As many scholars have already clarified, economic development and global standardization of education deliver opportunities for higher academic attainments for women as well as men (cf. Moock et.al. 2003; Nguyen 2006; Đặng 2007). However, most families living in less developed countries with meager financial resources must decide whether to spend money, and how much, for their daughters to go to school. Such a decision pertains not only to families' financial restrictions, but also to the estimated returns on a daughter's education. Specifically in East Asian countries, including the northern part of Vietnam, which are still strongly influenced by patriarchy, daughters tend to be accorded a lower priority in the family than sons. It has been claimed that gender-unequal practices have been revived in Vietnamese families, which have in turn influenced educational provision for children, especially daughters (Liu 2001; Barbieri & Bélanger 2009, 2; cf. Colclough et al. 2000; Bélanger & Liu 2004).

Despite a socialist regime for more than thirty years and despite feminist values, patriarchy—which dictates a preference for sons—survives strongly in the cultural values and practices of Vietnamese families (Haughton & Haughton

1995; Bélanger 2002). A Vietnamese proverb says, "A family who has a boy says, 'We have a child', but even a family who has ten girls says, 'We don't have a child'" (*nhất nam viết hữu, thập nữ viết vô*); another says, "Boys eat from the same tray, but girls eat from another tray" (*con trai ăn một mâm cơm, con gái ăn một mâm khác*). Both of these proverbs suggest a patriarchal ideology that strongly favors sons over daughters because sons offer security for their parents in old age, while daughters will be the "children of others" when they leave the natal family after marriage (Ahmed & Bould 2004, 1334; Bélanger & Pendakis 2009, 267). In fact, gender ideology has been maintained and even strengthened under modern socialistic institutions. Because of Vietnam's one-or-two-child policy, which was officially implemented in 1988 (Jones 1982, 795–97; Goodkind 1995a, 85–89), young parents have had to choose whether to have a son or a daughter. Therefore, the socialist policy—the fundamental purpose of which was to establish gender equality—instead preserved the cultural norm in Vietnamese families that favors sons over daughters, simply condensing it within a smaller family unit. Since the Đổi Mới policy was implemented in 1986, presocialist funeral customs and ancestor worship have returned (Luong 1993; Kleinen 1999). These developments have also resulted in reviving male-centered family norms and increasing gender inequalities in the postsocialist era in Vietnam (Pelzer 1993; Bélanger & Pendakis 2009, 273).

In addition, the centralized labor market during the period of the state-planned economy played an important role in preserving the social norms of gender. Like other socialist countries, Vietnam implemented a mandatory job-allocation system for university graduates (Marr & Rosen 1999; cf. London 2006). Because of the state committee's control over job allocation for at least fifteen years, the Vietnamese labor market was strongly influenced by socialist ideology concerning a gendered labor force. As we will see in the next section, even though the government of the Democratic Republic of Vietnam officially encouraged young women to obtain a higher education, it also specified "favorable" occupations, which were derived from gender. University graduates inevitably took these gendered paths, becoming the expected laborers with high academic skills. Vestiges of this system remain, even though it was demolished at the end of the 1980s and free-market principles introduced. Elson indicated that labor markets, which seem like a neutral arena in which buyers and sellers interact, are institutional "bearers of gender" (Elson 1999, 611). According to her, "certain social stereotypes associate masculinity with having authority over others in the workplace (being the 'boss'), and such stereotypes also dictate what is 'man's work' and 'woman's work'." The operation of labor markets is structured by formal and informal rules that deliver instantiations of the gender relations of the society in which the labor market is embedded (Elson 1999, 611–12).

In terms of functioning as a "bearer of gender," the Vietnamese labor market after the Đổi Mới policy should be considered as influenced by two different kinds of gender social norms: (1) patriarchy and (2) socialistic gender norms. In this chapter, I discuss the struggles of women with high academic backgrounds as they seek to shape a life for themselves, as well as their negotiations with the social norms of gender roles as they look for self-fulfillment. These women act as multilayered agents: they must be "good daughters" in terms of male-centered family norms, the "expected female workers," an expectation still strongly influenced by the pre–Đổi Mới job allocation system, and "modernized people" who have obtained substantial human resources as a result of individual efforts and merits.

To research this topic, I rely here on interview data derived mainly from women studying in universities in Hanoi.[1] These women came from rural areas to the city of Hanoi to pursue academic careers. Another narrative was used from a female teacher who was interviewed by the author in 2006 at Lào Cai province in the northern part of Vietnam, as well as statistical data analysis.

Gendered Academic Choice in the Pre–Đổi Mới Era

The national elites of the Democratic Republic of Vietnam (North Vietnam) imitated the Soviet Union's national education system, which was characterized by a dual public education system (vocational and academic track). In the 1974–75 academic year, North Vietnam had forty-one universities modeled on the Soviet system, with 55,700 students and 8,658 teachers (Bộ Giáo dục và Đào tạo 2004, 23).

---

1 In 2012 and 2013, I conducted interviews with twenty-four female students who were studying at a leading university in Hanoi. With a long history in Vietnam, it has many faculties, including humanities and natural sciences. I asked the Department of Student Management to provide a list of all students. The sample was randomly selected from a list of students who originated from different places in the northern part of Vietnam.

 A structured interview guide was used, with interviews lasting from half an hour to one and a half hours. The guide covered demographic variables, including birth year, ethnicity, number and gender of siblings, rural background, educational background, and parental background. It also covered the following main questions: (1) Why did you want to go to university? (2) How do you and the people around you—family, relatives, neighbors, and close friends—evaluate your higher education attainment? (3) What kind of job do you want to obtain after graduation, and where? All interviewees were female students born between 1987 and 1993. This means that they were educated during the upheaval of the transition economy.

TABLE 4.1 *Increase in the number of university students (long term) and percentage of female students from 1960 to 1969*

Year	Total (number)	Female students (number)	Female students (%)
1960	13,610	1,272	9.3
1961	15,908	2,059	12.9
1962	18,815	2,746	14.6
1963	20,611	3,176	15.4
1964	22,374	3,610	16.1
1965	23,900	5,386	22.5
1966	32,541	7,872	24.2
1967	42,909	11,845	27.6
1968	51,817	15,683	30.3
1969	61,885	19,434	31.4

SOURCE: TỔNG CỤC THỐNG KÊ 1970, 460.

The new national education system mobilized Vietnamese women from the narrow living spheres of their natal villages and brought them to school, to a new social space. According to the First Five-Year Plan for the national economy of North Vietnam in 1960, educating women to make them cadres was recognized as one of the important objects in that term (Unknown 1979, 17).

Owing to the education policy of North Vietnam's government, the number of female university students increased rapidly. While only 1,272 female students were going to university (long term) in 1960, the number more than quadrupled during the next five years (5,386 female university students in 1965), and had increased more than fifteen times within ten years (19,434 female university students in 1969). Table 4.1, which shows the increase in female university students from 1960 to 1969, reveals that the speed at which young women were being mobilized to obtain a higher education accelerated constantly and quickly.

Because of a lack of male laborers during the war, North Vietnam's government mobilized women to become highly educated laborers with technological knowledge (Trần 1995). However, the gender-equalization policy still provided women less freedom in their choice of academic field than men, in part because women were asked not only to move from a small living sphere in their rural villages but also to reorient themselves in a newly constructed, feminized space at school.

According to Instruction 88/TTG-VG from Prime Minister Phạm Văn Đồng on March 5, 1965, the political intent was to guide women to choose a "favorable" academic field to study:

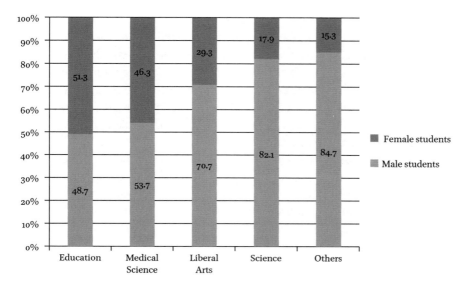

FIGURE 4.1 *Gender gap of university students by major, 1975–1976*
SOURCE: TỔNG CỤC THỐNG KÊ 1977, 189–90.

We need to pay attention to educating public officials for basic scientific fields and basic research fields. At the same time, more technical officials who work for industry, agriculture, forestry, economic management, and technical management should be educated. We need to have policies to mobilize women to enter into some specialized areas which are fit for them, such as medical science, pharmacy, culture, education, agriculture, and light industry, etc.

VIETNAMESE COMMUNIST PARTY 1979, 49

Because of the political intention to channel women into certain academic majors, more female than male students tended to choose to study the liberal arts (including education) and medical science.

Figure 4.1 shows the gender gap among university students by major in the 1975–76 academic year. While the rate of female students who majored in science was only 17.9 percent, almost half of the students who studied education or medical science were female.

In sum, the Vietnamese Communist Party's gender-equalization policy in education had a certain amount of success in quickly mobilizing women, especially young women, from their villages and bringing them into the wider (even nationwide) society to make them a productive labor force with high-level academic skills. However, in this same way, it also generated a newly gendered manner in the choice of academic majors. A female student might become a worker for the socialist state, but she might also be feminized by having to choose a "favorable" gendered academic major, such as education or medical science.

This public canalization for academic field by gender was closely related to the job allocation policy under the control of the state planning committee. For the sake of reunifying the nation and constructing a socialist state, North Vietnam's government policy was to distribute highly educated people into all fields, from the central to the local level (Chỉ thị 190/CT-TƯ 1979). In particular, it promulgated socialistic institutions in two places. One was the southern part of Vietnam, which had been "newly released," and the other was the northern mountainous area, where many ethnic minorities were still living with their own customs. Because of the severe lack of teachers and medical staff, young, single women with high-level academic skills were expected to move to these areas to help construct the socialist nation, and even to marry local people and settle there.

A teacher who graduated from a university of education in Thái Nguyên province in 1986 told me about the public expectations for young female graduates at that time.

> Just after graduating from university, I was informed that I would be sent to Tân Uyên High School in Lào Cai province as a teacher. I felt very sad and kept crying, even after I moved there. My parents said, "You should go because it was the government's decision." Actually, teachers who were distributed to mountainous areas, specifically female teachers, were expected to marry local people and make a new life there. Myself? I also married a local man when I was twenty-five years old.
>
> MS. TH, BORN IN 1968 IN THÁI BÌNH PROVINCE, GEOGRAPHY TEACHER

From this woman's narrative, we can see that young female university graduates were pressured to act as socialists by the government and even by their own parents. For them, attaining high-level academic skills not only provided a chance to move away from their villages, but also forced them to become part of the socialist labor force and to move to wherever they were sent, without their individual consent.

Educational Aspirations in the Đổi Mới Period

After the Đổi Mới period began, when the socialist distribution policy was abandoned, all people were free to choose their occupations and workplaces. At the same time, the universities, which had been centrally controlled by the national educational budget, were asked to manage both their finances and student quantity by themselves, and they attempted to enlarge their schools.

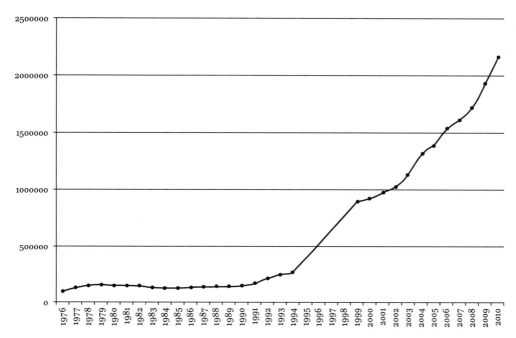

FIGURE 4.2 *Number of university and college students from 1976 to 2010*
SOURCE: BỘ GIÁO DỤC VÀ ĐÀO TẠO 1995; 2011.

In addition, with the establishment of many new universities (both public and private), even in local prefectural capital cities, the number of university students rapidly and explosively expanded.

Figure 4.2 shows the increase in the number of people who went to university and college. The number of postsecondary students (university and college) has risen dramatically since the early 1990s. Almost 2 million students went to postsecondary schools in 2009, which was double the number in 1999 (893,754 people) and fourteen times the number in 1989 (138,566 people).

Families interested in the educational investment of their children were behind this enthusiasm for higher education. Before the Đổi Mới policy was implemented, the Vietnamese government announced educational reform policies in the late 1980s that allowed private and semipublic schools to engage in market-based provision of informal and self-instruction activities. Moreover, students (or, rather, their families) were required to shoulder the financial burden of the substantial and rising cost of school tuition, fees, and supplies (Glewwe and Patrinos 1998; Korinek 2006, 60). This fiscal pressure required parents to consider carefully the costs and benefits of educating sons and daughters. As a result, Goodkind proposed that family investment policies towards the education of daughters might "be less valuable than before," because of the

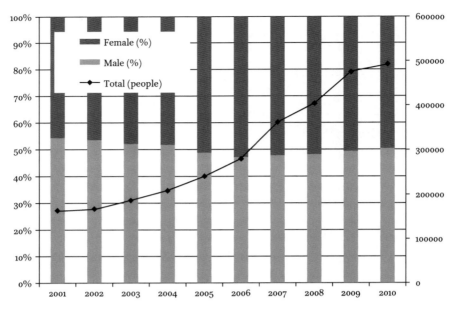

FIGURE 4.3 *The gender gap of students in postsecondary education from 2001 to 2010*
SOURCE: BỘ GIÁO DỤC VÀ ĐÀO TẠO 2012.

"recent increase in patrilocal residence following marriage" (1995b, 353). However, his prediction did not come true.

The gender gap of students has not experienced as big a shift during the rapid expansion period of post-secondary education. Although the proportion of female college and university students increased from 45.5 percent in 2001 to 52.8 percent in 2006, it decreased slightly, settling at 50 percent in 2010 (Figure 4.3).

This result is not surprising; the socialistic norms of education, which encouraged young women to enter higher education and become part of a highly skilled labor force for constructing the socialistic state before the Đổi Mới policy, still more or less influence people's perception of children's education. In Vietnamese society, people are influenced largely by Confucian philosophy, which emphasizes the importance of children's education, even if women are largely excluded (London 2011, 8); thus, it seemed that people could accept relatively easily the socialist idea that they should invest in their children's education. In addition, the tendency for parents to invest in educational opportunities for their sons more than for their daughters in the early 1990s, when the market-oriented economy was just being introduced (Liu 2001), gradually diminished as people became used to the idea of market-oriented rationalism. A female university student said,

TABLE 4.2 *Family expectations regarding children's employment (Data from Bình Lục District, Hà Nam Province, 2008)*

	Rich		Middle		Poor	
	Girls	Boys	Girls	Boys	Girls	Boys
Local farmer	0%	1.7%	2.3%	1.0%	0%	2.9%
Retail trade or other occupations	34.5%	35.0%	34.9%	38.8%	24.2%	29.4%
Government officials and workers	65.5%	63.3%	62.8%	60.2%	75.8%	67.6%
Total(People)	55	60	88	98	33	34

SOURCE: ĐẶNG 2011, 157.

My elder sister was born in 1981. She did not go to high school. My parents encouraged her to go study, but at her time, due to a social atmosphere that supposed a female should not go to school like the male, she decided herself it was not necessary to go to high school. Even now, such an atmosphere still remains; I think, however, it gradually has changed, since around the mid-1990s. Because of the economic prosperity that people began to perceive in rural areas, many people connect investment in their child's education with overcoming present poverty.

    MS. SA, BORN IN 1989 IN VĨNH PHÚC PROVINCE, SENIOR IN THE HISTORY DEPARTMENT

Families' Expectations for Daughters

Families' expectations for their children's educational attainment prevailed in all economic strata. Table 4.2, which shows family expectations for children's employment in the Bình Lục district of Hà Nam province, indicates that at all economic levels, regardless of gender, families aspire for their children not to engage in agriculture locally but to obtain occupations, probably with wages. We should especially focus on the fact that more families expected more girls than boys to become "government officials and workers," but this expectation is most pronounced for the poorest families (75.8 percent).

The category of "government officials and workers" should be treated carefully because of the possibility that the characteristics of each labor market are completely different. While the "government officials" category has basically continued from before the Đổi Mới period (even though it expanded to its lowest level [cấp xã] in the 1990s), the "workers" category is supposed to include the semiskilled local workforce in the light industries, which has developed in the globalized economy in Southeast Asia since the 1970s (King and Wilder 2003, 280). According to surveys on factories conducted by the Japan External Trade Organization (JETRO 2013), 8,339 companies were operating in 261 industrial parks in Vietnam as of 2010 in such places as Hải Phòng, Hưng Yên, and Nam Định in the North and Đồng Nai and Bình Dương in the South, with 1.6 million workers.

With a significant demand for workers in such industrial parks, families in rural areas tend to send daughters to these workplaces for one to two years to learn a trade, lessen the burden on the family, and earn some money before marriage (Nghiem 2004, 304). Considering the young people's new way of working, it is not surprising that families in the poor strata tend more to expect their children to join the new category of workers rather than become government officials. In particular, poorer families with daughters strongly desire that they work as "factory girls" and earn enough to send money back to their natal families.

The literature on factory girls acknowledges the difference between married and unmarried women owing to the patriarchal family system. As Bélanger and Pendakis (2009, 266) note, "A rural woman's marital status generally determines her sphere of belonging: a daughter 'belongs' to her natal family until marriage, then, after her marriage, she 'belongs' to her husband's family." Daughters' sphere of belonging seems to be expanding or multiplying gradually, regardless whether they marry out of their natal families. Ms. TH (born in 1992 in Bắc Giang province, freshman in the environment department) reported on her sister: "My elder sister has been a worker at a Canon factory since 2008. In 2012, she married a guy who is from the same province and also works in the same factory. However, she continues to send 2 million đồng per month to our [natal] parents." Thus, even though Ms. TH's elder sister now "belongs" to her husband's family rather than her natal family, she still sends a substantial amount of money to her parents. During Ms. TH's time in lower secondary school, her parents could not afford to support her elder sister's completion of secondary education. Therefore, the elder sister stopped going to upper secondary school and, after several years of living with her parents, decided to work for a foreign company in Bắc Ninh province. The factory attracted her because it provided a way of earning enough money to live away from home and relieved her feeling of being a burden to her parents (Bélanger & Pendakis 2009, 282). This case seems to reveal a typical trajectory for factory girls who leave their natal homes to work in unfamiliar places. She could have quit sending money to her parents after marriage, but she could (or did) not. It is possible that the period of daughters' belonging to their natal homes has been extended because of the aging population, combined with the diminishing number of children. Because of the birth-control policy imposed by the Vietnamese government, downsized families with only two children, even when both are daughters like Ms. TH's family, inevitably rely on the daughters' labor, even though they are supposed to belong to other families. In this process, daughters who earn a modest but stable wage by working in factories tend to keep strong ties to their natal families, even after they marry.

In contrast to "factory girls," women with high academic attainment seem to become more personalized. So that their daughters can attend good universities in metropolitan areas, parents encourage their children to "put their backs" into studying. This interviewee, the children felt that her parents had encouraged her to study hard not so she could support the family but for her own individual happiness.

> My mother told me that people used to think it was useless to invest in daughters going to school. While sons might pay back the investment for education to their parents by staying with the natal family after graduation, daughters might not do so because they would marry someone and move from the natal house to become a member of his family. However, my parents did not think so. They thought that investment for education would yield a return for the person herself, not for her family. I thank them because they have such a progressive way of thinking.
> MS. DU, BORN IN 1992 IN SƠN LA PROVINCE, FRESHMAN IN THE LITERATURE DEPARTMENT

However, female university students do not consider themselves as individuals apart from the expectation of parents. Rather, they seemed to suffer from complex emotions, such as whether they should try to realize their own dreams or to pursue a career according to what their parents might expect for a daughter's future.

> My parents encourage me to study hard. Maybe they want me to become a teacher. However, I want to go to the Police University, because this has been my dream since I was a child. Unfortunately, they didn't allocate a quota for female students in my province in the year when I had the entrance examination. I felt deep regret, because they assigned a female

quota for my province in the next year. However, I had already studied one year in this university, and I know it would put an extra burden on my parents if I quit this school and prepared for the re-entrance examination of the Police University. Therefore, I have no choice but to work hard in this university.

    MS. DU, BORN IN 1993 IN TUYÊN QUANG PROVINCE, FRESHMAN IN THE PUBLIC AFFAIRS DEPARTMENT

Another female student told the author that she had modified her dream according to her mother's ideas on "favorable" occupations for women.

Since I entered junior high school, I have dreamed of becoming a teacher. It was my mother who gave me this idea for the first time. She told me that teacher was an occupation fit for women because it was light (*nhẹ nhàng*) work with flexible hours. I had wanted to go to the Business University to be a businessperson, but my mother said that it would be too burdensome and competitive for girls to do such work, and then I changed my mind.

    MS. LY, BORN IN 1992 IN HÀ TÂY PROVINCE, SOPHOMORE IN THE MATHEMATICS, MECHANICAL AND INFORMATION SCIENCE DEPARTMENT

We can recognize here that the socialized gender norms for academic majors and occupations still greatly affect female university students' ability to determine their own paths. As discussed earlier in this chapter, "teacher" (or education major) was considered one of the favorable occupations for female students, and it was publicly canalized by North Vietnam's government during the pre–Đổi Mới era. Even though the job-allocation institution has since been abolished and people have the freedom to choose their occupations, this gendered public canalization has remained in Vietnamese society as a social norm.

More precisely, the social norm of the socialist gendered occupation strongly affected the parents' thought, in turn prescribing their daughters' behavior. By analyzing the narratives of female university students, we can see that the socialistic gender norms have been reproduced beyond generations from parents to children, specifically from mother to daughter.

This tendency is obvious in the ratio of female university students, who choose humanities majors much more than men do, even in recent years. In 2011, one of the top universities for humanities in Hanoi had 1,681 freshmen, 1,450 of whom were female (86.3 percent) (Figure 4.4).

FIGURE 4.4 *Female university students studying Japanese studies*
SOURCE: PHOTO BY ITO MIHO.

Hopes to Return to Hometown after Graduation

Female university students are supposed to experience a big moment of empowerment by taking the opportunity to obtain higher education. While one might think that they surely would be empowered by academic attainment, they still struggle with a glass ceiling that prevents freedom of choice in their own lives (sometimes against their own will) and the expectation from their parents to be a "good daughter." These aspects can be seen in their narratives about the workplace after graduation as well.

> After graduation, I want to be a journalist in Hanoi, but I know it will be hard to pull off. If I cannot become a journalist, I will have to get back to my hometown to become a junior high teacher or high school teacher there, even if this is against my will... I believe that I myself have the ability to find a job anywhere, but my parents want me to come back to somewhere nearby. To tell you the truth, I just dream of going to study abroad, if I cannot become a journalist in Hanoi.
> MS. TI, BORN IN 1990 IN THÁI NGUYÊN PROVINCE, LITERATURE DEPARTMENT

Though Ms. TI felt empowered by a high academic status and had her own dreams, she realized that she had to give up her dream to conform to her parents' expectations. Another female student also described mixed emotions concerning her parents' expectations regarding her work and even her marriage.

> I don't intend to keep living in Hanoi, and I want to return to my hometown after I graduate from university. While I'm studying as a mathematics major, there are no occupations relating to mathematics that are fitting for women, except for being a teacher. But I don't want be a teacher. Therefore I began to study Chinese at another school to become a Chinese translator, three months ago. Because my hometown is near the national border with China, there are many Chinese and Vietnamese tourists and businessmen. I want to work for a cross-border communications and logistics company. Actually, my returning to my hometown is my parents' expectation, partly. They have always said to me that I should marry someone as soon as possible after graduation. They might think that it would be better if I would take over the house, because my family has only two daughters. [Do you have anyone to love already?] Not yet! I don't have anyone yet. But my parents will introduce me to someone, maybe. I myself suppose that it will be better for me to marry at twenty-five or twenty-six years old, after working for some years.
> MS. HA, BORN IN 1992 IN LẠNG SƠN PROVINCE, SOPHOMORE IN THE MATHEMATICS, MECHANICAL AND INFORMATION SCIENCE DEPARTMENT

This narrative reveals the student's struggle with the social norm of "favorable" occupations for women and her parents' expectations. As a result, she plans to choose returning to her hometown to work and even marrying someone her parents would introduce to her.

According to the literature discussing the sexuality and morality of young Vietnamese girls who live in rural villages, young, single women control their curiosity and desire by staying at home, carrying out household chores, and doing their homework in order to demonstrate the good "morality" of women. These young women recognize that they should not be involved with a boyfriend but rather concentrate on their education in order to get high marks and a good job in the future (Gammeltoft 2002; Rydström 2006, 295). "Factory girls," on the other hand, who migrate for a while to work for wages, are subjected to the scrutiny of their family and neighbors during visits home. They suffer from the tension between their notions of themselves

FIGURE 4.5
A newly married couple in Yên Bái province
SOURCE: PHOTO BY ITO MIHO.

as faithful, hardworking daughters and their parents' perception that they may be too urbanized or worse, sexually "spoiled" (Nghiem 2004; Bélanger & Pendakis 2009, 274).

While young, single women who are studying to get a higher education or who work for wages at factories far from home experience conflict between their own desires and the well-established social norms of gender, female university students also experience a tension between their image as an empowered, high-achieving woman and the expectation to behave as a "good daughter" and "favorable female worker." From fear of seeming too urbanized, they tend to reveal a willingness to go back to their hometowns after graduation, explaining that they could not live in the city where everything is "too speedy," and therefore "not fit for me." (Figure 4.5 and 4.6)

Daughters Who Transgress the Social Norms of Femininity

Though most female students tend to choose humanities majors according to their "favorability" for female students, not all take the expected path. Ms. VA,

FIGURE 4.6
A female teacher giving a lecture for elementary students at temple of literature (Văn Miếu) in Hanoi
SOURCE: PHOTO BY ITO MIHO.

who was in her fourth year at the Department of Biology, voiced her desires for the future:

> Now, I suppose that I have two different things that I could do after graduation. One is to find a job immediately. I don't want to be a government official, however, because it offers a lower salary than non-governmental organizations do. The other one is to go to postgraduate school to obtain a master degree. After that, I will work somewhere for a few years, and then I will come back to postgraduate school again to gain a doctoral degree. That's my future plan. I never think of returning to my hometown. I cannot endure working in such a boring place. When I was a secondary-school student, I made up my mind to go to Hanoi to study and work.
>
> MS. VA, BORN IN 1989 IN THÁI BÌNH PROVINCE, BIOLOGY DEPARTMENT

In contrast to female students in the humanities, those who study the natural sciences seemed able to reveal their choices for their own futures more freely. This tendency may also be seen in female students in international studies.

I want to work for a nongovernmental organization after graduation. Because more and more foreign investors have concerns in Vietnam in recent years, I want to advertise Vietnamese ethnic culture for them so that they have more assistance. What I should do now, I suppose, is to have more experience, to study English, and surely to study hard at university... I don't talk to my parents on my dreams for the future yet. Probably they will say for me to go back to home. My mother wants me to become a teacher, while my father wants me to be a doctor. However, I think I am not fit for either one.

MS. DU, BORN IN 1991 IN LÀO CAI PROVINCE, SOPHOMORE IN THE INTERNATIONAL STUDIES DEPARTMENT

As mentioned earlier, the public canalization of occupation by gender continues to influence people's ideas on job selection. These notions also shape the goals of Vietnamese youth regarding higher education. Moreover, the recent increase in unemployment among university graduates increases the anxieties of female humanities students. Marr and Rosen (1999, 192–93) note that "because of the high unemployment rate of university graduates immediately after the economic reforms, most young people with a tertiary academic background worried about their future in the changing socio-economic conditions." As such, many university graduates and their families tend to follow the old public norms for occupation, which were established during the period when there were no problems of unemployment under central control, to seek stability. Even today, more than twenty-five years after the implementation of the Đổi Mới policy, most female humanities students express ambiguity concerning their futures, often showing a half-resigned face. While they are convinced that they are the luckiest and hardest working, they also realize that the perception that they are empowered to become whatever they want is not reality. As discussed in the beginning of this chapter, their belief that they will encounter a difficult time finding a good job but that they may get a good husband easier than some others reflects their struggles and negotiations with the social norms that relate to both socialist gendered occupations and traditional expectations for single daughters with self-confidence as those empowered by high-level academic attainment.

Conclusion

This chapter depicts female university students' struggles and negotiations with the social recognitions that were shaped both by North Vietnam's government in the pre–Đổi Mới period and the traditional patriarchal norm for young, single woman in Vietnam, specifically in the North. As many scholars have pointed out, in contrast to "factory girls" and most young women, who do not opportunities for upward mobility, these young women may now attain a higher education and career. Their moment of empowerment has come: they can survive in society and they have the self-confidence to become whatever they want (Nguyen & Thomas 2004). However, female university students, even those with high academic skills, still suffer from multilayered social norms, such as the choice of an occupation "favorable" for female workers and their parents' expectation that they should be feminine and behave as a "good daughter" of the family.

In their narratives, we find that female humanities students have positive as well as negative emotions when they return to their hometowns after graduation, even though they are still *seen* as vulnerable and passive agents of the multilayered gender ideologies. While they are not completely satisfied with going back to their hometowns, they also realize that doing so will bring them much a better life course than women with high academic careers find in Hanoi, due to a severe slump in the labor market for university graduates in recent years, particularly in large urban areas. Ms. TI stated, "I believe that I myself have enough capability to find a job anywhere." This indicates that while young female students have confidence in their ability to find work anywhere, they attempt to find the best way to maximize their own possibilities under the prevailing conditions. Choosing to go back to their hometowns does not necessary mean giving up their freedom or binding their activities into the gendered code of conduct; it provides them a space to lead better lives by strategically accepting these social norms. They struggle to survive in the changing socioeconomic situation and try to realize their own desires in the face of new opportunities by reframing, reconfiguring, and transgressing these public norms.

References

Ahmed, Sania Sultan, and Sally Bould. 2004. "'One Able Daughter Is Worth 10 Illiterate Sons': Reframing the Patriarchal Family." *Journal of Marriage and Family* 66: 1332–41.
Barbieri, Magari, and Danièle Béranger, eds. 2009. *Reconfiguring Families in Contemporary Vietnam*. Stanford, CA: Stanford University Press.
Bélanger, Danièle. 2002. "Son Preference in a Rural Village in North Vietnam." *Studies in Family Planning* 33(4): 321–34.
Bélanger, Danièle, and Jianye Liu. 2004. "Social Policy Reforms and Daughters' Schooling in Vietnam." *International Journal of Education Development* 24: 23–38.

Bélanger, Danièle, and Katherine Pendakis. 2009. "Daughters, Work, and Families in Globalizing Vietnam." In *Reconfiguring Families in Contemporary Vietnam*, edited by Magari Barbieri and Danièle Béranger, 265–97. Stanford, CA: Stanford University Press.

Bộ Giáo dục và Đào tạo. 1995. *Số liệu thống kê giáo dục và đào tạo 1945–1995*. Hà Nội: Trung tâm thông tin quản lý giáo dục [Statistics on Education and Training 1945–1990].

———. 2004. *Giáo dục Đại học Việt Nam*. Hà Nội: Nxb. Giáo dục [University Education in Vietnam].

———. 2011. *Niên giám thống kê Giáo dục Việt Nam 20 năm*. [Annual Statistics on Education in Vietnam during 20 Years].Internal document.

———. 2012. *10 năm phát triển giáo dục và đào tạo Việt Nam qua các con số 2001–2011*. Hà Nội: Nxb. Giáo dục Việt Nam. [Educational Development during 10 Years in Vietnam with Statistics from 2001 to 2011].

Colclough, Christopher, Pauline Rose, and Mercy Tembon. 2000. "Gender Inequalities in Primary Schooling: The Roles of Poverty and Adverse Cultural Practice." *International Journal of Educational Development* 20: 5–27.

Đặng Thanh Nhàn. 2011. "Định hướng nghề nghiệp cho con cái trong gia đình nông thôn" [Vocational Trends of Farm Families' Children]. In *Gia đình nông thôn đồng bằng bắc bộ trong chuyển đổi* [Changing Families in Rural Villages in the Red River Delta], Trịnh Duy Luân (chủ biên), 150–67. Hà Nội: Nxb. Khoa học xã hội.

Đặng Thị Hoa. 2007. "Thực trạng giáo dục và vai trò của cha mẹ trong giáo dục con cái ở nông thôn Việt Nam" [Current Situation of Education and Parents' Roles for Children in Vietnamese Villages]. *Kỷ yếu khoa học Tuyển tập các bài viết phân tích kết quả khảo sát chung* [Publications of Selected Research Papers], 125–48. Hà Nội: Nhà xuất bản khoa học xã hội.

Elson, Diane. 1999. "Labor Markets as Gendered Institutions: Equality, Efficiency and Empowerment Issues." *World Development* 27(3): 611–27.

Gammeltoft, T. 2002. "Seeking Trust and Transcendence: Sexual Risk-Taking Among Vietnamese Youth," *Social Science and Medicine* 55(3): 483–96.

Glewwe, P., and H. Patrinos. 1998. "The Role of the Private Sector in Education in Vietnam: Evidence from the Vietnam Living Standards Survey," *World Development* 27(5): 887–902.

Goodkind, Daniel M. 1995a. "Vietnam's One-or-Two Child Policy in Action." *Population and Development Review* 20(1): 85–111.

———. 1995b. "Rising Gender Inequality in Vietnam since Reunification." *Pacific Affairs* 68(3): 342–59.

Haughton, Jonathan, and Dominique Haughton. 1995. "Son Preference in Vietnam." *Studies in Family Planning*. 26(6): 325–37.

JETRO. 2013. "Country Report on Industrial Park in Vietnam, July 2013," https://www.jetro.go.jp/world/reports/2013/07001447.html.

Jones, Gavin W. 1982. "Population Trends and Policies in Vietnam." *Population and Development Review* 8(4): 783–810.

King, Victor T., and William D. Wilder. 2003. *The Modern Anthropology of South-East Asia: An Introduction*. London: Routledge.

Kleinen, J. 1999. *Facing the Future, Reviving the Past: A Study of Social Change in a Northern Vietnamese Village*. Singapore: Institute of Southeast Asian Studies.

Korinek, Kim. 2006. "The Status Attainment of Young Adults during Market Transition: The Case of Vietnam," *Research in Social Stratification and Mobility* 24(1): 55–72.

Liu, Amy Y.C. 2001. "Flying Ducks? Girls' Schooling in Rural Vietnam." *Asian Economic Journal* 15(4): 385–403.

London, Jonathan D. 2006. "Vietnam: The Political Economy of Education in a 'Socialist' Periphery." *Asia Pacific Journal of Education* 26(1): 1–20.

London, Jonathan D., ed. 2011. *Education in Vietnam*. Singapore: Institute of Southeast Asian Studies.

Luong, Hy V. 1993. "Economic Reforms and the Intensification of Gender Rituals in Two North Vietnamese Villages, 1980–90." In *The Challenge of Reform in Indochina*, edited by Borje Ljunggren, 252–59. Cambridge, MA: Harvard University Press.

Marr, David, and Stanley Rosen. 1999. "Chinese and Vietnamese Youth in the 1990s." In *Transforming Asian Socialism: China and Vietnam Compared*, edited by Anita Chan, Benedict J. Tria Kerkvliet, and Jonathan Unger, 176–203. New York: Rowman & Littlefield.

Moock, Peter R., Harry Anthony Patrinos, and Meera Venkataraman. 2003. "Education and Earnings in a Transition Economy: The Case of Vietnam." *Economics of Education Review* 22: 503–10.

Nghiem, Huong Lien. 2004. "Female Garment Workers: The New Young Volunteers in Vietnam's Modernization." In *Social Inequality in Vietnam and the Challenges to Reform*, edited by Philip Taylor, 297–324. Singapore: Institute of Southeast Asian Studies.

Nguyen, Bich Thuan, and Mandy Thomas. 2004. "Young Women and Emergent Postsocialist Sensibilities in Contemporary Vietnam." *Asian Studies Review* 28: 133–49.

Nguyen, Phuong L. 2006. "Effects of Social Class and School Conditions on Educational Enrolment and Achievement of Boys and Girls in Rural Viet Nam." *International Journal of Educational Research* 45(3): 153–75.

Nguyen-Vo, Thu-Huong. 2006. "The Body Wager: Materialist Resignification of Vietnamese Women Workers." *Gender Place and Culture* 13(3): 267–81.

Pelzer, C. 1993. "Socio-cultural Dimensions of Renovation in Vietnam: Đổi Mới as Dialogue and Transformation in Gender Relations." In *Reinventing Vietnamese Socialism: Đổi Mới in Comparative Perspectives*, edited by W.S. Turley and M. Seldon. Boulder, CO: Westview Press.

Rydström, Helle. 2006. "Sexual Desires and 'Social Evils': Young Women in Rural Vietnam." *Gender, Place and Culture* 13(3): 283–301.

Tổng Cục Thống Kê. 1970. *15 năm xây dựng nền kinh tế xã hội chủ nghĩa 1955–1969.* [15 Years of Construction of a Socialist Economy, 1955–69]. Hà Nội: Tổng Cục Thống Kê.

———. 1977. *Tình hình phát triển kinh tế và văn hóa miền bắc xã hội chủ nghĩa Việt Nam 1960–1975.* [Development of Economy and Culture in the Northern Part of Vietnam, a Socialist State, 1960–75]. Hà Nội: Tổng Cục Thống Kê.

Trần Hồng Quân ed. 1995. *50 năm phát triển sự nghiệp giáo dục và đào tạo (1945–1995)* [50 Years of Education Development and Training, 1945–95]. Hà Nội: Nxb. Giáo dục.

Vietnamese Communist Party. 1979. *Một số văn kiện của trung ương đảng và chính phủ về công tác đại học và trung học chuyên nghiệp (1960–1979)* [Documents of the Party and the Government on Policies for Universities and Colleges (1960–79)]. Hà Nội: Bộ Đại học và Trung học chuyên nghiệp.

PART 2

Transgressing Boundaries, Weaving Alternatives, and Putting Down New Roots

CHAPTER 5

The Limit of *Chia Sẻ* (Compassion): Interpretative Conflicts in the Collectivity of the Vietnamese Women's Union*

Kato Atsufumi

Introduction

This chapter examines the possibilities of forming alternative civic organizations based on the "collectivity" (*tính tập thể*) of the Vietnam Women's Union, an official organization in contemporary Vietnam. Joerg Wischermann and Nguyen Quang Vinh (2003, 186) define a civic organization in contemporary Vietnam as "a heterogeneous ensemble of non-state, voluntary, nonprofit-oriented societal organizations," including state-affiliated official mass organizations, without presupposing specific relationships between these secondary associations and the state. Based on their definition, this chapter refers to the realm of moral deliberation concerning the framework of a state-sponsored organization that functions as an arena of political debates on the official discourse on good civics, on the one hand, and a space of communication about personal feelings, personal connections, and mutual concern among peers in everyday life, on the other. The meanings of these civic organizations' collectivity are negotiated and reconstructed in the local context. The Women's Union is often considered to be either ineffective or simply a propaganda organ. I argue instead that the Women's Union has the potential to become an alternative space for rural women, namely a sisterhood (*chị em*) among the members, through their efforts in reinterpreting their collectivity.

This chapter focuses on conflicts between different local understandings of the collectivity of the Women's Union using data gathered through anthropological fieldwork on local self-governance in a village in Hà Tĩnh province, Central Vietnam (Figure 5.1), which I have been conducting since 2002.

First, this chapter analyses the idea of *chia sẻ* (compassion) to understand village women's motives for participating in the Women's Union. *Chia sẻ* means sharing another person's happiness and sadness by expressing one's sympathy

---

* This contribution is a revised version of a previously published article that appeared in Kato, Atsufumi ed. 2012. *Alternative Intimate Spheres for Women in Vietnam*, GCOE Working Papers (Next Generation Research) 71, Kyoto, Japan: Kyoto University Global COE Program for Reconstruction of the Intimate and Public Spheres in 21st Century Asia.

FIGURE 5.1 *Repairing footpaths between rice fields*
SOURCE: PHOTO BY KATO ATSUFUMI.

for that person. *Chia sẻ* may be expressed via visits, monetary offerings, or empathizing with another's situation and feelings. While male cadres in the village express compassion to villagers to win the hearts of their colleagues, female cadres consider *chia sẻ* the most important motivation for participation in collective activities.

The second part of this chapter closely examines a debate in a hamlet among members of the Women's Union over whether to help a pregnant woman with the harvesting process. Her family did not follow the national family-planning program and her husband has a drinking problem; therefore, her family does not meet the state's "cultural" (*văn hóa*) expectations. The local cadres of the organization does not allow members to provide in-depth assistance to fellow women when they are not viewed as practicing "cultural" civics; this case, then, shows the limits of *chia sẻ* for the sisterly members of the Women's Union. At the same time, the case also highlights the possibilities for women to express their solidarity based on the official organization's capacity to mobilize people.

In conclusion, I argue that the undertaking of forming rural women's solidarity is not a process to activate preexisting social relationships among women, but is local women's attempt to create an ideal sisterly relationship that has never existed before by appropriating the framework of an official mass organization as a source of social mobilization. I emphasize that the civic organization is one of the most effective channels to create an alternative sphere of commonality between the dichotomy of the public and private spheres in contemporary Vietnam, where official organizations have great influence on society. I suggest that the interpretation of collectivity can be the focal point in the construction of alternative civic organizations in Vietnam.

The Vietnamese case in this chapter can be contextualized in anthropological studies about the reconstruction of civil society in (post)-socialist countries and regions such as the former Soviet Union, Eastern Europe, and China. According to Chris Hann, in socialist states in Eastern Europe, state-affiliated organizations, such as labor collectives and cultural circles, played an important role in people's everyday lives as secondary associations between the state and individuals (Hann 1990a, 12–3; 1990b, 36). These secondary associations provided people with a locus for fostering egalitarianism and the "socialistic" morality (Hann 1990b, 39; Hann, Humphrey, & Verdery 2002, 10). These organizations, as a result, supported members' quality of life by producing relatively autonomous social spaces and cultivating the morality of mutual aid among members. They also provided a basis for the rise of civil society in transitional societies after 1991 (cf. Ashwin 1999). As the authors of *Post-Socialism* argue, it is necessary to reevaluate these ambiguous realms of social relations between the private and the state as "civil society" (Hann, Humphrey, & Verdery 2002, 9). Jean Oi makes a similar argument on post-collective villages in China. For Oi, the process of collectivization made Chinese villages local corporate groups in which political actions are made based on community interests that cannot be reduced either to the state's will or the networks of private interests (1989, 3). Even after the Open Door Policy, the Chinese villages' capacity for political mobilization for and against the state is still thriving.

Along with these case studies, the Vietnamese case in this chapter also helps us broaden the idea of "civil society" to better understand the plural possibilities of public-sphere reconstruction. In recent years, Vietnam has also experienced the appearance of many kinds of autonomous organizations. In rural areas, *dòng họ* (male-centered kinship groups) and traditional autonomous associations, such as Buddhist associations for women and alumni associations for men, have been revived since the Đổi Mới (the Renovation) in 1986 (Luong 2010, 231–33). On some occasions, these organizations, constitutive of alternative civilities in rural areas, provide local residents with the capacity for collective action and create "public dialogues" at the local level (Luong 2010, 246, 257).

However, to fully understand politics in rural areas of Vietnam, we need to look not only at autonomous associations but also at "official" channels for political participation (Kerkvliet 2005, 400). As Thaveerporn Vasavakul notes, popular organizations in contemporary Vietnam have the ability to represent particular interests and provide policy options alternative to those advocated by the party-state regardless of official status and affiliations (Vasavakul 2003, 53). In this respect, as I mentioned above, we need to consider Wischermann and Nguyen's (2003) use of the term "civic organization" to evaluate a wide range of secondary organizations in contemporary Vietnam that are characterized by their ambivalent status between their role as an agency of the state and that as the locus of the people's solidarity.

Public Sphere for Rural Vietnamese Women

In Vietnamese villages, women have many channels to influence political debates at the local level. This public sphere may include gossip among wives with cups of "fresh tea" (*chè xanh*) before going to the local market, or among women in the kitchen while preparing dishes for weddings. These spaces often become the locus of counterarguments against dominant official discourses in the village, where people can evaluate local cadres' virtues and their political behaviors, for instance. Religious organizations, especially

Buddhist temples, have also provided rural women with an alternative space in which they can support each other by following their own strict social order (Luong 2010, 231–3).

In contrast, official channels for rural women to participate in political debate are still limited in Vietnam. Though Vietnamese women's participation in the political arena was facilitated in the era of total mobilization during the Vietnam War, women had to give over their positions to male villagers who came back from the battlefields after the war (Houtart & Lemercinier 1984). Although affirmative action toward women's political participation was launched in 1994, the ratio of female leaders in political and administrative institutions is still low (Tran Thi Minh Thi 2012). In this context, the Women's Union has become one of the most important ways for rural women to participate in official politics.

The Women's Union in Thạch Châu Commune

The Vietnam Women's Union (Hội Liên Hiệp Phụ Nữ Việt Nam) is a state-affiliated official mass organization that functions as an interest group for women, as well as an apparatus for mobilizing women to adopt the directions of the Communist Party and state policies. As a unique political organization for women in Vietnam, the Women's Union has a network throughout the country with four administrative levels (central, provincial, district, and commune) and a total membership of more than 13 million, according to its website.

The Women's Union was founded in 1930, during the colonial period. During the period from 1955 to 1975, when the whole country was at war, the Women's Union initiated many emulation campaigns across the country. While the Women's Union functioned, since its early days, as an interest group for women in terms of policymaking and women's progress, it has also focused on reinforcing ideologies about Vietnamese women's roles and status in the family and society. The Union also mobilized women to participate in the war through its various campaigns. Such examples as the "campaign of five goods" and the "campaign of three responsibilities" encouraged women to take responsibilities in their labor, combat, and everyday family life.

Since the early stages of the Đổi Mới, the Women's Union has begun to attract local women again through the Communist Party's strategy of reactivating mass organizations as institutionalized means of governance (Endres 1999, 160). It has also emerged as a prime institution at the local level, introducing a new role for the household (Werner 2002, 43). There have been, however, important gaps between what the Women's Union aims to do—protect women's legitimate rights and strive for gender equality—and what it actually does—consolidate state power and influence the masses to advance the regime's interests. For instance, the Women's Union's contribution to the spread of birth-control awareness is unclear. By encouraging rural women to use contraceptives that are available at and distributed through the communal health centers, the Women's Union, in practice, acts as an agent of the state that interferes with women's choices (Endres 1999, 166; see also Gammeltoft 1999).

In Thạch Châu Commune in Hà Tĩnh province, Central Vietnam, where I have conducted anthropological field research, the Women's Union has become the absolute way for women to participate in official village politics. It is also assumed to be the absolute social space in which women build close relationships with each other, since all religious and traditional constructions in the commune, including all Buddhist temples, were destroyed during the Communist Party's campaign against conservative culture in the 1970s. As the wide range of regional variation in Vietnam makes countrywide generalizations problematic, the case study on the Women's Union in this chapter should be read as a specific case in a village in Northern Central Vietnam, where the revolution was strong and the former institutional structure of the village and kinship network were relatively weaker than those of villages in Northern Vietnam. Moreover, endogamy is not the norm here. Thus, in this village, women from outside the region married into the village community and formed bonds with other women through the Women's Union.

Thạch Châu Commune is located in a lowland area 10 kilometers from the capital of Hà Tĩnh province. The commune's population is approximately 5,600. The residents are Kinh, the ethnic majority of Vietnam. The majority of residents are small farmers.

To describe the activities of the Women's Union in the village, it is necessary to explain how the organization is integrated in the administrative structure in Vietnamese rural areas. In Vietnam, the commune ($xã$) is the lowest level of government in rural areas. A commune has a Communist Party cell, People's Assembly, People's Committee, and branches of official mass organizations, including the Women's Union. The communal executive committee of the Women's Union consists of three members, including the chairperson, who are elected by the representatives of the hamlet branches of the organization in the commune by following the recommendation of the Communist Party and the upper branch of the organization at the district level. The main activities of the Women's Union at the communal level include promoting the national birth-control campaign as well as managing various types of funds (Kato 2010).

Within the commune, there are quasi-administrative units. These units are called *làng*s in Northern Vietnam, and they were the lowest administrative village levels before the independent revolution in 1945. In certain regions, the unity of the *làng*s completely disappeared after the revolution, and *xóm*s, which were the hamlets under the former *làng*s, became the lowest units. In Thạch Châu Commune, *làng*s have lost their territorial and emotional unity; eleven hamlets, with around 500 residents in each, comprise the basic quasi-administrative units. In practice, hamlets in the commune are now required to act as agents of the communal government; under its guidance, the hamlet is responsible for collecting taxes, mobilizing villagers to participate in social-cultural campaigns, managing small-scale investment grants, and allocating social benefits. Each hamlet in Thạch Châu Commune has its party cell and a directional committee (*ban chỉ huy*) composed of a chief and two assistants who are elected by villagers. Typically, they hold the posts of executive committee members of the hamlet party cell. The hamlet organizes the villagers' assembly, which is open to all adult residents.

In Thạch Châu Commune, each hamlet has a branch of the Women's Union. The hamlet executive committee of the organization consists of three members who are elected by members in the hamlet branch, following the recommendation of the Communist Party and the communal Women's Union. As Endres (1999) notes, the Women's Union was reactivated in the 1990s as a state agent for local governance and a popular organization to provide members with economic interests by allocating foreign and national funds.

In 2009 and 2011, I interviewed sixteen male and female local cadres in Thạch Châu Commune to ask about their life stories, including four chairpersons of the Women's Union communal branch and two other female cadres (Appendix 5.1). Most cadres of the elder generations are assigned as chairs of the Women's Union after working for many years in the communal agricultural collective or the communal People's Committee, while cadres of the younger generations who started their careers in the 1990s are usually trained at the hamlet branch of the Women's Union and then recruited for positions at the communal level (Appendices 1 and 2). In nowadays, there are two types of female leaders at the hamlet level. One is a category of leaders who are enthusiastic about social and collective activities. They often have ambitions to be politicians in the commune. In recent years, most of the female members of the communal People's Assembly in the commune are recommended by the local Women's Union, if they are not local schoolteachers or nurses in the communal clinic. Some of the others are wives of local cadres and are imposed upon to work as leaders.

They often feel that their duty in the Women's Union is a burden and do not continue more than one term.

In Thạch Châu Commune, the Communist Party and the official organizations, including the Women's Union, have deeply penetrated villagers' collective lives as a substitute for the weakness of *làng*s' solidarity. The Women's Union, especially, is fairly active compared to other official mass organizations in Thạch Châu Commune. Although the Women's Union is a voluntary association, because the party and state strongly recommend that all citizens should participate in at least one official mass organization, almost all the adult women in the village participate, except some young unmarried women and elder women who moved to the Elders' Association. There were 270 adult women in H hamlet, where I have been conducting in-depth field research, and there were 74 members who were enthusiastic about participating in the organization's everyday activities. It organized hamlet membership meetings eighteen times between 2000 and 2002, when I first stayed in the village. Members of the Women's Union have to participate in the organization's everyday activities. If a member is absent from the organization's meetings too often, does not go to the organization's activities—such as repairing footpaths between rice fields, harvesting the organization's rice field, or cleaning up the alleys in the village—or does not take part in the state campaign for the improvement of the living environment, she would not be certified as an "exemplary" (*tiêu biểu*) member, which might result in her failing to receive benefits from the organization (Figure 5.2).

Indeed, participating in the Women's Union is a way for women to receive benefits, such as loans with low interest rates. One of the most significant activities of the Women's Union at the communal and hamlet levels is the management of various types of funds. According to the annual report of the H hamlet branch of the Women's Union in 2002, it held VND 108,500,000 (approximately USD 7,230) as funds that the Women's Union contributed to the hamlet (Figure 5.3). The hamlet branch is also allocated 500 square meters of agricultural land by the hamlet for raising funds.

For ordinary members, the Women's Union is also a mutual friendship association. Almost all the married women in the village are from different hamlets because endogamy is not the norm here, so participating in the Women's Union is an important opportunity for women to join in the social life of the village. In addition to the income from the allocated land, the H hamlet branch also raises funds by receiving harvesting contracts from members who do not have the time or labor power for rice reaping. This additional fund is used for recreational trips organized by the hamlet branch.

INTERPRETATIVE CONFLICTS IN THE COLLECTIVITY OF THE VIETNAMESE 149

FIGURE 5.2 *Taking attendance at the harvesting of the organization's rice field*
SOURCE: PHOTO BY KATO ATSUFUMI.

FIGURE 5.3 *The Thạch Châu Commune office of the women's union on a loan registration day*
SOURCE: PHOTO BY KATO ATSUFUMI.

In contrast to the Women's Union's intensive activities, in Thạch Châu Commune there are no active autonomous associations, such as the same-age associations and credit associations that are found in Northern Vietnamese villages (cf. Luong 2010, Chapter 7). There are four reasons for the weakness of villagers' autonomous associations in Thạch Châu Commune.

First, as I mentioned above, *làng*s have lost their territorial and emotional unity in Thạch Châu Commune and hamlets were merely territorial units within the *làng*s, without any constant administrative obligation before the revolution in 1945. At least in Thạch Châu Commune, the village solidarity was made by the socialist transformation (*cải tạo xã hội chủ nghĩa*). Under North Vietnam's collectivization of agriculture in the 1960s, each hamlet was organized as a productive brigade under the collective; they became places for everyday social activities for villagers, such as weddings, funerals, and childcare. According to villagers, they began to attend neighbors' funerals with each other quite often after the collectivization (Malarney 2002, 146). A villager also said that before the revolution, people did not care about conflicts in neighboring households. After the dissolution of collectives in 1993, the hamlets were reorganized as nonadministrative and autonomous villagers' associations under the commune. However, their collectivity is still artificial and based on the everyday practice of administrative practices, such as meetings of official mass organizations and funerals supported by the division of labor among the Communist Party, the Elders' Association, the Women's Union, and the Youth League at the hamlet level.

Second, agriculture in Thạch Châu Commune relies heavily on rainwater and there is no irrigation system; thus, people do not need to collaborate to control water. Furthermore, as agricultural productivity is comparatively low because of the limited irrigation system, people do not have deep attachment to their land. People do not want to invest in their land, but prefer investing in their children's education so that their children can find good jobs elsewhere and then help their parents and relatives in the future. Everybody takes the village as a tentative living space; it is difficult to make the village a permanent corporate group. That is one of the reasons why the communal agricultural collective dissolved very quickly in 1993 when the state changed its land policy. Though there have been several private and official attempts to establish corporative agricultural projects in the commune after 1993, they did not succeed in practice.

Third, as mentioned above, endogamy is not the norm in the village. A hamlet usually consists of two or three major lineage groups. However, one is not expected to choose a wife from the lineages in the village. Wives usually come from other hamlets in the commune or neighboring communes. Thus, the kinship network is not as dense as in villages in Northern Vietnam, where endogamy is the strong norm among villagers.

Fourth, as I also mentioned above, there is no basis for the reconstruction of traditional village communities, because the villagers of Thạch Châu Commune destroyed almost all traditional structures in the 1970s, along with other "feudal" (*phong kiến*) constructions such as communal houses and ancestral houses of lineage groups. Even now, religious activities and traditional festivals have not been revived. One reason why the villagers carried out the campaign thoroughly is their loyalty to the Communist Party. Hà Tĩnh was the birthplace of the Communist movement in Vietnam and it belonged to North Vietnam before 1975; for this reason, in general, the residents are sympathetic to the Communist Party. Perhaps, too, they also had to demonstrate their loyalty to the party, since a prime minister of the South Vietnam government during the Vietnam War was from this commune. In Hà Tĩnh province, the proportion of Communist Party members is 4.8 percent in 2000, higher than the national average (3.2 percent in 2001), and Thạch Châu Commune has an even larger proportion than the provincial averag, at 6.2 percent in 2001.

In sum, Thạch Châu's case is an "exceptional" one, in which the Women's Union, an official organization, plays a critically important role in the construction of a public sphere for women. However, Thạch Châu's case is also "typical" of Vietnamese villages that have constructed their public space by appropriating state influences upon the local society (Woodside 1971; Sakurai 1987).

Chia Sẻ (Compassion)

Female cadres recognize working for the Women's Union as an opportunity to connect to "society" (*xã hội*) and as a means for self-empowerment to gain social prestige among fellow women. *Chia sẻ* (compassion) is one of the key terms for understanding female cadres' explanations of their motives for devoting themselves to the organization.

Both male and female cadres emphasize the importance of expressing sympathy and compassion. However, there are gender differences in the discourse on compassion. Some elder male cadres in Thạch Châu Commune say that local leaders should get along with the masses (*hòa đồng với quần chúng*). Mr. Liệu (fictitious name), a retired male party secretary, commented that a cadre should behave as an "ordinary peasant" (*một người nông dân*) to let villagers talk about their needs.

> Local cadres have to get along with the masses. This means that, for example, although I am a party secretary, I also have to take my position

as an ordinary peasant in the village. Only by doing so can I understand people's feelings, desires (*tâm tư, nguyện vọng*), and problems for which they want to ask leaders for solutions.

He gave some examples of how to behave like a peasant. One is sharing tobacco with people:

> For example, I don't smoke. But, you know, people here often smoke *lào* tobacco [a kind of water pipe]. And whenever I find a group of people smoking *lào* tobacco, I also sit down with them for a while and smoke some. If I do so, even though I am a party secretary, I can build a spirit of consensus with them, and then they are willing to tell me what they really think. If I find them sitting together but just go by and don't say anything to them, they might feel a distance between me and them and would not tell me what they want to say. As cadres in the village at the grassroots level. ...I don't know how it is in Japan, but in Vietnam, cadres think like this.

As Shaun Malarney (1997, 911) notes, villagers expect a "good" cadre to express commonality with them and behave, "as if he were any other resident." It is recommended for leaders to participate in weddings, funerals, and other ceremonies in the village. Faithful attendance at these occasions is seen as the expression of a sentimental relationship (*tình cảm*) with villagers and as the leader's "expression of solidarity and equality with the people" (912).

For local cadres, the expression of commonality is necessary to gather correct information from villagers. Mr. Hà, a commune security chief for almost two decades, says that "relations" (*mối quan hệ*) with villagers are important to gathering correct information about conflicts in the village:

> If the relations become better, then they will give you much information. It all depends on the relations. If a party member has good relations with them and when they feel that he has enough prestige, enough capability, and enough trustworthiness, then they will share everything with him. This is true not only for the security section, but for everyone.

A female cadre also expressed the same idea. "For women, you must understand their psychology," said Ms. Hương, a former chairperson of the communal Women's Union. For her, *chia sẻ* is a way to win members' hearts.

> Our activities rely on members' family conditions. To be successful in the organization, first of all, I must understand cadres at the grassroots level.

> ...When I was in office, I had to convince people around peer cadres. This person was in a situation like this; another person was in a situation like that. I had to understand each case to manage cadres so that they were eager to work with me; then, I eventually gained success.

She continued,

> In those days, many of my fellow cadres were in difficulty, but I encouraged them. ...For example, the circumstances of Ms. Hằng in the First Brigade were very difficult then. She wanted to join the activities, but her husband did not allow her to do so. Besides, he was not a party member, but an ordinary citizen. So, I visited him and managed to get him to understand. I described the situation to the husband and encouraged him to let her participate in the activities. I analyzed those things for the husband to understand. I then requested for the cooperation of the members and encouraged them to contribute financially to help the family in difficulty. With a successful movement like this, at last, I could encourage him to agree with her completely, and eventually the activities in the brigade also improved.

Meanwhile, some female leaders mention that *chia sẻ*, in itself, is the main attraction of their jobs. For example, Ms. Vân, the present chairperson of the Women's Union, said that she likes her job because she can keep in touch with other women and "share grief and happiness" (*chia sẻ vui buồn*) with fellow "sisters" (*chị em*). In fact, female cadres usually know much about peer cadres' families and often told me proudly about the successes of their fellow female cadres' children.

For male cadres, the practice of sharing is initially an art of governance, to win the hearts and minds of the people and to gather information, while it is evident that practicing *chia sẻ* is a source of joy for female cadres.

As the case study in the next section shows, *chia sẻ* is not merely a cliché of local cadres but also a key to understanding ideal relationships for ordinary members of the Women's Union. However, this does not mean that people easily realize *chia sẻ* practices in the organization's activities.

Harvesting for a Pregnant Woman

In this section, I examine a 2005 debate among members of the Women's Union in H hamlet regarding the reasons for supporting a pregnant woman

(Ms. Hoa) whose husband (Mr. Tuấn) was defined by the state as not being a "cultured" citizen.

The situation was as follows: their son was injured and admitted to a hospital in Hồ Chí Minh City, and Mr. Tuấn had to leave the village to take care of him. Thus, there was no one who could harvest for their household. Though Vietnamese women tend to continue working until the month in which childbirth is expected, hard labor is usually avoided in the last few months. In addition, Vietnamese people prohibit new mothers from going outside for more than one month after childbirth. Therefore, especially in agricultural areas, support from surrounding familial and social networks is crucial for pregnant women. Female relatives from the husband's side as well as the wife's often come to assist with childcare and domestic work in the household as much as possible. There is no public harvesting service for families with pregnant women, though the quality of primary healthcare in rural areas has improved since the beginning of the 1990s (cf. Grossheim & Endres 1999, 185–6). Ms. Hoa and Mr. Tuấn's household could not afford to hire workers from outside the village for harvesting, either, a common practice when family members are busy. Villagers seem to prefer hiring workers to asking neighbors for help with harvesting because the cost of gratitude is much more complicated than paying a wage to strangers. However, hiring cost around 100 kilogram of paddy per 600 kilogram of harvesting at that time, and this was quite expensive for Ms. Hoa and Mr. Tuấn's household. In sum, Ms. Hoa and Mr. Tuấn could not expect support from the public service, nor could they afford to rely on the market economy for harvesting.

The ordinary members of the Women's Union proposed that the organization should mobilize to help the family with harvesting. However, the communal branch dismissed this proposal. Ms. Trung, a former chairperson of the communal Women's Union and a resident of H hamlet, said that it was inappropriate for an official organization to help any household defined as not being "cultured" by the state. Ms. Trung was concerned about the baby, which was to be the third child of Mr. Tuấn's household, a violation of the birth control campaign promoted by the state and the Women's Union. In addition, she criticized Mr. Tuấn's bad drinking behavior.

The Movement for Construction of Cultured Families (*Phong trào xây dựng gia đình văn hóa*) is a national campaign started in 1989. Local cadres and villagers are quite serious about the movement because the ratio of cultured families is one of the achievement criteria for their commune. To be certified as a cultured family, households must meet the following criteria: (1) success in family planning; (2) realization of a harmonious, happy, and advanced family; (3) solidarity with neighbors; and (4) fulfillment of civil obligations. In Thạch Châu Commune, candidates for cultured families are selected by voting among the residents of each hamlet. As noted above, it is an important mandate of the Women's Union to implement directions of the Communist Party and state policies. Ms. Trung rejected the members' proposal, interpreting the organization's political position quite strictly, though the rules of the Women's Union do not prohibit supporting members who have a third child.

Members opposed Ms. Trung's instructions, however, by saying, "Mr. Tuấn is a bit mentally ill" (*bệnh thần kinh*) and that "we should help them if we have a sense of mutual love and affection" (*tương thân, tương ái*).

In responding to these opinions, the former chairperson proposed a compromise. She said that there would be no problem if Women's Union members wanted to help Ms. Hoa's household personally, but "to help voluntarily" (*tự nguyện giúp*) and "to help collectively" (*tập thể giúp*) were different, and in this case, the Women's Union could not help collectively. She said that members could help the family if they had the "spirit of charity" (*hảo tâm*) and that the organization would not prohibit members from doing so. To "help collectively" would have involved, in this context, the Women's Union mobilizing members and officially supporting Ms. Hoa's household. On the other hand, *hảo tâm* usually means for better-off people to personally and voluntarily support people in difficulty. The former chairperson meant that members could help Ms. Hoa's household as a personal activity, but that the Women's Union, as an official mass organization, could not support the family.

Finally, the meeting confirmed that the organization would not prohibit members from personally supporting Ms. Hoa's household out of "mutual love and affection" (*tương thân, tương ái*) and "sentiment and duty among villagers" (*tình làng nghĩa xóm*), but decided that the Women's Union would not organize harvesting.

Discussion

This minor episode shows the possibilities for and difficulties of women's attempts to express their morality of *chia sẻ* based on the official organization's capacity to mobilize people. Though a close relationship based on the practice of *chia sẻ* is ideal for members, including its local cadres, it cannot be concluded that the Women's Union is, in fact, an autonomous mutual-aid association among sisterly women. The local leaders in the case study insist that the Women's Union is an official organization operating under the authority of the party and the state. Thus, beneficiaries of the organization's collective activities—or, in other words, the boundary of compassion—must be limited to "cultured" people. Ordinary members, on the contrary, view the organization as a friendship association of local women and placed more emphasis on mutual aid among members, seeing the organization as a locus of "mutual love and affection."

This episode reveals the conflicting position of the Women's Union as a state-affiliated mass organization. In the case study, the Women's Union functioned, after all, as an apparatus to reinforce state ideology concerning the "cultured" family, as indicated by its failure to support Ms. Hoa's household. The working of the Women's Union is, however, more complicated. First, the ideology of the local Women's Union cadres is not, in fact, aligned with the organization's official policy. At least, the Women's Union has never expressed the aim to exclude "uncultured" families as objects of the organization's activities. Instead, the local cadres in the case study insisted on the interpretation of the organization's policy in a rigid manner. Even with this state-oriented role, the Women's Union functions through the complex process of interpretation and appropriation at the local level; thus its reinforcement of the idea of the "cultured" family cannot be reduced simply to its upholding of state interests.

Also, the case shows that the Women's Union still has the potential to become an alternative "civic organization" for women based on women's negotiations for the collectivity of villagers. In the case I discussed above, ordinary members tried to provide support for Ms. Hoa's household as a collective activity of women in the village, not as a private activity. They tried to make harvesting for Ms. Hoa's household an obligation of village women, in other words, as a "collective" activity, although they could have supported her household personally, as Ms. Trung asserted, if they had just wanted to help Ms. Hoa based on their close relationships with her.

What is interesting here is that it is the Women's Union, a framework for mobilization provided by the state, on which local women rely to create the category of village women as agents of compassion and mutual support among peer members. The collective agency of village women in the case of Thạch Châu Commune is, in practice, based on the institutional capability of the Women's Union instead of the existing framework of the village community. The ordinary members' proposal was the start of the process of creating village women's agency based on an alternate morality, which contrasts with the state's definitions of civility. To put it more abstractly, the collectivity of village women, which claimed mutual support for Ms. Hoa's household, did not exist before the arguments among members of the Women's Union for its collective action. What ordinary members tried to do was to appropriate the collectivity of the Women's Union for the collectivity of village women.

However, we need to reemphasize that the village women's attempt to appropriate the collectivity of the Women's Union can be dangerous sometimes. These women have at least partially bought into state discourses—to mobilize private resources to undertake community projects through the Women's Union, which, ultimately, promoted the "socialization" (*xã hội hóa*) of welfare in Vietnamese administrative terminology. The villagers also accept and even support the state discourse on "cultured" families as filtered through the local cadres of the Women's Union. In fact, as the case study shows, even though ordinary people were skeptical about the ideology of the "cultured" family, which distinguishes between beneficiaries of the organization's official support, they still unconsciously focused on supporting a family as a unit instead of supporting a woman in a problematic family. Evidently, the alternative civic organization based on the Women's Union is vulnerable.

Also, emphasizing the importance of a women's agency in providing mutual support may easily lead to gendering welfare issues. In a sense, *chia sẻ* can be seen as a gendered practice. In Vietnamese society, women are expected to "share grief and happiness" with their "sisters," as this is expected as appropriate behavior for women. Though both men and women are expected to respect sentimental relationships (*tình cảm*), women are expected to display greater sensitivity to emotional relationships in the process of socialization (Rydström 2003). Some kinds of social problems, such as family planning, childcare, and farming would be categorized as issues that women should solve by themselves through the village women's practice of creating solidarity.

The case study in this chapter should be read not as a mere example of confrontation between the state apparatus and the morality of the people, but as a story of women's struggle to reframe their own relationships to create an alternative sphere within the authorized public/private divide in contemporary Vietnamese political discourse. The case study shows that in contemporary Vietnam, where official organizations influence society greatly, the possibilities of forming alternative civic organizations for women are linked to women's capacity for interpreting collectivity such that a sphere of compassion and mutual solidarity is created between the public/private dichotomy.

Appendices

APPENDIX : TABLE 5.1 *List of interviewees*

No.	Name (fictive)	Birth year	Career	Education (years)	Military	Siblings
01	Nguyễn Xuân	1928	SPCC (1966–75, 78–88)	04 (*yếu lược*, elementary school)	None	Eldest child of 4
02	Ms. Giang	1938	CVWU (1968–1984)	07/10	None	Eldest child of 7
03	Phan Huy Hưng	1944	SPCC (1991–2000)	04/10	None	Only child
04	Hoàng Văn Tùng	1945	SPCC (1989–1990)	10/10	1967–75, wounded	NA
05	Lê Đại Liệu	1948	SPCC (2002–2008)	07/10	1967–78, 1979–81	Youngest child of 7
06	Lê Văn Chích	1948	CVFF	10/10	1967–1969, wounded	Youngest child of 4
07	Ms. Hường	1949	CVWU (1984–1999?)	07/10	None	Eldest child of 8
08	Ms. Lê Thị Trung	1950	CVWU (1996–2006)	07/10	the volunteer army service corps	Youngest child of 6 (no brothers)
09	Phạm Thái Sang	1951	CCPC	08/10	None	Second child of 6 (one elder sister)
10	Lê Mai Hà	1951	The head of the local security police contingent	07/10	1968–72, provincial force	Second child of 7 (one elder sister)
11	Trần Văn Hạnh	1960	SPCC (2001–2002)	10/10	1979–83	Eldest child of 4
12	Lê Quang Huy	1964	VSPCC (2008–)	12/12	None	Eldest child of 4

13	Le Thị Lam	1967	A member of the VWU communal committee (1995a–2003)	07/12	None	Fourth child of 5
14	Nguyễn Tiến Tân	1968	SPCC (2008–)	12/12	1985–89	Youngest child of 8
15	Le Thị Vân	1972	CVWU (2006–)	12/12	None	Eldest child of 3
16	Phạm Thị Tâm	1972	VCVWU (2011–)	12/12	None	Second-youngest child of 9

SPCC: Secretary of the Party's Communal Cell;
VSPCC: Vice Secretary of the Party's Communal Cell;
CVFF: Chair of the Vietnamese Fatherland Front;
CCPC: Chair of the Communal People's Council;
CVWU: Chair of the Vietnamese Women's Union;
VCVWU: Vice Chair of the Vietnamese Women's Union.

APPENDIX 2   Profiles of the female cadres in Thạch Châu Commune

02. Ms. Giang, born in 1938

Born in Thạch Châu Commune, the eldest child of seven sisters, Ms. Giang's parents were ordinary farmers who also raised silkworms and spun silk. She joined the August Revolution Boy and Girl Scout group (*Đoàn Thiếu Nhi Tháng Tám*) and played an active part in the chorus group. She joined the Mass Education Movement (*phong trào bình dân học vụ*) as a junior-high-school student and taught small children to write (*dậy vỡ lòng*). After finishing the seventh grade, she married a student from a sports university. She was nineteen years old at that time. She lost her husband in the war against the United States in 1968 (she received his death notice in 1977). She has a disabled son to support. She joined the Vietnam Women's Union and worked at the hamlet level. She joined the Communist Party in 1966 and subsequently was appointed chair of the communal branch of the Women's Union. She studied at the Women's Union school in Vinh City for two years. She also studied at a financial school for forty-five days and was then appointed cashier of an agricultural collective in the commune. Later, she became the cashier of the United Agricultural Collective of the commune. In 1986, she resigned from the collective administration because she wanted to concentrate on economic activities. She said it was natural for her to be active in the Women's Union because social activities had been her "environment" since her days in the scouts. At present, her only grandson works as a member of the communal committee of the Youth League. She said that being good at "taking care" (*lo lắng*) of directions from above and that the happiness of the association's members is a distinct feature of the female cadres' way of working.

07. Ms. Hương, born in 1949

Ms. Hương was born in a neighboring commune, the eldest child of eight brothers and sisters. After finishing the seventh grade, she dropped out of school because of financial problems. She joined the Civil Engineer Brigade, the coastal Defense Service, and Irrigation Team No. 202 when she was sixteen years old. She was assigned as the vice-chief of an agricultural collective when she was seventeen years old. According to her, the Communist Party kept her from leaving the commune because it was short of young cadres. She got married at seventeen and lost her husband on the battlefield. She joined the Communist Party when she was eighteen and was assigned as the sub-chief of the communal Youth League, then was reallocated to work as the chairperson of the communal Women's Union when she was twenty years old. She successively held positions as the assistant for the communal People's Committee and vice-secretary of the communal party branch. She married an elementary-school teacher in 1981 and moved to her second husband's house in Thạch Châu Commune. At that time, she had an adopted daughter and her second husband had five children.

She had two children with her second husband. She was assigned to positions as a committee member of the hamlet branch of the Women's Union in 1981, vice-chair of the communal branch of the Women's Union in 1983, and chairperson in 1984. In 1999, her position transferred to a successor and she moved down to the position of vice-chair in charge of a financial project for women in the commune. She resigned from the office in 2001. When she first moved to her second husband's village, she experienced difficulties with her husband's relatives, who were opposed to her working in "society" when her husband also worked. However, encouraged by cadres in Thạch Châu Commune, she overcame these challenges and worked for the Women's Union.

08. Ms. Trung, born in 1950

Ms. Trung was born in Thạch Châu Commune, the youngest of six sisters. Her parents were classified as middle-class peasants during the land-reform period. After finishing the seventh grade, she joined the Youth League. At that time, meetings were often held in each hamlet, rather than in schools as they are now, so group activities were very cheerful. They always sang songs and played games, even during bombings. She also joined shooting practices and the coastal Defense Service with other young women in the commune. She also voluntarily taught little children to write in her hamlet. She got married in 1968, when she was eighteen years old. However, she had to wait until 1973 to organize the wedding party because, when her husband returned from the South in 1971, she had to travel there as the vice-company commander of the volunteer army service corps (*dân câng hỏa tuyến*). She had her first son in 1974 and now has five sons, all of whom have graduated from universities. After the war, her husband went to Laos for military-political duties and came back to the village after demobilization. She said her husband was a hardworking man and often supported the people around him. She talked eagerly about education for children, saying that a mother should be an "accompanying friend" of her children and observe children's social relationships and everyday behavior. She was assigned as sub-chief of the local security police contingent in charge of the census resister. In 1986, she was allocated as vice-chair of the communal branch of the Women's Union and the cashier of the United Agricultural Collective of the commune concurrently. In 1996, she was assigned as the chair of the communal Women's Union. She has many memories of the integration of hamlet nurseries into the communal kindergarten and of credit projects for women. She thinks female cadres are usually better trained in their duties than men, especially when they start a new pilot project, and are not over-confident in organizing. She is proud of the children of fellow cadres, who study well and have good jobs. Her husband died in 2009, and since then she has often stayed at her eldest son's house in Hanoi. Her husband's younger brother is successful in political life and held important posts such as the secretary of the district Party branch and vice-chair of the provincial branch of the Vietnamese Fatherland Front.

13. Ms. Lam, born in 1967

Ms. Lam was born in Thạch Châu Commune, the fourth child of five brothers and sisters. After finishing the seventh grade, she dropped out of school because she could not pass the exam to enter high school. She joined the Youth League when she was fifteen years old. The main activities were coaching, singing, and dancing for small children, which was a very cheerful (*soi nổi*) experience for her. She also joined the irrigation team with her friends. She is regretful that the Youth League these days has become more and more like an "economic" activity instead of a "movement," like it was in her days. In 1985, she was assigned as leader of the hamlet Youth League. She joined the Communist Party in 1988 and got married in the same year. Her husband was an executive member of the communal Youth League at that time, and then successively held positions in the local government. He now works at the district party branch in charge of personnel. Ms. Lam had her first son in 1990. She has two children. She joined the Women's Union in 1992 and was assigned by the party as the leader of the hamlet branch in 1993. She became a member of the executive committee of the communal branch of the Women's Union in 1995 and held an additional post as person in charge of the population and families of the commune in 2001. She was reassigned to work as an official for administrative affairs in the communal People's Committee in 2004. According to her, the Women's Union became more active once it started to have credit funds and was able to provide members with material benefits. She claims not to have any feeling about the activities of the Women's Union. She rather insists on her preference for art performance activities in the village.

15. Ms. Vân, born in 1972

Ms. Vân was born in Thạch Châu Commune, the eldest of three brothers and sisters. Her father ran away when she was a child. After finishing high school, she decided to stay at home to support her mother even though she had enough ability to go to university. She was assigned as the subleader of the communal Youth League in 1988 and was selected as the leader in 1989. In 1994, she got married to a son of a former chairperson of the communal People's Committee. Her husband was successively selected as the chair of the hamlet branch of the Farmer's Association and the chief of H hamlet, but he had to resign from the position because of health problems. After having a daughter, Ms. Vân was successively assigned as the chair of the hamlet branch of the Women's Union in 1997, an executive member of the agricultural service collective of Thạch Châu Commune and the person in charge of population and families in the communal People's Committee in 2002, an executive member of the communal branch of the Women's Union in 2004, and the chair of the communal branch of the Women's Union in 2006. She still holds this position. She said she loves "political" activities more than "economic" activities. According to her, female cadres often take much more care (*lo lắng*) in their tasks than male cadres do; thus, they always plan ahead and take care of the outcomes.

16. Ms. Tâm, born in 1972

Ms. Tâm was born in Thạch Châu Commune, the eighth child of nine brothers and sisters. After retiring from a forestry office in Hà Tĩnh province, her father returned to the commune and worked as the chief of the communal stockbreeding collective. After graduating from high school, she did not continue studying because of laziness and started a small business at local markets with her parents' capital, then married a man in the commune. He worked at a lumber mill in the South at that time. She has two children. After having her first daughter in 1994, she joined the Women's Union. She was recognized for her ability by the chair of the hamlet branch of the Women's Union at that time, and was assigned as a member of the executive committee of the hamlet branch in 1998. She was assigned as chair of the hamlet branch in 2004, as a member of the executive committee of the communal branch in 2006, as the person in charge of the accounting for the agricultural service collective and electricity collective of the commune in 2007, and as the person in charge of keeping the agricultural collective store. She became the vice-chair of the communal Women's Union in 2011. She finally gave up her small business when she was assigned as vice-chair, though she had tried hard to keep working at the market since her youth. She said that although activities in the Women's Union give her political experience, they do not have anything to do with economic stability, at least working with a contract at the hamlet level.

References

Ashwin, Sarah. 1999. "Redefining the Collective: Russian Mineworkers in Transition." In *Uncertain Transition: Ethnographies of Change in the Postsocialist World*, edited by Michael Burawoy and Katherine Verdery, 245–71. Lanham, MD: Rowman & Littlefield.

Endres, Kirsten W. 1999. "Images of Womanhood in Rural Vietnam and the Role of the Vietnamese Women's Union: A Microscopic Perspective." In *Vietnamese Villages in Transition*, edited by Bernhard Dahm and Vincent J. Houben, 155–74. Passau, Germany: Department of Southeast Asian Studies, University of Passau.

Gammeltoft, Tine. 1999. *Women's Bodies, Women's Worries: Health and Family Planning in a Vietnamese Rural Community*. Richmond, VA: Curzon Press.

Grossheim, Martin, and Kirsten W. Endres. 1999. "The Development of the Educational Sectors and Recent Trends in Primary Health Care at the Village Level." In *Vietnamese Villages in Transition*, edited by Bernhard Dahm and Vincent J. Houben, 175–96. Passau, Germany: Department of Southeast Asian Studies, University of Passau.

Hann, Chris M. 1990a. "Introduction." In *Market Economy and Civil Society in Hungary*, edited by Chris M. Hann, 1–20. London: Cass.

———. 1990b. "Second Economy and Civil Society." In *Market Economy and Civil Society in Hungary*, edited by Chris M. Hann, 21–44. London: Cass.

Hann, Chris, Caroline Humphrey, and Katherine Verdery. 2002. "Introduction: Postsocialism as a Topic of Anthropological Investigation." In *Postsocialism: Ideologies and Practices in Eurasia*, edited by Chris M. Hann, 1–28. New York: Routledge.

Houtart, Francois, and Genevieve Lemercinier. 1984. *Hai Van: Life in a Vietnamese Commune*. London: Zed Books.

Kato, Atsufumi. 2010. "Tính Đa Thanh của Chính Sách: Một Quá Trình Lý Giải về Chương Trình Tín Dụng Quy Mô Nhỏ ở Vùng Nông Thôn Hà Tĩnh" [Polyphonic Policy: A Case Study of a Microcredit Project in the Rural Ha Tinh]. In *Hiện Đại và Động Thái của Truyền Thống ở Việt Nam: Những Cách Tiếp Cận Nhân Học* [Modernities and the Dynamics of Tradition in Vietnam: Anthropological Approaches] vol. 1, edited by Lương Văn Hy et al., 151–64. Thành Phố Hồ Chí Minh: Nxb. Đại Học Quốc Gia Thành Phố Hồ Chí Minh.

Kerkvliet, Benedict J. 2005. *The Power of Everyday Politics: How Vietnamese Peasants Transformed National Policy*. Ithaca, NY: Cornell University Press.

Luong, Hy V. 2010. *Tradition, Revolution, and Market Economy in a North Vietnamese Village, 1925–2006*. Honolulu: University of Hawai'i Press.

Malarney, Shaun Kingsley. 1997. "Culture, Virtue, and Political Transformation in Contemporary Northern Viet Nam." *The Journal of Asian Studies* 56 (4): 899–920.

———. 2002. *Culture, Ritual and Revolution in Vietnam*. Honolulu: University of Hawai'i Press.

Oi, Jean C. 1989. *State and Peasant in Contemporary China: The Political Economy of Village Government*. Berkeley: University of California Press.

Rydström, Helle. 2003. *Embodying Morality: Growing Up in Rural Northern Vietnam*. Honolulu: University of Hawai'i Press.

Sakurai, Yumio. 1987. *The Formation of Vietnamese Villages*. Tokyo: Sobunsha. [桜井由躬雄『ベトナム村落の形成——村落共有田=コンディエン制の史的展開』創文社].

Tran Thi Minh Thi. 2012. "Social and Family Roles of Working Women in Transitional Vietnam." In *Alternative Intimate Spheres for Women in Vietnam*, GCOE Working Papers (Next Generation Research) 71, edited by Kato Atsufumi, 87–103. Kyoto: Kyoto University Global COE for Reconstruction of the Intimate and Public Spheres in 21st Century Asia.

Vasavakul, Thaveeporn. 2003. "From Fence-Breaking to Networking: Interests, Popular Organizations and Policy Influences in Post-Socialist Vietnam." In *Getting Organized in Vietnam: Moving In and Around the Socialist State*, edited by Ben J. Tria Kerkvliet, Russell H.K. Heng, and David W.H. Koh, 25–61. Singapore: Institute of Southeast Asian Studies.

Werner, Jayne. 2002. "Gender, Household, and State: Renovation (*Đổi Mới*) as Social Process in Viet Nam." In *Gender, Household, State: Đổi Mới in Viet Nam*, edited by Jayne Werner and Danièle Bélanger, 29–47. Ithaca, NY: Cornell Southeast Asia Program Publications.

Wischermann, Joerg, and Nguyen Quang Vinh. 2003. "The Relationship between Civil and Governmental Organizations in Vietnam: Selected Findings." In *Getting Organized in Vietnam: Moving In and Around the Socialist State*, edited by Ben J. Tria Kerkvliet, Russell H.K. Heng and David W.H. Koh, 185–233. Singapore: Institute of Southeast Asian Studies.

Woodside, Alexander. 1971. *Vietnam and the Chinese Model: A Comparative Study of Nguyen and Ching Civil Government in the First Half of the Nineteenth Century*. Cambridge, MA: Harvard University Press.

CHAPTER 6

Living in Intimacy: A Case Study of Women's Community at a Caodaist Temple in Hanoi*

Ito Mariko

Introduction

Recent studies have pointed out the significance of a new perspective on the notion of community (Cohen 1982; Anderson 1983; Wenger 1998; Amit 2002; Delanty 2003). In this chapter, I will critically reconsider Wenger's (1998) idea of "community of practice" which is essential to understanding the relationship between the community and practice in religious activities for women in Vietnam. The concept "community of practice," focuses on the cognitive processes in which people commit to and identify themselves within a community, by participating in the practical process of building new knowledge and skills. Tanabe (2002; 2008), however, criticizes Lave and Wenger's theory, arguing that it does not fully consider the process through which community members affect changes through their group participation, which forms new relations among the members and creates a new style of knowledge and practice. In addition, Tanabe emphasizes that group participation among community members breeds self-confidence that enables them to better apply their skills in broader society. Thus, Tanabe (2002) suggests that the term "community" implies a space or a situation in which the affectional and social relations of individuals are constructed by everyday practices. Based on Tanabe's arguments, Hirai (2012) also suggests an idea of "community as practice" that is completely different from the traditional view of community as an affiliation based on birthplace and kinship relations. To this end, Hirai indicates five key points concerning the "community as practice" approach as follows: (1) People are thrown and throw themselves into a community, (2) a community is always reconstructed through practices, (3) relationships within a society are inherent in the community, (4) modes of knowledge and practice are realigned recursively, and (5) the community pays attention to affectional conjectures (Hirai 2012, 16–18). Community,

---

* This contribution is a revised version of a previously published article that appeared in Kato, Atsufumi ed. 2012. *Alternative Intimate Spheres for Women in Vietnam*, GCOE Working Papers (Next Generation Research) 71, Kyoto, Japan: Kyoto University Global COE Program for Reconstruction of the Intimate and Public Spheres in 21st Century Asia.

FIGURE 6.1 *The Caodaism Hanoi Temple*
SOURCE: PHOTO BY ITO MARIKO.

in this sense, connects affection with the community in settings where people create alternative "intimate spheres" for individuals (Tanabe 2008, 122–25).

In this chapter I focus on the religious community of the Caodaist Hanoi Temple (Thánh Thất Thủ Đô Hả Nội), which might also be regarded as an example of a community *as* practice. The Hanoi Temple is a subgroup of the Ban Chỉnh Đạo sect, the second-largest sect in Caodaism, and it is the only Caodaist institution of that sect in central Hanoi. At present, almost all the members of this temple community are women, in particular middle-aged and elderly women who have experienced suffering in their lives. They are involved in most of the temple activities as core community members. These activities are shaped by a unique relationship shared by these women. They describe this relationship using the word *thân mật*, which can be translated into Chinese as 親密 and into English as "intimate." In this chapter, I examine the possibility of an alternative intimate sphere through the analysis of the *thân mật* relationships among these women gathering at the Hanoi Temple (Figure 6.1).[1]

---

[1] I conducted long-term field research in two phases. The first was from September 2000 to October 2001, and the second was from April 2004 to October 2005. I recorded not only women's daily practices, including their religious activities at the Hanoi temple, but also the life stories of ten women. I frequently visited the women's houses to conduct these interviews.

Community as Intimate Sphere

In a patriarchal society like Vietnam, "womanhood" has been directly connected to the reproduction of kinship relations. As Keith Taylor (2002, 7) suggests, there is a traditionalized ideal of the patriarchal family where all women marry, all women remain virgins until then, everyone lives in a three-generation household, and divorce and separation are not acknowledged as viable options (Werner 2002). An unmarried and childless woman is located at the periphery of society because she does not have agency in the reproduction of patrilineal kinship. A war widow's life is often understood as socially disadvantaged. In this sense, the women I focus on are regarded as having deviated from the ideal of womanhood in Vietnamese society. In fact, the female community members meeting at the Hanoi Temple are preoccupied with situations related to their marital status—whether unmarried, divorced, or widowed by the Vietnam War—or are concerned with suffering in their family, such as a son who died young or an ill husband. Though the social status of women changed dramatically during the Vietnam War, it also appears that the traditional notion of womanhood has been reproduced through the modern form of family advocated by government policy after the Đổi Mới (Renovation) era in the late 1980s (Eisen 1984; Gammeltoft, 1999; Rydström 2003; Drummond and Rydström 2004).

What I focus on here is the emergence of a social relationship among women who have different experiences and difference native places. Each woman moved from her native village to Hanoi for different reasons. They all happened to meet and form a religious community, constructing relationships through interactions with each other. They have been creating a new "community as practice" through interactions based on religious activities in the community.

In order to look closely at the relationships created by practices and interactions among individuals in the community, I reexamine a series of discussions about intimate spheres. Japanese scholars have been reconsidering the intimate sphere, with reference to Hannah Arendt's (1958) views on examining the relationships among individuals in a new type of community. Arendt regarded the intimate sphere of modernity as a space of resistance against "the social." The intimate sphere is thus a space characterized by privacy or internal actions and is distinguished from the public space, open for all people in society. She calls this public space the "space of appearance," in which people connect with others through their own actions and speech. She also explained that "appearance" is something being seen and heard by others as well as by ourselves, which constitutes the real world of relatedness (50). Based on Arendt's argument, Saito Jyunichi (2003, 92–99), a Japanese political scientist, suggests that it is not only the openness of the public sphere that enables the space of appearance but also that the "shadowiness" of the intimate sphere fosters another kind of space of appearance. Saito goes on to redefine the intimate sphere as a medium through which people care for and are interested in "specific others." According to Saito, intimacy is connected to inter-subjective relationships "in between" specific others who have bodies and personhood; meanwhile the "space of appearance" can be redefined as a space where people can derive each "appearance" by receiving others' affection in relation to specific others, though there are always differences and dilemmas (Saito 2000, 92–93). Moreover, Saito emphasizes that the intimate sphere is a space of discourse as well as a space of affection. In the intimate sphere, people are encouraged to present themselves through acts and words without the fear of being ignored. Also, in the intimate sphere, people empathize with one another's feelings and difficulties (99).

Tanabe (2008, 113–25), a Japanese anthropologist who has been conducting field research on a community of HIV patients in Thailand, refers to Arendt and Saito, specifically about the significance of intimate relationships created in communities formed by individuals who have suffered in life. In the community on which Tanabe focuses, HIV patients and nonpatients are engaged in the work of managing the community together. They talk about their life histories to other community members as part of the daily routine. According to Tanabe, they create a relationship based on intimacy through labor and care as well as the sharing of stories about life. The community also creates a social space for HIV patients and nonpatients through shared practices and values. Thus, the community members share common emotions with each other. The intimate relationship manifest in this community is completely different from any family or kinship relationship.

These discussions of intimate spheres provide a new perspective to reconsider the lives of women dealing with suffering in contemporary Vietnamese society. On the following pages, I will consider the intimate relationships within the Hanoi Temple community through analysis of community members' practices and interactions. First, I review the features of Caodaism and briefly look at the present situation at the Hanoi Temple. In the next section, I ethnographically describe the daily life of Priestess Hoa, the representative of the Hanoi Temple, and examine her understanding of the temple community through an analysis of the interrelation between her religious practice and the laywomen's attitudes toward her. Then I consider the laywomen and their practices and interactions to examine their relationships with one another. Finally, I argue the possibility of creating an alternative intimate sphere for laywomen through an examination of the *thân mật* relationship within the temple community.

Caodaism as the Epitome of Religion in Vietnam[2]

Caodaism was organized in the Southern region under French rule in the 1920s, then expanded rapidly. Caodaism is a syncretic religion, with practices and ideas derived from popular Vietnamese beliefs as well as from major world religions and ideologies such as Buddhism, Taoism, Confucianism, and Christianity. The Caodaist pantheon of gods is composed of Confucius, Buddha, Laozi, Guanyin, Ly Po, Jesus Christ, and others, all under the Jade Emperor as the Creator of the world. The doctrine was also codified as being God's words communicated through the Jade Emperor and Ly Po, via the medium of *phò loan*, which was a popular intermediary method among people in the Southern region at the time Caodaism became institutionalized. In Caodaist doctrine, the worldview of Caodaism is represented by the *đạo*. The *đạo* is related to the sense of values among Vietnamese people in general, which I will explain in detail in the next section.

The founders of Caodaism—who were from the upper middle class, including government officials, land owners, and intellectuals—got legal permission for religious activities from the French governor in 1926. They initiated their religious activities at a Buddhist pagoda called Go Ken in Tây Ninh province. After a while, they built huge plantations there. A large number of local residents, mostly peasants and workers living in and around the Mekong delta, participated in the construction of these plantations. They embraced Caodaism in the hope that it might give them relief from poverty and oppression from authority. In other words, Caodaism manifested itself as millennialism (Ho Tai 1983). At the same time, the Caodaists did work for welfare, including organizing and enabling employment, education, and medical treatment for their followers. The founders separated the initial organization into several sects in the 1930s. Seven sects were created, each administered by one of the founders; these were active in the Central and Southern region until the 1960s.

Each Caodaist sect had an administrative system that was similar to the political system of the state. In particular, the Tây Ninh sect had a military

---

2   Previous studies on Caodaism have discussed its origin, history, and tenets, the hierarchical structure of the organization, and its sociopolitical aspects with regard to nationalism and millennialism (Gobron 1949; Fall 1955; Hickey 1964; Smith 1970; Oliver 1973; 1976; Werner 1976; Ho Tai 1983; Blagov 2002).

setup that could mobilize half a million people. Their activities grew into a large religious-social movement and became connected to the national liberation movement as a counter to French rule. Other sects, such as the Tiên Thiên and Ban Chỉnh Đạo sect, also engaged in their own political activities. Since Caodaism was seen as a strong political force operating against French rule, all the sects were oppressed by political authorities. After 1975, all religious and ritual activities were rigorously controlled by the Communist government. The government intervened in the activities of various sects of Caodaism and even closed down their facilities, in accordance with its policy on religion. After the Đổi Mới era started in the late 1980s, the government permitted eleven sects to conduct their own activities, operating as official organizations. Now there are more than 3 million Caodaist believers in Vietnam and elsewhere.

If someone wants to be a Caodaist, he or she has to undergo the rite of passage (*lễ nhập môn*) at a local temple. After the ritual, he or she usually belongs to a basic group called *họ đạo*, which has a role similar to that of a parish in Christianity. All the members belonging to a *họ đạo* are required to take part in religious activities under the Caodaist doctrine. A *họ đạo* is administered by one main representative and several of its members. An individual who has renounced the world may often become the representative of a *họ đạo*. Laypersons who belong to a *họ đạo* have to obey the representative because he/she has rights and responsibilities with regard to all activities. When a *họ đạo* gets over five hundred members, they are permitted to build their own temple called *thánh thất*.[3]

Caodaists are basically divided into two categories. The first category is that of the renouncers (*thượng thừa*). After renouncing the world, a renouncer usually lives in a *thánh thất*. He/she spends his or her whole life at the temple following Caodaist doctrines, such as the five commandments, and taking part in religious activities, including services to the Supreme Being (Ông Trời) four times each day and eating only vegetarian meals. Such a renunciant may become the representative of a *họ đạo* and direct religious activities at the temple. The second category is that of laypeople (*trung thừa/hạ thừa*), who normally live in their own houses and meet at temples to participate in rituals and other religious activities.

Caodaists worship the Supreme Being, called the Jade Emperor or Đức Ngọc Hoàng Thượng Đế.[4] He is represented as the creator of the universe and the

---

3 After 1975, each organization needed to have permission from the government for all activities.
4 Đức Ngọc Hoàng Thượng Đế is familiar to Vietnamese people as the guardian deity of each village. It is worshipped at the communal house (*đền*).

FIGURE 6.2 *Participating in a ritual in the Hanoi temple*
SOURCE: PHOTO BY ITO MARIKO.

father of human beings. The Goddess, called Diêu Trì Kim Mẫu, is represented as the mother of human beings.[5] All human beings in the world are viewed as their children, and followers identify each other as brothers and sisters. For example, followers belonging to the Ban Chỉnh Đạo sect consider the sect founder, Nguyễn Ngọc Thương, as the eldest brother and rank themselves by seniority within the organization (Figure 6.2).

The Concept of *Đạo*

The term *họ đạo* consists of two terms: *họ* and *đạo*. *Họ* is a term relating to kinship, and it signifies a family or a clan. In ordinary usage, Vietnamese people usually employ the term *họ* to represent their own kinship, as in *dòng họ*, for instance. Thus, *họ* is not a term unique to the followers of Caodaism.

---

5 Goddess worship is the most familiar religious practice in Vietnam. The Đức Ngọc Hoàng Thượng Đế is situated at the top of the pantheon of gods and goddesses, called *thánh mẫu* or *công chúa* (see Endres in this volume).

Đạo is translated into Chinese as 道, which means "way" or "ism." Vietnamese speakers usually use the term *đạo* to represent religion or belief. They refer to *đạo* Nho, *đạo* Phật, or *đạo* Cao đài, which respectively mean Confucianism, Buddhism, and Caodaism. For instance, when asking someone about their religion or belief system, they may say, "*Anh/Chị theo đạo nào?*" This means, "What religion/belief system do you follow?" Moreover, in the broader sense of the term, *đạo* signifies morality and ethics, which generate the social order. The terms *đạo đức* and *đạo lý* are translated as "morality" and "ethics," which are understood as an order including what is good and social norms among the people. For instance, *đạo con* means "morality of the child," that is, an individual worships his own deceased mother with veneration and his own deceased father with respect (Gammeltoft 1999, 173).

In the Caodaist context, the *đạo* is based on the doctrine or worldview of Caodaism. In this sense, the term *họ đạo* signifies an ideal relationship of a fictive kinship group among the followers of Caodaism. The meaning of *họ đạo* includes not only a parish based on geographical regulation, but also a created kinship formed by individuals sharing the *đạo* to organize their personal lives. *Thánh thất* is regarded as a fictive home, and the followers try to visualize an ideal relationship among peer members of the community who share the same *đạo*.

The Caodaist Hanoi Temple

Caodaism was propagated in the northern region of Vietnam in the late 1920s. The first propagator was a male layperson of the Tây Ninh sect. Then, some priests sent from headquarters founded a *họ đạo* and built their own temple, the Thăng Long Temple (Thánh Thất Thăng Long) in Hanoi (Lê Quang Tấn 1956). In the 1930s, Nguyễn Ngọc Tương, the founder of the Ban Chỉnh Đạo sect, and a young renouncer named Pho, who became the representative of the Hanoi Temple later in life, started to propagate Caodaism in the North. In 1939, they founded the *họ đạo* of the sect with its own temple in Northern Vietnam (Lê Anh Dũng 1993). From this period up to the late 1980s, there were two *họ đạo* belonging to different Caodaist sects in Hanoi.

After Pho returned to the headquarters in Bến Tre province, three male renunciants set up the Hanoi Temple *họ đạo*.[6] They had initial difficulties

---

6 Bến Tre province is located in the Mekong delta. Nguyễn Ngọc Tương seceded from the Tây Ninh sect at the beginning of the 1930s and then created the Ban Chỉnh Đạo sect in Bến Tre province.

obtaining basic shelter and food, but they eventually borrowed a room in a suburb of Hanoi and kept working to propagate Caodaism among the inhabitants of the area. Moving several times within the city from the foundation period until 1945, they continued their work. At that time, most of the followers were workers, traders, and migrants originally from other Northern provinces.

Since 1945, when the Democratic Republic of Vietnam was founded, the situation of the Hanoi temple *họ đạo* has changed under the socialist reformation. For instance, in 1945, the community moved to another place and built its own temple in what is its current location. In 1946, Hồ Chí Minh visited the temple, and after his visit, the Hanoi temple was recognized (*công nhận*) as an official religious organization by the government in 1947. At the same time, its religious activities were put under the control of the government. Under the war regime, the Hanoi Temple engaged in the patriotic movement in cooperation with the Thăng Long Temple. They organized a committee to support the War Front for the Unification of the Homeland and opened their temples to the general public for use as spaces for social and cultural activities.

The activities of the temple's community members during the war (from the mid-1950s to 1975) are unknown. According to Priestess Hoa, representative of the Hanoi temple from 1998 to 2010, almost all laypeople were evacuated to other provinces, leaving only Priest Pho at the temple, where he worked with the Red Cross.[7]

The Hanoi Temple restarted its religious activities after the Vietnam War ended. From 1975 to the 1990s, twenty-one people, including most of the present core members, became Caodaists there. Currently, the Hanoi Temple is the only Caodaist organization in the center of Hanoi.[8] As of 2010, Priestess Hoa and approximately fifty laypeople belonged to the Hanoi Temple. About 80 percent of the laypeople are middle-aged and elderly women in their fifties to eighties, and there are thirteen core members who support temple activities. The core members are widows who lost their husbands during the Vietnam War, unmarried women, divorcees, and women with some sort of family problem. They share the experience of embracing Caodaism after migrating to Hanoi from their birthplaces in neighboring provinces during the Vietnam War.

---

7 Priest Pho received an official commendation for supporting the patriotic movement through participation in the rescue operations of the Red Cross.
8 Two *họ đạo* had been jointly working under socialism from 1945 to 1986. In 1986, the two temples *họ đạo* unified into one organization under the Ban Chỉnh Đạo sect.

Imagining a Familial Community: The Daily Practice of the Priestess Hoa[9]

Until 2010, all activities within and outside the Hanoi Temple were conducted under the leadership of Priestess Hoa. She had lived in the Hanoi Temple for fifty-nine years, ever since she renounced a social life at the age of twenty. She became the representative of the Hanoi Temple in 1998 when her predecessor, Priest Pho, passed away. Hoa continued religious practice based on Caodaist doctrines until she passed away in 2010. In this section, I focus on her daily practice and the interactions between her and other laywomen to examine Hoa's usage of *họ đạo*. Usually, *họ đạo* signifies a parish under a particular sect of Caodaism and also a family constituted by members of the same parish who share a common *đạo*. In the Hanoi Temple, Priestess Hoa brought the term into use by to emphasize an ideal family relationship in the temple community.

Priestess Hoa was born in Hanoi in 1931. She was the eldest in a family of five children. After graduating, she became a teacher in an elementary school in Hanoi. When she was nineteen years old, Hoa fell ill suddenly and developed a curious ability to cure diseases. After she recovered, she also became able to predict other people's futures. Priestess Hoa described this: "One day, I cured a boy completely. His disease was regarded as incurable by the doctor. Then, many neighbors came to my house and asked me to treat them."

Her ability to cure sickness was gradually recognized and accepted by neighbors. Their attitude toward Hoa changed further after she had a mysterious experience.

> One day, a woman came to my house. She said to me repeatedly, "You're a child of God, you're a child of God." After that, the woman rushed away. Then I dreamed of a religious facility that I had never seen. I went around Hanoi for a whole year to find the religious facility and finally found the place I had dreamed of. It was the Caodaist Hanoi Temple. Then, neighbors began to avoid me because they saw my behavior as strange. I also had a boyfriend who had promised to marry me, but I could not marry him because I was regarded as a child of God.
> INTERVIEW WITH PRIESTESS HOA, MAY 8, 2001

Hoa said that after she found the Caodaist Hanoi Temple, she realized that the God the unknown women had talked about in her dream was the Jade Emperor. Hoa asked Priest Pho about Caodaism. Then she decided to renounce normal

---

9 I interviewed Hoa about her life from October 2000 to August 2001 and then conducted additional interviews during my secondary long-term research.

life and live at the Hanoi Temple. After she renounced the world, her mysterious powers and dreaming disappeared completely.

According to Hoa, at the time when she became a renouncer, several renouncers, including Priest Pho, lived together at the temple. During the Vietnam War, three female renouncers migrated to other countries. Other renouncers had already passed away. After Priest Pho died in 1998, two female renouncers, Priestess Hoa and Ms. Miên were left at the temple. Ms. Miên had no specific status in the Hanoi Temple họ đạo. She simply took care of Priestess Hoa's daily needs. In 2000, Ms. Miên went back to her birthplace after losing her eyesight, and she passed away in 2001. Priestess Hoa lived alone at the Hanoi Temple for nine years until she passed away in 2010.

Priestess Hoa spent her life continuing the worship of the Supreme Being four times a day. She usually got up at four o'clock in the morning, then dressed in a white robe (aó dài trắng), the Caodaists' costume for ritual, and arranged her long hair for the daily worship service of the Supreme Being at five o'clock. After that, she would enter into the room called the "palace" (bửu điện), and start to chant the sutra of Caodaism in front of the altar. After chanting, she would move to the office and eat some fruits, offerings from the altar that had started rotting. She sometimes went outside to participate in official meetings of the district-level Fatherland Front and the Women's Union.[10] She also often visited the houses of ill laypeople. At around ten-thirty in the morning, she came back to the temple for another worship service at eleven o'clock. In the evening, she usually spent time in the temple reading books, telephoning headquarters, and, if necessary, cleaning the yard.

Priestess Hoa maintained the "strictness" of đạo in her daily practice, which helped shape her extremely simple and modest life. The Hanoi Temple management budget included living expenses for Hoa, which were covered by offerings from laypeople and Hoa's pension from when she was a teacher. According to two core members who maintain the accounts, the Hanoi Temple is not at all well-endowed. There are funds for temple activities.[11] However,

---

10 The Vietnamese Fatherland Front (Mặt Trận Tổ Quốc Việt Nam) was founded in 1977. As an umbrella group of a pro-government mass movement in Vietnam, it has close links to the Communist Party and the Vietnamese government. The Fatherland Front is an amalgamation of various social and political associations, including the Communist Party itself (http://www.mattran.org.vn/index.htm). The Women's Union (Hội Liên Hiệp Phụ Nữ Việt Nam), founded in 1930, is an association under the Fatherland Front. It has been given roles in various antipoverty, healthcare, and education programs geared toward women (http://hoilhpn.org.vn/; see also Kato's chapter in this volume).

11 I could not verify the amount of expenses in detail, but a core member who was an accountant had recorded expenses for the temple activities.

there were only minimal living facilities at the temple until 2010. For instance, there were no electrical appliances, such as a television or refrigerator, which were used in ordinary households, because Hoa did not agree to have those facilities. The priestess disapproved of even changing a small light bulb. She rarely bought anything for herself. She usually ate vegetarian meals in keeping with the *đạo*, which core members delivered out of concern for her health, as she was not preoccupied with getting all her meals. Her daily clothes were well worn and had been used for many years, and she washed and mended them carefully by herself. Hoa usually saved money for temple activities, for donations to other *họ đạo* and the headquarters, and to give to people who were ill.

Hoa's daily practice based on the *đạo*, which she had learned during her more than fifty years of life at the temple, might be called "habitus." She was aware of herself as a renunciant who deviated from the secular norm, and she recognized the Hanoi Temple as "home" for her entire life. Hence, she paid attention to all temple activities, however insignificant or menial.

Họ Đạo as a Private Space, a "Lonely" Space

To understand Priestess Hoa's usage of *họ đạo*, I look at her attitude toward ritual days at the Hanoi Temple, when she guided laywomen in conducting the ritual. The laywomen followed her directions. After the ritual, Hoa preached as follows:

> We, the Hanoi Temple *họ đạo*, are practicing affection, caring for each other as brothers and sisters under the eldest brother Nguyễn Ngọc Thương. You have to come back to the temple on ritual days and solemnly participate in a service to the Supreme Being in order to face everyday life with appreciation and calmness, because the Supreme Being is our father, and we, *họ đạo*, are his children. It is the *đạo* that children respect their parents. And children have to care for each other as brothers and sisters. If someone becomes ill, we visit him or her. If someone has a serious problem, we have to join hands with each other to solve the problem. That is the *đạo* we have to follow.
> PRIESTESS HOA'S PREACHING, AUGUST 14, 2004

Priestess Hoa usually preached about the relationships among members belonging to the *họ đạo*—the relationship of members following the *đạo*. Moreover, she emphasized that each layperson should have responsibility as a member of the Hanoi Temple *họ đạo*, and required them to gather at the temple frequently to give each other mutual help and support as in a familial community. Her preaching was aimed at enhancing their identity and self-awareness

FIGURE 6.3 *Women gathering at Priestess Hoa's preaching*
SOURCE: PHOTO BY ITO MARIKO.

as members of the Hanoi Temple *họ đạo*. For instance, she ensured that every layperson could offer fruits and sweets at the altar on ritual days. By doing so, she tried to indicate her respect and compassion for all members as well as shape the Hanoi Temple *họ đạo* into a harmonious and moral collective thorough these attitudes (Figure 6.3).

However, laypeople did not respond as Hoa intended. A core member talked about this in an interview:

> Going to the temple often does not matter. We are in different situations with different daily routines. It is not the same as things used to be in the past. Now, we do not need to make an effort to find time to go to the temple. It is unavoidable that we do not have much time to waste on temple activities. What is more important for us is to follow the *đạo* by ourselves. That is our own moral, *đạo mình*.

The term *đạo mình* usually refers to layperson's own *đạo*, that is, their belief in Caodaist religious ideas. I will explain this further in the next section. Core members had interacted closely with Priestess Hoa because they were involved in assisting all activities of the Hanoi Temple. These members understood her views on *đạo* and *họ đạo*. However, if laypeople had responded to all of Hoa's demands in accordance with the requirements of the *đạo*, they would have spent a great amount of time on temple activities. It was clear that there were differences between the ways in which the priestess and the lay community interpreted *đạo*. In fact, laypeople usually did not go to the temple except for sutra recitations and ritual days. Moreover, they also did not have a common understanding of the doctrine. They did not know any details about the pantheon of gods because they felt that they had insufficient time to study Caodaist doctrine. Additionally, the Caodaist altars that laypeople have in their homes took different forms based on each family's economic situation. They reinterpreted some basic knowledge of Caodaist doctrine that was essential to the Caodaist world view. Laypeople understand these religious acts as accumulation of good deeds for themselves, which is referred to as *tâm công*. *Tâm công* includes not only mutual help given by community members, such as visits to the ill or elderly, but also attendance at all temple activities, including rituals. However, as I mentioned above, most of the laypeople did not visit the Hanoi temple except on some specific ritual days, and their knowledge of Caodaist doctrine did not match Priestess Hoa's *đạo* practice. Priestess Hoa frequently complained about attitudes toward activities in the Hanoi Temple *họ đạo*.

> I do not know why all members in my *họ đạo* are so lacking in knowledge. It is the ritual day for Lê Bá Trân, who was the founder of the Ban Chỉnh Đạo sect, but no one remembers that. It is certain that they do not know who Lê Bá Trân is. There is no one who studies *đạo* in my *họ đạo*. There is also no one who practices *đạo* in my *họ đạo*. There is no one who worries about the Hanoi Temple *họ đạo*'s future.
> PRIESTESS HOA, PERSONAL COMMENT

In fact, when there were no religious activities like rituals or sutra recitations going on, nobody visited the temple. The temple was usually very quiet. Priestess Hoa's daily life at the temple was lived out in solitude and silence. She often muttered to herself: "I am alone in the temple every day because nobody comes to the temple. Can you imagine what I'm thinking in this silence every day? I do not want to eat anything alone any more. It is sad to live alone here."

In the more recent past, conflicts between the priestess and the lay community became more serious. In particular, the core members found interacting with Hoa quite stressful. Some members had a rebellious attitude toward her. However, they did not refuse to meet at the Hanoi Temple and did not treat Hoa with contempt. They continued to go to temple and participate in specific rituals. The core members also kept caring for Priestess Hoa and assisting her with daily tasks in spite of the conflicts. They avoided increasing the intensity of the conflicts by talking about Hoa with each other and thus releasing their stress.

In their discussions, core members expressed various emotions, including resentment and compassion toward the priestess. For instance, a core member said that Hoa had learned not only *đạo* but also a suitable attitude toward outsiders who were not members of the Hanoi Temple *họ đạo*. According to some laywomen, Hoa treated outsiders such as government officers and guests from other sects with suitable respect and hospitality. They regarded her behavior as essential to a representative of the *họ đạo*. It seems that the respect for Hoa among members was maintained not only by the *đạo* practice, but also because of her understanding about how to behave toward outsiders.

On the other hand, since she insisted on strictly following the *đạo*, laywomen regarded her with pity. A core member told me, "Priestess Hoa has been living alone at the Hanoi temple. She renounced the world, so she did not marry and has no family of her own. That is her commitment as a renunciant. But how painful it must be to live alone at the temple! Her life must be so full of suffering and distress." This description shows that Priestess Hoa was regarded as a marginalized woman who deviated from traditionalized womanhood connected to the reproduction of family and kinship. As I mentioned above, she demanded that laywomen should engage in *đạo* practice, conforming to strict rules to construct a *họ đạo* as a familial community. When preaching after rituals, Hoa often emphasized the image of family with harmony and order. It seems that Hoa attempted to create her own family through *đạo* practices.

Đạo Mình and *Thân Mật* Relationships

Laypeople belonging to the Hanoi Temple are divided into two categories. The first one is that of laypeople with some status (I have called them core members), and the other is that of those who do not have any status (ordinary followers). Core members in the Hanoi Temple comprised thirteen women and two men until 2010, when Priestess Hoa passed away. They played a pivotal part in the religious activities, including the preparation for and execution of rituals and meeting Priestess Hoa's daily needs. Ordinary followers, on the other hand, just took part in some specific rituals (Figure 6.4).

There were differences in attitudes toward ritual activities between core members and ordinary followers, though most of the laypeople had no common understanding of *đạo* with Hoa, regardless of whether they were core members or ordinary people. They referred to their religious activities using *đạo mình*, which means "our own morality."

FIGURE 6.4 *Participating in a ritual in the Hanoi temple*
SOURCE: PHOTO BY ITO MARIKO.

Đạo mình practices among laypeople are supported by the relationships among them. Here, I examine their relationship, described as the *thân mật* relationship, among core members. *Thân mật* is the opposite of the *họ đạo* emphasized by Priestess Hoa. For instance, a core member mentioned, laughing:

> When we have some problems with Hoa, we talk about her with each other. In doing so, each member gradually feels better. If someone talks about a conflict between Hoa and herself, others who have had a longer relationship with Hoa can tell her what would be a suitable attitude to take in the situation. Because we are in a *thân mật* relationship in which we know each other well, we can get along with Priestess Hoa.

The core member explained that the *thân mật* relationship is constructed among members who know each other well. This indicates that the relationship is created through close interactions among peer members.

Rituals provide a space in which interaction among laywomen is prominent. In the ritual space, they chat about private affairs, including their life histories. I introduce the life histories of three women who are core participants in temple activities. L was born in 1943. She is single. Her father died when she was two years old. Her mother remarried after a few years, leaving L in her parents' care.

Thus, L was brought up by her maternal grandparents. She has been ill since childhood and was later diagnosed as infertile. She did not hope to marry and decided to enter the Youth League of the Communist Party. In her twenties, she moved to Hanoi with other members of the Youth League and enrolled in college, with the support of the party. After her graduation, she started to work as a clerk at the transportation bureau. Colleagues in the office introduced her to the temple community. She became a Caodaist in 1974 and has continued to take part in temple activities as a layperson (Interview with L, May 10, 2004).

L seems to be a woman removed from not only patrilineal kinship but also from marriage. She was stigmatized by being infertile. "After my maternal grandparents died when I was in my teens," she said, "I stayed at my stepfather's house. He and my mother had four children. The family was poor, and I could not assist in the hard cultivation work because I was in bad physical condition. The purpose I had in deciding to participate in the Youth League was not only to serve the revolution, but also to live by myself. To be a Caodaist was also my decision."

Another personal story presents the experience of a childless woman. H was born in 1932. When she was in her teens, she got married to a man who lived in the same village. She became pregnant four times. However, because of hard work in the paddy fields, she miscarried every time. When she was forty years old, her father-in-law brought a second wife for her husband. The second wife soon got pregnant and had a baby. Her husband's family made H agree to a divorce; she then moved to Hanoi, where her elder brother was stationed as a soldier. She knew the Hanoi Temple since her brother's daughter participated in activities there. She accompanied her niece to the temple and decided after a few years to be a Caodaist (interview with H, August 14, 2005).

"There was no choice," H said,

> That was my fate. A woman who cannot have a child is no use to her husband's family. After the divorce, I became dependent on my elder brother living in Hanoi. I moved to Hanoi and came to know about Caodaism. That was also my fate. I have female friends who met at the temple. We know each other very well. We have spent a long time together since I first encountered them. Our relationship is similar to that of siblings.

Within the Hanoi Temple community, there are also widows who lost their husbands in the Vietnam War. The story below is that of a widow who enthusiastically participates in activities at the temple.

D was born in 1934. When she was in her thirties, her husband died in the Vietnam War. Her husband's remains could not be retrieved and sent home, as his exact place of death could not be determined. She did worry about how and where he had died. However, she had no time to find information about her late husband at that time. Her husband's parents were deceased and D was left with five children to bring up by herself. She decided to move to a mountainous area in the northern part of Yên Bài province, where her relatives had migrated following the collective migration policy. However, her relatives were not in a good position to take in her and her five children. D and her children then moved to Hanoi, relying on her elder sister for help. The family settled in Hanoi and gradually reconstructed their lives. When D turned fifty years old, she had the time to think about her late husband and herself again. Following a common Vietnamese custom for women, she started to participate in religious activities at Buddhist temples but did not feel comfortable. Eventually, she visited the Hanoi Temple and decided to join in the activities. Now, she is a kind of leader among the core members of the Hanoi Temple community (Interview with D, March 8, 2004).

D said:

> All my children are married already. They have settled down in life. I do not worry about my children at all. But I have been worrying about my husband's death for long time. I decided to adopt Caodaism to give my husband's soul some rest and peace. The mortuary rituals of Caodaism are more rigorous than those of Buddhism. The laypersons' behavior during rituals is also supposed to be in keeping with a single norm that must be adhered to strictly. I also found the relationship among the laywomen to be comforting. My responsibility is to give my husband's soul some peace and to find the place where he died, so I devoted the time I have left in life to the temple activities. I cannot die until I fulfill my responsibility.

Although chatting among women is common behavior in daily life, women who gather at the temple acquire the unique sense of being with specific others by hearing one's words spoken within the *thân mật* relationship.

Followers of Caodaism take part in the monthly rituals, called *lễ sóc vọng*, on the first and fifteenth of every month. At the Hanoi Temple, laypeople also attend rituals to pray for peace in the family. They pray to the Supreme Being and other gods under Priestess Hoa's direction. There are also other kinds of rituals: annual rituals throughout the year for each deity, remembering events in the history of Caodaism, and rites of passage for followers. Out of all of these, however, laypeople belonging to the Hanoi Temple only take part in a few specific rituals. Because most of the rituals are held on weekdays, almost all of the members do not have time to visit the temple. Because of personal commitments, such as their jobs, housework, caring for grandchildren, and so on, they attend only the rituals that have great significance for them.

One of these is the Goddess Ritual. Of all activities, the busiest ritual during the year at the Hanoi Temple is that dedicated to the Goddess, which is held on the fourteenth and fifteenth of August. In Caodaism, the Goddess Diêu Trì Kim Mẫu, or Phật Mẫu, is the most familiar deity for women. They call the Goddess "mother" (*mẹ*) and take themselves as her "child" (*con*). They pray to her for their own health and happiness and for that of their family. Most of the laywomen assemble at the Hanoi Temple and enjoy the ritual as well as the preparation for it.

The Goddess Ritual attracts the largest number of participants of all rituals at the Hanoi Temple. One reason is because of the peculiar features of the Goddess Ritual. First, the preparation process is unique. In addition to the special altar of the Goddess set up for the ritual at the *bửu điện*, the place for the altar of the Supreme Being, they also prepare special incense. Offerings, such as several kinds of special fruits, are prepared for the Goddess, too. Core members start these preparations several days before the ritual. Priestess Hoa would call core members to the Hanoi Temple to begin preparations. Core members gathered early in the morning to clean the temple thoroughly before setting up the altar at the *bửu điện*. This work for the Goddess Ritual was apparently directed by Priestess Hoa. However, core members actually engaged in this work based on their own *thân mật* relationship. They completed tasks one by one, sharing information on preparations for the Goddess Ritual while chatting about their own lives, families, and health. Working together for the ritual and talking about their own lives among themselves made this a space in which to come to know each other and to create relationships of intimacy.

The second feature is a specific aspect of the ritual. Laywomen of the Hanoi Temple spent a long time together and repeated a single specific action in the temple during the period of the Goddess Ritual. This action is called *hầu* and means "to serve" in English. During the ritual process, laywomen stand and chant sutras several times, taking turns, on the side of the goddess altar. A laywoman said, "The Goddess Ritual is for women. We conduct *hầu* many times taking turns and enjoy chatting while waiting for the next time we have to conduct *hầu*. We wait eagerly for the day of the Goddess Ritual more than we do for all the other rituals." While waiting for their turns, they sit in a small room. They share one bed, with a few women sitting or lying down on it, and they talk about various topics. Through these collective experiences of the Goddess Ritual, laywomen interact closely and construct specific relationships.

Mortuary rituals for the dead members of the community are also very important for laywomen. There are also three memorial service rituals: *lễ cầu* siêu, *lễ tiêu tường*, and *lễ đại tường*. Funerals are held by the chief mourner of the deceased community member's family at their house. Many mourners attend, including non-Caodaists who were relatives, neighbors, and friends. The memorial service rituals are held at the temple and were previously under the direction of Priestess Hoa. Participants in memorial service rituals are members of the Hanoi Temple and the family of the deceased. On the ninth day after the funeral, laypeople gather in the Hanoi Temple, acting as kin, in order to give peace to the soul of the dead. One of the memorial service rituals, *lễ cầu siêu*, is held nine times every nine days after the funeral. Laypeople, especially core members, attend all of these rituals. Each participant wears a white robe, chants the sutra, and prays at the altar of ancestors; this is repeated for over an hour. After the ritual, participants move to their room to change clothes. In that room, some begin to talk about their memories of the deceased. Through these narratives, they share emotions toward the death with peers.

Participating in all these rituals is not an obligation, but an ideal attitude of a Caodaist following *đạo*. However, laywomen belonging to the Hanoi Temple reinterpret *đạo* to explain why they have to participate in some of these rituals. In particular, core members put greater emphasis on the Goddess Ritual and

FIGURE 6.5
Praying widows
SOURCE: PHOTO BY ITO MARIKO.

FIGURE 6.6
Volunteer cooking activity
SOURCE: PHOTO BY ITO MARIKO.

the preparation, such as the cleaning of the temple, setting up the altar, choosing offerings, and cooking vegetarian meals to offer on the altar (Figure 6.5 and 6.6). Mortuary rituals provide a place for sharing emotions about the death of a "specific other" and to confirm their relationship with both the ancestors and with the other laywomen (cf. Suenari 1998, 338).

In this sense, the relationships in the Hanoi Temple community give opportunities and places for laywomen to find a space of social protection which differs from the kinship or social relationships in their home villages. Moreover, it seems that these activities create a "community as practice" for individuals through close interactions during these rituals.

Being "Specific Others"

The two rituals discussed above indicate that laywomen are constructing intimate relationships through sharing in religious activities. Their interaction is also developed through daily practices outside the temple.

I introduce two core members' interaction with other members outside the Hanoi temple. Each core member has been interacting closely and maintaining contact with the others outside of the temple. They sometimes talk on the phone about not only the activities associated with the temple, but also about their private affairs.

Case 1

An unmarried sixty-four-year-old woman named L has been an earnest follower and temple community member for over thirty years. L is the woman whose life history was presented in the first section. Recently, she has had no time to attend rituals at the Hanoi temple because she is looking after a baby. The baby is her younger sister-in-law's son. Her sister-in-law is also a single woman, over forty years old, who became pregnant after an extramarital affair. She had the baby as a single mother in her native village. Being a single mother in Vietnam is unusual, especially as L's sister-in-law lives in a conservative rural society typical of Central Vietnam. Her elder brother and relatives were ashamed of her pregnancy and treated her as an immoral woman. She also needed to care for her bedridden mother. Therefore, her relatives in the village did not agree to her caring for the baby by herself there. L, who lives in Hanoi, which is far from the village, adopted the baby to bring up as her child. She talked only to two core members of the temple community about this. They are worried about L and sometimes call her to see how she is managing everything.

She did not talk about acting as a foster parent with other core members, including Priestess Hoa for a fixed period, because her sister-in-law's child was born out of wedlock, which was against *đạo*, even though her sister-in-law is not Caodaist. L talked about this with only two women from among the core members, D and Tr. D is a leader among the core members; D and Tr find L trustworthy because of her character and personality. L often consults D on the phone. Also, D often calls L because she is concerned about L's health. In recent years, L has not participated in temple activities as before, but she still communicates with D and Tr on the phone occasionally.

Case 2

This is the case of D, the same woman as in case 1, a widow, whose life history was also presented in the preceding section. D has been an earnest lay member of the community for more than twenty-five years. Her husband died in the Vietnam War when he was still in his mid-thirties. Vietnamese people believe that the remains of a dead person are essential to hold a funeral and give peace to the soul of the dead. However, D did not hold a formal funeral for her late husband, because she had no information about when and where her husband had died and could not identify his body. After the Vietnam War, many people went to fortunetellers to find the remains of their own family members.[12] D has been talking to members of the temple community, including Priestess Hoa, about her feelings regarding her late husband. However, she has also secretly visited a fortuneteller to find his remains, and a few members know about this.

D consulted a core member and neighbor named T on this matter. T is also a war widow. They participated in the Hanoi Temple *họ đạo* together in the 1990s. D did not open up about her private affairs to any of the other members.

According to T, she met D over forty years ago. D runs a small business, and T has sometimes visited D as a customer. They have developed a close relationship through this interaction in daily life. Because both women were war widows, they exchanged some information about a compensation scheme. Their family members have also come to know each other. The crucial point of their relationship was becoming Caodaists together. After that, they were involved in the Hanoi Temple's activities for more than twenty-five years together. They always visited the temple and went back home together.

Both cases were related to extremely private affairs, not easy to talk about with others. However, the women confessed these concerns to a limited number of core members, with whom they not only share social experiences but also have constructed intimate relationships through the practices at the temple.

Conclusion: Creating an Alternative Intimate Sphere

In this chapter, I assert that the practices that inform the *thân mật* relationship among women gathering at the Hanoi Temple create an alternative "intimate sphere." I shed light on the concepts of *họ đạo* (religious kinship) and *đạo mình* (our own morals), which women of the Hanoi Temple community often refer to in religious activities. Although both *họ đạo* and *đạo mình* are used by women in the Hanoi Temple community to distinguish themselves from outsiders, each term has a different usage in practice. *Họ đạo* usually means "a parish that belongs to a particular sect of Caodaism" and also "a family constituted by members who share a common *đạo* (Caodaist doctrine)" in the same parish. The term was brought into use by Priestess Hoa, the representative of *họ đạo*, to emphasize the ideal of familial relationships to the Hanoi Temple community. On the other hand, *đạo mình* usually refers to laywomen's own

---

12 The government permitted possession rituals only to find the places of death and the remains of those dead in the war.

đạo, or their own beliefs in Caodaist religious thought. Through a close analysis of daily usage, it becomes clear that *đạo mình* has some interesting connotations. This term is often used by women to convey certain ideas, feelings, and acts such as passive or negative feelings, attitudes toward the Hanoi Temple community, and extramarital affairs, which do not directly stem from orthodox Caodaist doctrine. Their heterodox usage of *đạo* does not necessarily indicate direct disobedience to either Caodaist doctrine or to the parish. It implies a reinterpretation of the meaning of *đạo* so that these women can share pain, make their lives more tolerable, and reconstruct their own morals according to the various issues they have confronted in the course of their lives. This practice has raised internal conflicts with the priestess in various situations throughout temple life, but these women nevertheless continued to participate in the Hanoi Temple community.

In conclusion, I emphasize the possibility of creating an alternative intimate sphere through the examination of the *thân mật* relationship among women in the Hanoi Temple community. Previous gender studies in Vietnamese society have focused on the gendered inequalities between men and women, and in particular emphasized the ways in which female bodies and sexuality are burdened by the responsibility to reproduce the patrilineal system (cf. Gammeltoft 2002; Nguyễn-Võ Thu-Hương 2002). Subsequently, the lives of Vietnamese women have been exclusively understood within this limited paradigm of family and sexuality. As such, single women and childless women, on whom I focus in this chapter, have not only been considered as "deviating" from the norm or being on the "social periphery," but their very existence as subjects worthy of inquiry has not been fully recognized in previous studies.

In this chapter, I describe through ethnography how women who do not share common backgrounds such as birthplace and kinship ties, developed connections with specific others through activities at the Hanoi Temple community, in a relationship referred to as *thân mật*. In considering this relationship, Arendt's idea of the "space of appearance" provides a relevant point of view:

> In the acting and speaking, men show who they are, reveal actively their unique personal identities, and thus make their appearance in the human world, while their physical identities appear without any activity of their own in the unique shape of the body and sound of the voice. This disclosure of "who" in contradistinction to "what" somebody is—his qualities, gifts, talents, and short-comings, which he may display or hide—is implicit in everything somebody says and does... This revelatory quality of speech and action comes to the fore where people are with others and

neither for nor against them—that is, in sheer human togetherness. (Arendt 1958, 179)

Laywomen gathering at the Hanoi Temple are constructing the groundwork for *thân mật* relationships through shared experiences of religious activities. They come to care for and become interested in specific members at the temple through talking about their own lives and emotions with each other. In their togetherness, the *thân mật* relationship seems to be the space to find out "who," in contradiction to "what." In this sense, the *thân mật* relationship could be regarded as the "space of appearance" for women in the Hanoi Temple.

Saito (2003, 219) argues that the public sphere can be distinguished from the intimate sphere analytically, but they do overlap with each other in real life. He redefines the notion of an intimate sphere by focusing on the human body and personhood. Moreover he suggests that an "alternative intimate sphere" creates the "space of appearance," which allows a way of life and the experience of a life that has not been previously deemed by society as "normal" and/or "fair."

Laywomen such as L and D talked about their own private affairs with "specific others." In so doing, they acquired a space of appearance where their own lives and experiences were accepted. Through the practice of *đạo mình*, laywomen in the Hanoi Temple constructed a specific relationship that allows them to share even the most private affairs with each other. It seems that the specific relationships among those women who have a common background and are situated on the periphery of patriarchal society can generate an alternative way of securing the social ease that had been lost by deviating from their traditional kinship relations.

The Hanoi Temple community provides an intimate sphere open to women alienated by patriarchy and the traditional notion of womanhood. For these women, this space produces an intersubjective relationship that rests "in between" the specific other and a new kind of living space in which to reconstruct the order of their daily lives, and through which we might be able to reach a holistic understanding of the social world of women in Vietnam.

References

Amit, Vered. 2002. "Reconceptualizing Community." In *Realizing Community: Concepts, Social Relationship and Sentiments*, edited by Vered Amit, 1–20. London: Routledge.

Anderson, Benedict. 1983. *Imagined Communities: Reflections on the Origin and Spread of Nationalism*. London: Verso.

Arendt, Hannah. 1958. *The Human Condition*. Chicago: University of Chicago Press.
Blagov, Sergei. 2002. *Caodaism: Vietnamese Traditionalism and Its Leap into Modernity*. New York: Nova.
Cohen, Paul. 1982. "Belonging: The Experience of Culture." In *Belonging: Identity and Social Organization in British Rural Culture*, edited by Paul Cohen, 1–20. Manchester: Manchester University Press.
Delanty, Gerard. 2003. *Community*. London: Routledge.
Drummond, Lisa, and Helle Rydström. 2004. *Gender Practices in Contemporary Vietnam*. Singapore: Singapore University Press.
Eisen, Arlene. 1984. *Women and Revolution in Vietnam*. London: Zed books.
Fall, Bernard B. 1955. "The Political-Religious Sects of Viet Nam." *Pacific Affairs* 28 (3): 235–53.
Gammeltoft, Tine. 1999. *Women's Bodies, Women's Worries: Health and Family Planning in a Vietnamese Rural Community*. Richmond, VA: Curzon Press.
——— 2002. "The Irony of Sexual Agency: Pre-Marital Sex in Urban Northern Viet Nam." In *Gender, Household, State: Đổi Mới in Viet Nam*, edited by Jayne Werner and Danièle Bélanger, 111–28. Ithaca, NY: Cornell University Southeast Asia Program.
Gobron, Gabriel [1949] 2010. *Histoire du Caodaisme: Bouddhisme Rénove*. Paris: Dervy.
Hickey, Gerald. C. 1964. *Village in Vietnam*. New Haven: Yale University Press.
Hirai, Kyonosuke. 2012. "Introduction." In *Community as Practice: Immigration, State and Movement*, edited by Hirai Kyonosuke, 1–37. Kyoto: Kyoto University Press. [平井京之介「イントロダクション」、平井京之介編『実践としてのコミュニティ』京都大学出版会、1–37頁].
Ho Tai, Hue-Tam. 1983. *Millenarianism and Peasant Politics in Vietnam*. Cambridge: Harvard University Press.
Lê Anh Dũng. 1993. *Lịch Sử Đạo Cao Đài Thánh Thất Hà Nội* [The History of the Caodai Hanoi Temple]. Thành phố Hồ Chí Minh. [Ho Chi Minh City].
Lê Quang Tấn 1956. *Đạo Cao Đài Phổ Truyền Ra Bắc Việt (Hà Nội), 1935–1945*. [Missionary of Caodaism in Northern Vietnam (Hanoi), 1935–1945]. Tây Ninh: Tòa Thánh Tây Ninh. [Tây Ninh: Tây Ninh Cathedral].
Nguyễn-Võ Thu-Hương. 2002. "Governing Sex: Medicine and Governmental Intervention in Prostitution." In *Gender, Household, State: Đổi Mới in Viet Nam*, edited by Jayne Werner and Danièle Bélanger, 129–52. Ithaca, NY: Cornell University Southeast Asia Program.
Oliver, Victor, L. 1973. *Caodaism: A Vietnamese Example of Sectarian Development*. Ph.D. dissertation, Syracuse University, Syracuse, NY.
——— 1976. *Caodai Spiritism: A Study of Religion in Vietnamese Society*. Leiden, Netherlands: Brill.

Rydström, Helle. 2003. *Embodying Morality: Growing Up in Rural Northern Vietnam*. Honolulu: University of Hawai'i Press.

Saito, Junichi. 2000. *The Publicness*. Tokyo: Iwanami Shyoten. [斉藤純一『公共性』岩波書店].

———. 2003. "Politics of Intimate Sphere and Security." In *The Politics of the Intimate Sphere*, edited by Saito Junichi, 211–36. Tokyo: Nakanishiya Syuppan. [斉藤純一「親密圏と安全性の政治」、斉藤純一編『親密圏のポリティクス』ナカニシヤ出版、211–236頁].

Smith, Bernard R. 1970. "An Introduction to Caodaism II: Beliefs and Organization." *Bulletin of the School of Oriental and African Studies* 33: 573–91.

Suenari, Michio. 1998. *Ancestor Ritual in Vietnam: Social Life in Trieu Khuc*. Tokyo: Hukyosya. [末成道男『ベトナムの祖先祭祀―潮曲の社会生活』風響社].

Tanabe, Sigeharu. 2002. "Introduction: Imagined and Imagining Communities." In *Imaging Communities in Thailand: Ethnographic Approaches*, edited by Sigeharu Tanabe, 1–19. Chiang Mai: Mekong Press.

———. 2008. *Community of Care: The Opening Up of the Self-Care Group in Northern Thailand*. Tokyo: Iwanami Shoten. [田邊繁治『ケアのコミュニティ―北タイのエイズ自助グループが切り開くもの』岩波書店].

Taylor, Keith. 2002. "Introduction: Gender and Việt Nam Studies." In *Gender, Household, State: Đổi Mới in Việt Nam*, edited by Jayne Werner and Danièle Bélanger, 7–12. Ithaca, NY: Cornell University Southeast Asia Program.

Wenger, Etienne. 1998. *Communities of Practice: Learning, Meaning and Identity*. Cambridge: Cambridge University Press.

Werner, Jayne. 1976. "The Cao Đai: The Politics of Vietnamese Syncretic Religious Movement." Ph.D. dissertation, Cornell University, Ithaca, NY.

———. 2002. "Gender, Household, and State: Renovation (Đổi Mới) as Social Process in Viet Nam." In *Gender, Household, State: Đổi Mới in Việt Nam*, edited by Jayne Werner and Danièle Bélanger, 29–47. Ithaca, NY: Cornell Southeast Asia Program Publications.

CHAPTER 7

Imperious Mandarins and Cunning Princesses: Mediumship, Gender, and Identity in Urban Vietnam*

Kirsten W. Endres

In Vietnam's postreform era, religious beliefs and practices that were once attacked as wasteful and superstitious have (again) become a conspicuous feature of contemporary urban and rural life (Malarney 2003; Taylor 2007). Four Palace mediumship, an intrinsic part of the so-called Mother Goddess Religion, Đạo Mẫu (see Ngô Đức Thịnh 1996, 2004; Fjelstad & Nguyen 2006; Endres 2011), is one case in point. Whereas in the heyday of socialist construction, most notably during the 1960s and 1970s, spirit mediums had to conduct their ritual possessions in secluded privacy for fear of being arrested by local authorities, they have gradually managed to reassert their place in the public realm since the launch of the reform policy in the late 1980s. Besides being performed in private temples established by individual master mediums, as well as in public temples recognized and managed by the state as "historical and cultural vestiges" (*di tích lịch sử văn hóa*), in the past ten years Four Palace possession rituals (called *hầu đồng*, "a medium's service" or *lên đồng*, "mounting the medium") have even been performed on open stages on festival occasions and enhanced with video, sound, and lighting effects (Endres 2011, 158, 182–3). In January 2012, the Vietnamese Women's Museum launched an exhibition entitled "Worshipping the Mother Goddess: Pure Heart—Beauty—Joy" aimed at raising public awareness of the religion's key values and cultural significance.[1] Representatives of various government and academic bodies even debated the prospects of the Mother Goddess Religion receiving official state recognition, as well as the nomination of *hầu đồng* possession rituals for inscription on the UNESCO world Intangible Cultural Heritage list (Phạm Gia Khánh 2012).

Spirit mediums of the Four Palaces perceive the world as divided into four distinct domains or palaces (*phủ*)—Heaven (Thiên Phủ), Earth (Địa Phủ), Water (Thủy Phủ), and Mountains and Forests (Nhạc Phủ)—that are "supervised" or governed by the Mother Goddesses. Associated with these palaces is a

---

* This contribution is a revised version of Chapter 5 of my book, *Performing the Divine: Mediums, Markets and Modernity in Urban Vietnam* (Endres 2011).
1 See http://www.baotangphunu.org.vn/en/gii-thiu/news-a-events-/184-13122012.html (accessed September 8, 2012).

hierarchically ranked pantheon of male and female deities with different characteristics and powers (Figure 7.1). During a possession ritual (called *lên đồng*, *hầu bóng*, or *hầu thánh*), a select number of these deities are invited to descend from their palaces to the world of humans and "mount" their mediums in a prescribed order while a group of *chầu văn* musicians chant their legends, composed in poetic verse (Norton 2009).

Just like in other possession religions, the initiation into Four Palace mediumship often relates to critical moments in human life. A "yin illness" (i.e., an illness perceived as caused by spiritual powers; see Nguyễn Thị Hiền 2008), a continuous streak of bad luck in business or personal affairs, or haunting dreams may all be an indication that the deities (or spirits) are calling a person into a life of service as a medium. It is important to note that a person qualifies as a ritual practitioner not because of his or her free will, but because that person has a "spirit root" (*căn*), meaning that he or she is fated for mediumship. This spirit root is often associated with one or several deities of the pantheon. A person can have the root of, for example, the Seventh Prince (*căn* Ông Hoàng Bảy) or the Third Princess (*căn* Cô Bơ). This root is believed to have been "implanted" during a previous life (*kiếp trước*) and usually implies the idea of a debt owed to the deities of the Four Palaces that needs to be repaid by serving the spirits in this life and becoming a medium. As a minimum requirement,

FIGURE 7.1 *Altar dedicated to the pantheon of the Four Palaces. Hanoi, 2011*
SOURCE: PHOTO BY KIRSTEN W. ENDRES.

a medium has to hold one *lên đồng* ritual per year, during which she or he becomes a "seat" (*ghế*) for the deities to sit upon (Nguyễn Thị Hiền 2007). The ritual performance is considered as efficacious when the medium reaches a state of "self-forgetfulness" that allows the deities to come into presence (Lambek 2010). In line with possession idioms in other parts of the world, Four Palace mediums commonly construe their state of divine embodiment as a displacement of their human agency by the agency of the possessing deity. Paradoxically, though, mediums generally feel empowered by these encounters, with their "ontological reality of a supernatural presence" (Endres & Lauser 2011a, 12). Besides being perceived as efficacious in curing illnesses and reducing mental distress, possession practices may also enable mediums to achieve material well-being and exert social power (Boddy 1994).

Initiation into Four Palace mediumship is commonly performed by a master medium, a *đồng thầy*.[2] Whereas knowledge and learning (*hiểu biết*), performative skills and moral virtue (*đức*) rank high on the list of vital qualities a master medium should possess, the reputation and authority of a *đồng thầy* also derives from dominant gender ideologies in Vietnamese society. Infused with patrilineal principles and Confucian ideals, these ideologies are "configured by virtue of a strict oppositional and heterosexual structure in which a male is seen as masculine in terms of being essentially superior, active, aggressive and powerful and a female as feminine, in terms of being essentially inferior, passive, submissive and receptive" (Rydström 2006, 335). This binary conception of gender is further underlined by the Daoist principles of yin and yang (*âm* and *dương* in Vietnamese), with yin representing the "female" principle associated with passivity, darkness, and cold, and yang representing the "male" principle associated with activity, light, and heat. The cosmic duality of yin and yang also entails the idea of two complementary realms: the yin realm of spiritual agents (*thế giới âm*) and the yang world of the living (*thế giới dương*).

As I shall show in this chapter, Four Palace mediums transgress this binary conception of gender in a number of ways: by deviating from socially proscribed norms of masculinity and femininity, by ritually embodying deities of the opposite gender, and, more generally, by acting as mediators between the yin world of divine beings and the yang world of humans. Based on anthropological

---

2   Any medium with at least ten years of ritual experience, sufficient knowledge, and a private temple may proclaim him- or herself as a master. In contrast, a "normal practitioner" who has undergone the initiation ritual is referred to as a "child of the spirits" (*con nhà thánh*) and a "follower" or "disciple" (*con nhang đệ tử*) of a master. Because a *lên đồng* is essentially self-therapeutic in purpose, "regular" mediums have to bear all costs associated with their ritual activities by themselves.

fieldwork among urban spirit mediums in Hanoi, I will explore the gendered and gendering dimensions of Four Palace mediumship from two different but interrelated angles: the general bias toward belief in male superiority, and the construction of alternative gender identities among Four Palace mediums.[3] Their views draw on a diverse range of "traditional" and "modern" concepts and suggest that mediumship has evolved as a creative space in contemporary Vietnamese society within which both male and female spirit mediums may, privately as well as publicly, enact identities that move beyond the restricting frames of hegemonic social norms and gender binaries.

"Gender Trouble" in the World of Mediums

If we look at the ratio of male to female mediums in contemporary Hanoi, two trends become evident. First, women clearly constitute the majority of Four Palace adherents. Second, master mediums with large followings and thriving temples seem to be predominantly male. In contrast, sources dating back to the French colonial period hardly mention male mediums in Four Palace mediumship (Giran 1912; Durand 1959). Instead, they suggest a gendered separation between the female domain of the Four Palaces (or the Chư Vị Cult, as it was then referred to), and the male sphere of the Saint Trần Cult. Nguyễn Văn Khoan, a Vietnamese scholar associated with the École Française d'Extrême Orient, distinguishes between the following three "popular cults":

> Three main popular cults share the favor of the masses: the Chư Vị Cult, the cult of Trần Hưng Đạo's generals, and the cult of the infernal spirits and patrons of sorcerers. The priests of the Chư Vị Cult are the *bà đồng* [female mediums], the ones of Trần Hưng Đạo's generals are the *ông đồng* [male mediums] or *thày pháp* [masters of magic formulae], and those who worship the spirits of hell are the *thày bùa* [masters of amulets] or *thày phủ-thủy* [masters of amulets and waters].
> NGUYỄN VĂN KHOAN 1930, 109, my translation

The male mediums of Trần Hưng Đạo (called *ông đồng* or *thanh đồng*) were apparently held in higher esteem than the female mediums (called *bà đồng* or

---

3   In-depth research was carried out from January to December 2006 as part of a research project funded by the German Research Foundation (DFG).

đồng cốt) of the Four Palaces (Do 2003, 97–105; Pham 2009; Phan Kế Bính [1915] 1995, 239–240). Whereas the male cult was associated with the superior morality of Saint Trần, whose mediums were considered capable of exorcising demons and evil spirits from possessed (and predominantly female) individuals, the female Chư Vị Cult was associated not only with marginalized women (such as widows and childless divorcees) but also with a morally inferior spirit world. As Paul Giran (1912, 293, my translation) remarks: "Among the Chư Vị [assembly of spirits], there are many subaltern spirits, male or female, that are tolerated by the Holy Mothers even though they cause a lot of trouble for people." Many of the possessed, Giran continues, turn to Saint Trần in order to get rid of these malevolent entities. Contrary to what these early accounts suggest, it may be safely assumed that the two spirit possession cults have always overlapped with each other to some extent. Since the resurgence of spirit mediumship in the Đổi Mới era, however, these formerly distinct ritual realms have opened up and intermingled in complex ways.

While on the one hand, female mediums nowadays actively participate in the ritual embodiment of Saint Trần (Pham 2009, see Figure 7.2), male mediums now seem to dominate the ranks of masters in Four Palace mediumship. This development may also have informed the pronounced emphasis on the importance of knowledge and learning, because biases rooted in persisting Confucian gender norms perceive male intellectual abilities as superior to those of women and link knowledge and leadership roles with masculinity (Luong 1992, 70; Soucy 1999, 228). However, when I raised the issue of male superiority in Four Palace mediumship for discussion, I received an interesting range of replies that reflect and challenge persistent gender ideologies in society.

First of all, there is a strong bias against women's bodily functions and the social roles associated with them. During menstruation, women are generally considered unclean and thus are prohibited from entering sacred places and participating in ritual activities. A female master who has not yet gone through menopause would therefore be severely constrained in her work. Moreover, if a woman fulfills the social expectations of getting married and having children, her family is seen as her first and foremost obligation. One of my informants, whom I shall call Master Cảnh, argues that these constraints are the main reason why there are more male than female masters. He explains, "A medium's job is very hard, and female mediums cannot act in the same ways as men." As an example, he cites that, before a palace-opening ritual, a master has to abstain from sexual intercourse for at least one week in order to be "pure."[4] A master who initiates many followers thus has to live a largely celibate life.

---

4 "Regular" mediums also have to follow this rule, but usually only for one day.

FIGURE 7.2 *Ritual embodiment of Saint Trần by a female medium. Hanoi, 2006*
SOURCE: PHOTO BY KIRSTEN W. ENDRES.

Cảnh maintains that whereas men have no problem being "chaste" (*sic*), women in their fertile age cannot withdraw from their "conjugal duty" unless they decide to abandon their husbands. He even mentions the case of a female master who had given birth to her youngest child at the age of fifty, which had apparently caused a major uproar in the *lên đồng* scene. "The news that the old hag N. had given birth flashed through the whole of Hanoi with lightning speed!" Cảnh laughed and scornfully added, "Who would trust a female master if she is [still sexually active] like that!"

The "impurity" issuing from a woman's body is a general concern among female worshippers, and it entails that most women have already passed menopause when they decide to operate as masters. One of my female interlocutors, Master Nga, related how the deities helped her to overcome the issue:

> The deities had made me go [on a pilgrimage] to the temple of the Fifth Lady. At that time I was just over forty. On the way I started [to menstruate], I went to the river and took a bath, and then I pleaded to the deities for help. I said, "Praise to you, my [heavenly] parents have conscripted me into their service, and now this just happened to me naturally. It was not

my own will, it just happened and now I feel so miserable. I shall go back home!" From that day on [my menstruation] stopped. Everyone said I was clean early. Many women still [menstruate] until they are over fifty. I'm telling you, the people distinguish between men and women, but the deities provide for all, no matter if man or woman.

In contrast to Master Cảnh's assumptions, the self-confident octogenarian master asserts that women are, in fact, morally more virtuous than men. Men, she argues, are more lecherous. They booze, enjoy talking dirty, and still lust after women when they are well over fifty years old. Yet she admits that women, too, tend to have extramarital affairs: "Many male mediums have affairs with their followers. Their families crumble and this is not good; but women also do that." However, this inclination toward licentiousness, the upright master argues, is limited to "female mediums whose root of mediumship is light."[5] Here, a light root (căn) of mediumship refers to women who have the root of a lesser deity in the Four Palace pantheon. In contrast, a heavy root is related to the morally superior deities, such as the Great Mandarins or even Saint Trần. "If a woman has a root of Saint Trần," Master Nga reasons, "she would not dare to do anything dishonest or immoral, or else she'd be punished immediately."

The *căn* of a Four Palace medium is often of the opposite gender—i.e., many male mediums have the root of a female deity and many female mediums that of a male deity. Female master mediums who have the *căn* of a Great Mandarin sometimes argue that their *căn* is higher (*cao hơn*) than a male master's *căn*. While the root of an imposing male deity certainly lends authority, it does not necessarily grant the *bà đồng* a higher status or more prestige than that of a male master. Female mediums are often considered hot-tempered (*nóng tính*) or hard to please (*khó tính*). Although these traits do not conform to female ideals, they are not seen as particularly male characteristics either. Master Thiền, for example, is a rather loud and boisterous woman who enjoys leading people and organizing ritual events. But she also has a flaring temper that often offends other people's sensibilities. According to her associate, a spirit priest (*thầy cúng*) named Hiền, male masters generally do not display this kind of hot temper. He elaborates, "Men do not fly into a temper like that. Mrs. Thiền's disposition is very intimidating; she is often angry for trifles and resents petty mistakes." Compared to female masters, Hiền argues, "Male masters are more big-hearted (*quảng đại hơn*); they say, 'let's not talk about this anymore', whereas women have to reprimand, to scold and speak out because this is how

---

5   Master Nga's attitude is concordant with the view of colonial-era sources (i.e., Lộng Chương [1942] 1990; Nhất Lang 1952) that depict Four Palace mediums as women of loose morals.

they think." Master Thuận, himself a professed homosexual with the *căn* of a Princess Deity, sees it differently. He says, "Female mediums are more bighearted than men, and it has to be said that if you want to follow the right path in religion (*đi theo chính đạo*), women are more trustworthy than men." While he thinks that female masters have greater powers (*uy lực*) than males, he says male masters are more illustrious (*oanh liệt*) and imposing (*hoành tráng*). As both male and female interlocutors have confirmed to me, this assessment applies first and foremost to their performative skills in *lên đồng* ritual and explains why male masters usually gain more fame in the world of mediums. Furthermore, Thuận says, "Men are more successful as masters because they are more flexible and tricky (*éo le*)." The latter traits are consistent with his characterization of the Four Palace deities, whom he describes as cunning and artful, even to the point of being ruthless. According to this logic, the greater appeal and success of male masters is not based so much on any ideal hegemonic male characteristics as on the morally dubious features of female deities who prefer to plunge their roots into male human beings. In contrast, a female master's prestige would sprout from the root of the morally superior male spirits within the Four Palace (or the Saint Trần) system. These transgender aspects have gained greater prominence in Four Palace mediumship in recent years and therefore deserve particular attention.

Princesses, Queens and Imperial Concubines

Forms of "ritual transvestism" have been known in Southeast Asia (and beyond) since ancient times. Ritual transvestites, or "transgendered ritual specialists," a term I borrow from Peletz (2006), were "individuals who in the course of priestly or shamanic functions 'switched' genders or took on 'gender-ambiguous' roles as they interceded with spiritual beings on behalf of human subjects" (Blackwood 2005, 849). Following Blackwood and Peletz, I use the term "transgender" to denote a rather broad range of gender-transgressive practices and identifications that pass beyond culturally defined gender categories of "man" and "woman." Such a wide understanding would, for example, incorporate the ambiguously gendered hermaphrodite as well as the cross-dressing drag queen or the masculine "butch" lesbian.[6] In a ritual context, transgender practices may be temporary (i.e., in the case of a ritual practitioner who transgresses the

---

6 Contrary to what prevailing connotations of the term may suggest, however, transgendering does not in any case entail same-sex relations (Peletz 2006, 311).

established gender boundaries only during ritual performance) or part of a permanent transgender identity of the ritual practitioner. Throughout Southeast Asia, transgendered ritual specialists were most often "male-bodied individuals who dressed in female attire while performing certain rituals associated with royal regalia, births, weddings, and key phases of agricultural cycles" (Peletz 2006, 312). Among the best known examples are the *bissu* among the Bugis of South Sulawesi (Andaya 2000), the *basir* (male) and *balian* (female) of the Ngaju Dayak of Kalimantan (Blackwood 2005), and the Burmese *nat kadaw* (Brac de la Perrière 1989).

In contrast to these rather well-documented cases, very little is known about transgendered ritual specialists in early modern and colonial Vietnam.[7] To my knowledge, there is no historical record of their existence, with one faint exception. A French colonial source discusses the frequency of hermaphrodites among the Vietnamese in Cochinchina. It mentions a certain "class of individuals, the *muabum*, whose trade is to perform dances and diverse other entertainments and who pass themselves off without exception as hermaphrodites" (Gaultier de Claubry 1882; quoted in Proschan 2002a, 445).[8] The term *muabum* is most probably a malapropism for the *múa bóng*, a Southern Vietnamese ritual dance (that also involves acrobatic feats) performed by male transvestite performers (see Taylor 2004, 174). Until now, however, this Southern Vietnamese form of ritual transgenderism has not received adequate attention in the research literature. Another indication of the religious role of transgendered individuals in Southern Vietnam is found in Heiman and Le's (1975, 3) 1970s reference to "hermaphroditic witches." Set off in quotes throughout the article, they are described as male cross-dressers who "are trained in their career as healers from childhood" and "believe that they are inhabited by female spirits and that they are spiritually female." Outside the ritual context,

---

7 In the French colonial imagination, however, Vietnam (or rather "Indochina") stood out "as a site of homosexuality, and more particularly as characterized by physical androgyny" (Yee 2001, 270; see also Proschan 2002a; 2002b). In turn-of-the-nineteenth-century literary texts, the "androgynous young male" was a figure of beauty as well as a symbol of moral and sexual depravity. Women, on the other hand, were often portrayed as lacking grace and femininity (see Proschan 2002a). These colonial constructions of Vietnamese genders not only displaced anxieties about gender identity "from the imperial centre to the geographical periphery of empire and from the centre of (French) identity to the Other" (Yee 2001, 279), but also constituted an important part of the rationale for justifying French colonial rule in Indochina.

8 The Vietnamese term for hermaphrodite is *ái nam ái nữ* which literally means "love man love woman." The term is also used to indicate androgyny and bisexuality; see http://vietqueer.net/glossary.

many of these "witches" apparently lived "normal lives" and did not dress in female clothing.

In the early twentieth century, modern Vietnamese intellectuals scorned Four Palace mediumship. In his 1942 novel *Hầu Thánh*, the writer Lộng Chương provides a wealth of fascinating details about the world of mediums that are absent from scholarly works (e.g., Durand 1959). Although transgressive gender practices did not escape the author's attention, the issue did not factor significantly in his writing. Of particular interest are several references to female same-sex pairings between Four Palace mediums of complementary spirit roots, e.g., the root of a Great Mandarin and that of a Princess Deity. This practice was called *kết căn* (tying the roots) and, according to Lộng Chương, indicated that "two ladies have bonded as husband and wife." One of the characters in his novel is Bà Đào, the widow of a school teacher, who "seeks the affectionate caress of a strange love with another woman," a capricious temple owner named Châu. Interestingly, Bà Đào's same-sex attraction is not condemned as an aberrant deviation from traditional gender norms. Rather, it is explained from a social-psychological perspective. Social restrictions against the remarriage of widowed females would "not leave any other choice for a young widow to satisfy the strong desires of her heart" (Lộng Chương [1942] 1990, 53).

In contrast to this rather sympathetic attitude, male-bodied mediums who display effeminate mannerisms (*ông à ông ẹo*) only receive a marginal but scornful note: "[Like the female mediums], these effeminate men also dance and whirl around, they also tie their roots as 'wives' and 'husbands', they are also jealous in love, and sometimes even dress as women" (Lộng Chương [1942] 1990, 135, my translation). In his reportage "Mediumship (Đồng Bóng)," published in the satirical journal *Phong Hóa* (*Customs and Mores*), Trọng Lang explores the issue in greater detail:

> Besides the *bà đồng* there are the *cô đồng*, most of whom are men. They say they are *cô đồng* because their destined aptitude matches the Princesses, like that of husband and wife. In order to express their dedication to the Princesses, they do not get married and stay sexually chaste. Maybe this is a precondition for the Princesses to possess their bodies and help them earn money by telling fortunes or soul-calling.
>
> TRỌNG LANG 1935, VOL. 166, my translation

Trọng Lang then offers an intriguing explanation why the *đồng cô* are generally unable to take a wife (*lấy vợ*). It is, he argues, because they suffer from the "failing-in-love" disease (*họ có bệnh "thất tình"*), and this would make them become *ái nam*. In the strict sense, the Vietnamese term *ái nam ái nữ* designates a hermaphrodite, but in general usage it also refers to male homosexuality. Trọng Lang's remark could thus be an attempt to, first, link male effeminacy in spirit mediumship to homosexuality and, second, explain this "deviancy" in terms of a reaction to an unfulfilled (heterosexual) love life.

In earlier scholarly works, transgenderism was most often treated as an outlet for homosexuality. Moreover, transgendered ritual spaces were seen as providing a culturally accepted niche for homosexual males, an assumption that Blackwood (2005) refers to as the "homosexual niche theory." At first glance, the striking presence of gender-transgressive males in contemporary Four Palace mediumship seems to corroborate this argument. As Prochan has noted, "The role of the transvestite medium seems to offer an occupational niche to men whose sexuality does not conform to heteronormative expectations" (Prochan 2002, 463n40). However, as I will elaborate below, this view is much too narrow. Recent studies have called attention to the connection between gender-transgressive ritual practices and sacred cosmologies in Southeast Asian cultures (Errington 1990; Johnson 1997; Andaya 2000; Blackwood 2005). The theme of an original cosmic oneness manifest in dual-gendered or ambiguously gendered deities can be found across island Southeast Asia. In this perspective, transgendered ritual specialists appeared as "a metaphor for cosmic unity and incorporation" (Johnson 1997, 26) and were thus often seen as potent mediators between the world of divinities and the world of humankind. In contrast to these well-documented cases, Vietnamese cosmology does not provide a consistent, singular explanation for gender-transgressive behavior. Rather, it seems that gender-transgressive Four Palace mediums draw on a variety of spiritual conceptions in order to construct their identities.

Lộc and Kỳ, for example, conceptualize themselves as heavenly fairies (*tiên*) sent down to earth in a male human body: "According to the intent of the creator (*tạo hóa*) we ought to be females; in the West you wouldn't put it in these terms but here we say we are creatures of heaven." As immortal beings, fairies may be sent down to earth as a punishment for any misdeed committed in the heavenly palace. The most famous example is Princess Liễu Hạnh, who was expelled from heaven for breaking a jade cup and transformed into a powerful deity after serving a lifetime of hardship on earth.[9] According to Lộc and Kỳ's

---

9 Dror (2002, 67) mentions that Princess Liễu Hạnh sometimes disguised herself as an old woman and sometimes as a beautiful young lady. According to popular imagination, however, Liễu Hạnh, during her second life on earth, appeared in many places both as a woman (when she encountered men) and as a man (when she encountered women) in order to "tease" them. While this kind of gender crossing is not mentioned in the *Vân Cát Thần Nữ*

conceptualization, many of these fairies come down to earth "in the guise of males, but their characteristics and preferences are those of females." The reason for this disguise is linked to their task in life, which is "self-cultivation" (*tu*) by leading a (chaste) religious life.[10] If the fairy-in-disguise manages to practice self-cultivation "until the end of this incarnation," then she or he would be able to "escape the eternal cycle of birth" and "leave this world of dust to return to the other side" (*về bên kia*). But why, we may ask, does a fairy need the guise of a male body in order to practice self-cultivation? Lộc and Kỳ explain:

> If the fairies came [down to earth] in the guise of a woman, they could not practice self-cultivation; this is why the council of Buddhas and Saints decreed that they have to be born with a male body. The world is full of temptations in many respects; this is why the fairies need the guise of men in order to practice self-cultivation.

The notion that a fairy in the body of a (young and graceful) woman would not be able to live a chaste religious life is largely consistent with Master Cảnh's claim that a woman of childbearing age could not abstain from having sexual relations (for reasons of a woman's uncontrollable desire or because it is regarded as her conjugal duty). Yet Lộc and Kỳ admit that their male disguise does not always prevent the fairies from succumbing to mundane temptations: "Of course it is very difficult—the fairies are put to a test (*thử thách*), but it is their own responsibility [to pass it], and this is why not all of them can practice self-cultivation. Is there a difference, then, between a *đồng cô* (a gender-transgressive male medium with a female spirit root) and a gay[11] man?" I ask.

Truyện, Đoàn Thị Điểm's story relates that Liễu Hạnh crossed the gender boundary in her official deification by the Lê dynasty, when she was conferred the title Chế Thắng Hòa Diệu Đại Vương (Great King who grants victory and peace). Thus, the last part of the *Vân Cát Thần Nữ Truyện* refers to her not as a female deity, but as a male king (see Dror 2002, 72).

10   According to Thien Do (2003, 133), "The meaning of the word *tu* (Chinese: *hsiu*—to correct, repair, reform, improve) has long entwined the Confucian trajectory of *tu thân* (self-correction, perfectibility), or *tu tâm* (cultivate the heart-mind), with the Daoist *tu luyện* (training—as in various meditative arts including alchemy and magic) and with the Buddhist *tu niệm* (perfecting thought and imagination)."

11   There are various terms that indicate homosexuality, and "gay" has been adopted most recently into Vietnamese lingo. The colloquial word *pê đê* has apparently been adopted from the French *pédéraste*, whereas *ái nam ái nữ* confers the meaning of "half man half woman," or, more literally, "love man love woman," which is also the title of a documentary by Nguyen Trinh Thi (2006). Blanc (2005, 665) mentions the expression *lại cái,*

"The two are absolutely different from each other," Kỳ asserts. "According to the Vietnamese understanding, homosexuality—both male and female—is regarded as a kind of illness. In contrast, being a *đồng cô* is a completely spiritual matter (*việc tiên thánh*). After all, it is not our free will, but the deities have chosen us and bothered us in order to let us know we have a predestined affinity for the Buddhas and Saints."

In Vietnamese public opinion, male same-sex sexual behavior has for a long time been perceived as either a sexual deviancy incompatible with traditional morality and customs, a disease (*bệnh*) in need of treatment or, still worse, a sign of mental disorder (Colby, Cao, & Doussantousse 2004; Pastoetter 2004; Blanc 2005). Another common attitude perceives homosexuality as an "import" of debauched Western lifestyles and fashions. In this regard, Vietnam's most famous sexologist, Trần Bồng Sơn (1941–2004) distinguished between "genuine" (*thật*) homosexual men and "fake" (*giả*) ones, the latter being "lured by fashion or experimentation into trying homosexuality" (Colby, Cao, & Doussantousse 2004, 48). Although recently the media seem to have taken a more balanced view (e.g., Nguyễn Thành Như 2005), these highly prejudiced perceptions of male homosexuality are still reiterated today (see, for example, Nguyễn Thuận Thành 2005; *VnExpress* 2006). Many of these stereotypes are even perpetuated in the "identity discourse" of male gender-transgressive Four Palace mediums.

This becomes apparent in the motley concepts presented by the protagonists of Nguyễn Trinh Thi's recent documentary *Love Man Love Woman* (hereafter: LMLW) that portrays one of the most prominent Four Palace master mediums in contemporary Hanoi. Master Đ. makes no secret of his homosexual inclination, which he thinks of as a half-blessing, half-curse. From a spiritual perspective, he argues that the performative skills of *đồng cô* are always superior to that of "genuine women" because, he says, "it seems like the gods and spirits look for male mediums to descend into because men are perceived to be cleaner than women in every aspect. So the gods perhaps prefer men" (LMLW). From a more dispassionate perspective, however, Master Đ. perceives his female spirit root as a punishment from heaven. "This is against nature's law. And it's also against the morality by society. I know that—how could I not know that? But this is my fate—what can I do about it? There's nothing I can do about it" (LMLW). The way he perceives his own effeminate demeanor and

---

translated as "penetrated by the female spirit" and most probably used in the South rather than in the North of Vietnam. For official usage, the term *đồng tính luyến ái* has been adopted. According to Pastoetter (2004), the term is a literal translation of the Chinese word for "homosexuality" that came into use in the 1930s.

preference for same-sex relations clearly reflects the wider social ambivalence about homosexuality. In one scene of the documentary, Master Đ. reminisces that he had demonstrated an affinity for female pursuits like knitting and embroidering from his early childhood. Yet, in another scene, he perceives homosexuality as a "contagious disease" that he contracted as a teenage boy when he was seduced by his mathematics tutor:

> I have a feeling that this disease is contagious. When I was fifteen or sixteen there was a guy who worked close by and came here often. He asked me to come visit him and that he would tutor me with math. He did tutor me, decently, for a few days. Then, from the fourth or fifth day he started with his hanky-panky. At the beginning I was scared... Then suddenly I found it fun. And I felt I liked it. Then I started to like the guy. That's it. From then on it was getting worse... Then later some of my friends—first they didn't know. They were [genuine] men. And I was fond of them. Then suddenly, they got infected as well. You see! Then one led to a series of others.
> LMLW

In answer to the filmmaker's cheeky question of whether Master Đ. had ever tried to get "cured," he passionately exclaims: "I don't want to get cured! I don't want to get cured to be a total man. Because I still find love, I still find fun with people of the same sex. What on earth do I have to get cured for?" Despite the ambivalence in his opinions, Master Đ. does not clearly distinguish between Vietnamese "traditional" conceptions of male gender-transgressive behavior and contemporary "secular" constructions of male homosexualities. However, another male gender-transgressive master interviewed in the documentary sees things differently. He argues that "in the old days" there had been only a few *đồng cô*, but recently their numbers had grown significantly because of exposures to Western ideas and culture:

> First we had the *đồng cô*. Then we got exposed to the West. There are gay people in the West. Now it's spreading into Vietnam... Being gay is for a [different] class of people—for those men who like being playboys. Spirit mediums like us are different. They should be differentiated.
> LMLW

Besides the conceptualization of gender-transgressive males as *đồng cô*, Vietnamese culture also offers another explanation for effeminate behavior in male-bodied individuals. Human beings are believed to possess two different kinds of human souls: three "spiritual souls" called *hồn*, and seven (for men) or nine (for women) "material souls" called *vía* or *phách* (Nguyen Van Huyen [1945] 1995, 237). According to this concept, an effeminate male may be perceived as having eight *vía*—one more than a normative man and one less than a normative woman.[12] Even more compelling than the notion of a female spirit root, the idea of eight *vía* emphasizes a transgender identity outside the binary system of male and female. This third gender is seen as particularly efficacious in mediating between humankind and the spirit world.

For Master Cảnh, there is no difference between a female spirit root and homosexuality: "Here they say the female spirit root is too heavy. We don't refer to it as homosexuality, but in actual fact it is homosexuality, isn't it? Someone who [sexually] desires men and boys is homosexual, what else?" In his opinion, male effeminacy and homosexuality is the result of a disrupted equilibrium between the complementary "male" and "female" forces of yin and yang that needs to be balanced out in order to achieve harmony. Four Palace mediumship,

FIGURE 7.3
The đồng cô *are perceived as particularly talented ritual performers. Lạng Sơn, 2006*
SOURCE: PHOTO BY KIRSTEN W. ENDRES.

12 In popular usage, this concept generally relates to gender-transgressive men. In contrast, women with "male characteristics" are not said to have eight *vía*.

Master Cảnh argues, can be an effective way to restore this equilibrium—or, in his words, to "clear the psyche" (*giải tỏa tâm lý*): Four Palace mediumship "can clear the psyche. It means that after entering into mediumship [male effeminacy] lessens. That is, it raises their masculinity. In the West you have ways to change your gender. But in Vietnam we sneak into the temples to clear the psyche".

Whereas many male mediums would in fact be classified as homosexuals, others strictly deny that their demeanor indicates any (sexual) interest in other men. Cường, for example, feels offended because his slightly effeminate behavior is perceived as a homosexual trait in mainstream Vietnamese society:

> [As a child], one learns how to speak and then later I develop my way of speaking, so how can this be changed later? The language, voice, manner and bearing are also related to fate, to my spirit root. They cannot be changed..., we are how we are from early childhood, we are born like that. But alas! Many people say, "This guy behaves effeminate, womanish, and even transgendered (*ái nam ái nữ*)."... If people talk like that it kind of hurts my self-esteem. Sometimes I think if I could behave as dignified as a normal person others wouldn't say all these spiteful words, but [being like I am] is my fate and I have to accept it.

By tracing his *đồng cô* characteristics to the spirit root of the Little Princess, Cường now enjoys recognition within a group-network of fellow mediums that comprehends his personality in different terms than the vast majority. Like many other gender-transgressive male spirit mediums, he has fulfilled social expectations by getting married and fathering children. According to Confucian teachings, the failure to produce offspring is considered the greatest sin against filial piety (see also Nguyen Van Huyen [1945] 1995, 29). Not conforming to expected heterosexual norms by openly assuming a gay identity or, as Lộc and Kỳ have suggested, practicing self-cultivation and living a celibate life is not an option many pursue. Rather, as one of my interlocutors put it, they choose to have "one leg in each world" (*kiêm chi đôi nước*) and only act out their transgender identities in the safe space of Four Palace mediumship.

As mentioned above, the *đồng cô* are often perceived as exceptionally talented and dexterous in ritual performance (Figure 7.3). For Master Thuận, artistic skillfulness is an innate or essential characteristic of transgendered people that he (in stark contrast to Master Cảnh!) links to a greater balance of the male and female element: "All over the world, transvestites and homosexuals are more skillful than normal people, because...the unity of yin and yang always brings forth people of talent beyond the normal." But while, on the one hand, *đồng cô* are seen to make the Four Palace religion (Đạo Tứ Phủ) prosper, some of them are concerned that certain *đồng cô* may also bring in negative things that may smear the religion's image:

> Despite their skillfulness, most *đồng cô* don't take the right path in the religion. Eighty-five percent of them follow the wrong path (*đi theo tà đạo*), i.e., they are stubborn, deceitful, untruthful, dishonest and chaotic. It is perhaps difficult to make them improve their conduct, but it is these people who have made the spirit religion (*thánh đạo*) prosper. Without the *đồng cô* the religion cannot develop.
> INTERVIEW WITH MASTER THUÂN, MAY 10, 2006

For the octogenarian Master Nga, the *đồng cô* are, at best, a bunch of nonsensical liars and pleasure seekers, and at worst a gang of drug dealers. Based on what she has learned from the media, Master Nga rails against their alleged immoral and sinful conduct, although she herself has initiated many *đồng cô* into ritual practice.

One of her followers is assistant Lâm, who was twenty-four at the time of this research and apparently no longer as obedient to his old master as he used to be when he was initiated at the tender age of fourteen:

> When he was seventeen or eighteen years old, he often drove me crazy, and then I gave him a good scream and he didn't dare to do it again. But now that he is grown up I said to him, "I'm not following you [in person] but I'm following [the likes of] you on television, they call you 'queens' (*bà hoàng hậu*) and 'imperial concubines' (*bà cung phi*), right? Just watch out what kind of gangs you're hanging out with. Whether or not someone respects you, trusts you, feels compassion for you, or hates you—it all depends on your own conduct, so whatever you do, you better not commit a sin!"
> INTERVIEW, FEBRUARY 20, 2006

As I have shown in this section, gender-transgressive males are creatively drawing from and (re)combining a diverse range of "traditional" and "modern" concepts in order to forge their transgender, bisexual, or homosexual identities within and across various social and ritual spaces. However, Master Nga's condescending attitude toward the contemporary *đồng cô* also shows that "'modern' ways of being homosexual threaten not only the custodians of 'traditional' morality, they also threaten the position of 'traditional' forms of homosexuality, those which are centred around gender nonconformity and transvestism"

(Altman 2001, 88). Whereas, on the one hand, the "queering" of Four Palace mediumship can be attributed to a greater tolerance of gender-transgressive behavior in Vietnamese society at large, there also seems to be a need to conceive of nonnormative gender (and sexuality) in a way that marks it as inherent to Vietnamese culture rather than as a Western-influenced (debauched) fashion.

Constructing Unique (Female) Identities

In contrast to the *đồng cô*, gender-transgressive women are much less evident in the world of mediums.[13] However, women too carve out alternative identities in the *lên đồng* world that not only reach beyond the normative boundaries of gender appropriate behavior, but also exceed the breadth of Four Palace mediumship in what we might call its conventional form. Master Thiền, for example, is an ambitious woman who seeks to establish a reputation for efficacy and integrity. This includes offering her followers a diverse range of ritual services outside the established responsibilities of a Four Palace master: for example, the ritual cutting of a karmic bond that may undermine a woman's marriage prospects in this life (*lễ cắt tiền duyên*), rites for settling karmic debts (*lễ trả nợ tào quan*), as well as various rites relating to the souls of the ancestors (*lễ gia tiên*). These rituals require the expertise of other ritual specialists such as diviners, spirit priests and soul-callers (*người gọi hồn*), i.e., people who act as vessels for the souls of the dead.

The souls of the dead are, in fact, a serious concern in Vietnamese society. If not properly cared for, they may become hungry, potentially malevolent ghosts who can cause all kinds of misfortune to the living. This is particularly true if death has occurred under violent circumstances, as this will cause the soul to remain eternally trapped in the traumatic memory of mortal agony, a condition Kwon (2006, 120–36) describes as "grievous death" (*chết oan*). This entails the precarious possibility for these souls to be unable to make the transition into the Otherworld. Instead, they may "angrily roam the earth looking for any food and care they can find" (Malarney 2002, 180). The vast number of

---

13 Only one of my female interlocutors, a spirit medium in her early fifties named Yến, told me that she had behaved "like a boy" as a child. She had her hair trimmed short and wore trousers. When Yến grew up, she let her hair grow and behaved in a feminine way. However, when I tried to press the topic a bit and asked her whether she had felt as if she had been born in the wrong body, like some *đồng cô* would claim, she explained that only her character is "like a man's" and that otherwise she was not "deviant" (*lệch lạc*).

Vietnamese war dead who lost their lives during the so-called American War, estimated at one million, suggests that innumerable "ghosts of war" still haunt the country in both a figurative and a literal sense (Hirschman, Preston, & Vu 1995; see also Kwon 2006; 2008; Gustaffson 2009). While the official state commemoration of war dead glorifies the deceased soldiers' contribution to the national cause of reunification and independence, it does not resolve the most pressing concern for the bereaved: the fate of the war martyrs' souls (Malarney 2001). This is where Master Thiền's most ambitious spiritual project comes in. As the events have been described in detail elsewhere (Endres 2008; Endres & Lauser 2011b), I shall limit myself here to a brief summary of the most essential points.

In November 2006, Master Thiền mobilized her network of supporters and followers to raise funds for the organization of a major ritual to be held at Đồng Lộc Junction in the central province of Hà Tĩnh (Figure 7.4). During the American War, this intersection was a strategically and logistically important part of the legendary (so-called) Hồ Chí Minh Trail because virtually every supply truck heading south had to pass through it. In an effort to destroy the logistical network, American aircraft heavily bombarded the area. Among the victims of the carpet bombings was a squad of ten young volunteer girls who had been leveling bomb craters to keep the junction open to traffic. The girls were buried near the place where they had met their premature death. In the early 1990s, the area was declared a historical site (*khu di tích*) and various memorials in honor of the war dead were constructed. The graves holding the remains of the ten girls were upgraded and currently constitute the most important site of commemoration at Đồng Lộc Junction. Because they were ten in number when they sacrificed their lives at one single stroke (the number ten implies completeness) and their bodies were found intact and undamaged by the bombing, the ten girls are believed to possess divine powers that may be summoned for the benefit of the living. The Mông Sơn Ritual organized by Master Thiền (and performed by Thầy Hiền and his apprentices) had a twofold purpose. It pertained to the general aim of bringing peace and salvation (in terms of escaping the cycle of rebirth and attaining nirvana) to the wandering souls of Đồng Lộc Junction, and it served the specific purpose of smoothing the process of the ten girls turning into benevolent deities (*biến thành những vị thiên thần*). With untiring fervor, Master Thiền collected donations worth 18 million Vietnam đồng, of which 14 million were used to buy votive paper offerings (e.g., paper shirts with matching ties, paper military uniforms, hats, and shoes). The ritual was held at the memorial site and subsequently followed by a series of soul-calling rites that enabled Master Thiền's followers to establish direct contact with the girls and ask for their assistance and advice. But the ten girls also pursued their own agenda and asked for more rituals to be held at various war cemeteries along the Hồ Chí Minh Trail. Master Thiền complied with the demands of the girls' souls and committed herself to raising funds for another ritual dedicated to the liberation of the national war martyrs' souls. In December 2007, on the sixty-third anniversary of the Vietnamese People's Army, she organized an even bigger Mông Sơn Ritual at Trường Sơn National Cemetery, which contains more than ten thousand graves of fallen soldiers. Her wealthy supporters had contributed over 40 million đồng, most of which went up in flames in order to cater to the war martyrs' needs in the Otherworld (Figure 7.4).

Master Thiền's efforts at healing the wounds of war are timely and seem to meet an urgent need in contemporary Vietnam (Gustaffson 2009; Schlecker & Endres 2011). During his trip to Vietnam in February 2007, the exiled Vietnamese Zen monk Thích Nhất Hạnh held several "requiem ceremonies to untie the knots of great injustice" (*lễ giải oan*). Like the Mông Sơn Ritual, a *giải oan* ceremony is intended to liberate the souls of those who died unjustly or whose bodies were never found. Master Thiền, however, is not a Zen Buddhist monastic. As a *bà đồng* of the Four Palace religion, she offers her followers and supporters a wide range of ritual services and remedies that pertain to "this-worldly"

FIGURE 7.4 *Preparations for the Mông Sơn Ritual. Đồng Lộc Junction, 2006*
SOURCE: PHOTO BY KIRSTEN W. ENDRES.

concerns, rather than to the Buddhist aim of detachment from the world. Although some of her "ritual management strategies" are certainly entrepreneurial in character (Endres 2010), she is not a businesswoman and therefore depends on her followers' generous contributions in order to finance ritual projects. However, through her activities, she gives her (predominately female) supporters the chance to reconcile their spiritual needs with patriotic sentiments and to re-moralize their wealth by remembering their moral debt (*nhớ ơn*) to those who sacrificed their lives so that others could live in peace and prosper (Jellema 2005). Moreover, she constitutes her own identity as a "scientific medium" who is skillful in organization and efficacious in securing divine benefits for her supporters by exploring (and inventing) new ways of tapping into supernatural powers.

Conclusion

My interlocutors in the world of Four Palace mediumship have often emphasized that "nobody is alike" (*không ai giống ai*) and that, in the world of mediumship, it is important to distinguish oneself from others. For an aspiring master in contemporary Hanoi it is particularly crucial to set him- or herself apart from others, because he or she has to outperform a growing number of competitors on the *lên đồng* scene. When I started comparing the palace-opening rituals of several masters, I found a puzzling variety of detail where I had least expected it. But rather than reinventing the wheel, most of them develop their own style by watching other masters' performances and choosing certain elements over others. Master Thiền, besides refining her ritual style, has not only expanded her specialization as a *bà đồng* to include ritual services that reach further into the public and national sphere, but also her supernatural network of divine beings that can be approached for favors and blessings. Master Đ. has firmly established his standing as the most skillful (*giỏi nhất*) master in contemporary Hanoi (if not in the whole of Northern Vietnam) and tries to integrate his spiritual path as an illustrious *đồng cô* with his openly gay lifestyle. Master Cảnh, in turn, builds his reputation on his "superior" masculine qualities and on his moral integrity as a male master medium who enjoys a happy family life besides fulfilling his religious duties. Despite having carved their own niche, master mediums carefully watch each other's steps. From ritual lapses to scandalous rumors, news usually spreads like wildfire in the world of mediums, and everybody is careful not to become the target of criticism and mockery. The contradictory contestations involved in the contemporary fashioning of Four Palace mediumship, however, are not just a matter of fierce competition in the religious marketplace. As I have illustrated in this chapter, Four Palace mediumship also provides a creative alternative space in which non-normative, and sometimes transgressive, gender identities are constructed, negotiated, and performed in the rapidly changing social and economic context of contemporary Vietnam. As such, the religious sphere also reflects the shifting gender dynamics in contemporary Vietnamese society that empower women as well as gay and transgender men to exercise greater agency in both the private and the public realms.

References

Altman, Dennis. 2001. *Global Sex*. Chicago: University of Chicago Press.

Andaya, Leonard Y. 2000. "The Bissu: Study of a Third Gender in Indonesia." In *Other Pasts: Women, Gender and History in Early Modern Southeast Asia*, edited by Barbara Watson Andaya, 27–46. Honolulu: University of Hawai'i Center for Southeast Asian Studies.

Blackwood, Evelyn. 2005. "Gender Transgression in Colonial and Postcolonial Indonesia." *Journal of Asian Studies* 64(4): 849–79.

Blanc, Marie-Eve. 2005. "Social Constructions of Male Homosexualities in Vietnam: Some Keys to Understand Discrimination and Implications for HIV Prevention Strategy." *International Social Science Journal* 57: 661–73.

Boddy, Janice. 1994. "Spirit Possession Revisited: Beyond Instrumentality." *Annual Review of Anthropology* 23: 407–34.

Brac de la Perrière, Bénédicte. 1989. *Les rituels de possession en Birmanie: du culte d'Etat aux cérémonies privées*. Paris: ADPF (Recherche sur les civilisations).

Colby, Donn, Nghia Huu Cao, and Serge Doussantousse. 2004. "Men Who Have Sex with Men and HIV in Vietnam: A Review." *AIDS Education and Prevention* 16: 45–54.

Do, Thien. 2003. *Vietnamese Supernaturalism: Views from the Southern Region*. London: Routledge Curzon.

Dror, Olga. 2002. "Đoàn thị Điểm's 'Story of the Vân Cát Goddess' as a Story of Emancipation." *Journal of Southeast Asian Studies* 33: 63–76.

Durand, Maurice. 1959. *Technique et panthéon des médiums Viêtnamiens*. Paris: École Française d'Extrême-Orient.

Endres, Kirsten W. 2008. "Engaging the Spirits of the Dead: Soul-calling Rituals and the Perfomative Construction of Efficacy." *Journal of the Royal Anthropological Institute* 14: 755–73.

———. 2010. "'Trading in Spirits'? Transnational Flows, Entrepreneurship, and Commodifications in Vietnamese Spirit Mediumship." In *Travelling Spirits: Migrants,*

Markets, and Moralities, edited by Gertrud Hüwelmeier and Kristine Krause, 118–32. New York: Routledge.

———. 2011. *Performing the Divine: Mediums, Markets and Modernity in Urban Vietnam*. Copenhagen: Nordic Institute of Asian Studies (NIAS) Press.

Endres, Kirsten W., and Andrea Lauser. 2011a. "Introduction: Multivocal Arenas of Modern Enchantment in Southeast Asia." In *Engaging the Spirit World: Popular Beliefs and Practices in Modern Southeast Asia,* edited by Kirsten W. Endres and Andrea Lauser, 1–18. New York: Berghahn.

———. 2011b. "Contests of Commemoration: Virgin War Martyrs, State Memorials, and the Invocation of the Spirit World in Contemporary Vietnam." In *Engaging the Spirit World: Popular Beliefs and Practices in Modern Southeast Asia,* edited by Kirsten W. Endres and Andrea Lauser, 121–143. New York: Berghahn.

Errington, Shelly. 1990. "Recasting Sex, Gender, and Power: A Theoretical and Regional Overview." In *Power and Difference: Gender in Island Southeast Asia,* edited by Jane Monnig Atkinson and Shelly Errington, 1–58. Stanford, CA: Stanford University Press.

Fjelstad, Karen, and Nguyen Thi Hien eds. 2006. *Possessed by the Spirits: Mediumship in Contemporary Vietnamese Communities*. Ithaca, NY: Cornell University Southeast Asia Program.

Giran, Paul. 1912. *Magie et religion annamites. Introduction à une philosophie de la civilisation du peuple d'Annam*. Paris: Librairie Maritime et Coloniale.

Gustafsson, Mai Lan. 2009. *War and Shadows: The Haunting of Vietnam*. Ithaca, NY: Cornell University Press.

Heiman, Elliott M., and Cao Van Lê. 1975. "Transsexualism in Vietnam." *Archives of Sexual Behavior* 4: 89–95.

Hirschman, Charles, Samuel Preston, and Vu Manh Loi. 1995. "Vietnamese Causalities during the American War: A New Estimate." *Population and Development Review* 21: 783–812.

Jellema, Kate. 2005. "Making Good on Debt: The Remoralisation of Wealth in Post-Revolutionary Vietnam." *Asia Pacific Journal of Anthropology* 6: 231–48.

Johnson, Mark. 1997. *Beauty and Power: Transgendering and Cultural Transformation in the Southern Philippines*. Oxford: Berg.

Kwon, Heonik. 2006. *After the Massacre: Commemoration and Consolation in Ha My and My Lai*. Berkeley: University of California Press.

———. 2008. *Ghosts of War in Vietnam*. Cambridge: Cambridge University Press.

Lambek, Michael. 2010. "Traveling Spirits: Unconcealment and Displacement." In *Traveling Spirits. Migrants, Markets and Mobility,* edited by Gertrud Hüwelmeier and Kristine Krause, 17–35. New York and London: Routledge.

Lộng Chương. [1942] 1990. *Hầu Thánh. Tiểu thuyết trào phúng* [Serving the Deities. A Satirical Novel]. Hanoi: NXB Hà Nội.

Luong, Hy Van. 1992. *Revolution in the Village: Tradition and Transformation in North Vietnam, 1925–1988.* Honolulu: University of Hawai'i Press.

Malarney, Shaun K. 2001. "'The Fatherland Remembers Your Sacrifice': Commemorating War Dead in North Vietnam." In *The Country of Memory: Remaking the Past in Late Socialist Vietnam,* edited by Hue-Tam Ho Tai, 46–76. Berkeley: University of California Press.

———. 2002. *Culture, Ritual and Revolution in Vietnam.* London: Routledge Curzon.

———. 2003. "Return to the Past? The Dynamics of Contemporary Religious and Ritual Transformation." In *Postwar Vietnam: Dynamics of a Transforming Society,* edited by Hy Van Luong, 225–56. Boulder: Rowman and Littlefield.

Ngô Đức Thịnh, ed. 1996. *Đạo Mẫu ở Việt Nam* [The Mother Goddess Religion in Vietnam]. Hanoi: NXB Văn Hóa-Thông Tin.

———. 2004. *Đạo Mẫu và các Hình Thức Shaman trong các Tộc Người ở Việt Nam và Châu Á* [The Mother Religion and Forms of Shamanism among Ethnic Groups in Vietnam and Asia]. Hanoi: Social Science Publishing House.

Nguyễn Thành Như. 2005. "Đồng tính luyến ái có phải là bệnh?" [Is Homosexuality a Disease?] *VnExpress.* http://www.vnexpress.net/GL/Suc-khoe/Gioi-tinh/2005/05/3B9DE1E5/. Accessed January 29, 2011.

Nguyễn Thị Hiền. 2007. "'Seats for Spirits to Sit Upon': Becoming a Spirit Medium in Contemporary Vietnam." *Journal of Southeast Asian Studies* 38(3): 541–58.

———. 2008. "Yin Illness: Its Diagnosis and Healing within Lên Đồng (Spirit Possession) Rituals of the Việt." *Asian Ethnology* 67(2): 205–321.

Nguyễn Thuận Thành. 2005. "Đồng tính, đồng cô & đồng bóng [Homosexuality, Effeminacy, and Mediumship]." *Kinh tế & Đô thị Online,* http://www.ktdt.com.vn/default.asp?thongtin = chitiet&id = 35173. Accessed February 24, 2005.

Nguyễn Trinh Thi. 2006. *Love Man Love Woman.* Documentary film, http://nguyentrinhthi.wordpress.com/2012/09/29/song-to-the-front-2/.

Nguyen Van Huyen. [1945] 1995. *The Ancient Civilization of Vietnam.* Hanoi: Gioi Publishers.

Nguyễn Văn Khoan. 1930. "Essai sur le đình et le culte du génie tutélaire des villages au Tonkin." *Bulletin de l'Ecole française d'Extreme-Orient* 30: 107–39.

Nhất Lang. 1952. *Đồng Bóng* [Mediumship]. Hanoi: Nhà In Lê-Cường.

Norton, Barley. 2009. *Songs for the Spirits: Music and Mediums in Modern Vietnam.* Chicago: University of Illinois Press.

Pastoetter, Jakob. 2004. "Vietnam." In *International Encyclopedia of Sexuality,* edited by Robert T. Francoeur and Raymond J. Noonan, http://www.kinseyinstitute.org/ccies/vn.php.

Peletz, Michael G. 2006. "Transgenderism and Gender Pluralism in Southeast Asia since Early Modern Times." *Current Anthropology* 47: 309–40.

Phạm Gia Khánh. 2012. "Hội thảo về Đạo Mẫu-những vấn đề đặt ra trong công tác quản lý nhà nước [Conference on the Mother Goddess Religion—Emerging Issues in State Management]." http://daomauvietnam.com/index.php/tin-tuc/827-hoi-thao-ve-dao-mau-nhung-van-de-dat-ra-trong-cong-tac-quan-ly-nha-nuoc.html. Accessed September 8, 2012.

Pham Quynh Phuong. 2009. *Hero and Deity: Tran Hung Dao and the Resurgence of Popular Religion in Vietnam*. Chiang Mai: Mekong Press.

Phan Kế Bính. [1915] 1995. *Việt Nam Phong Tục* [Vietnamese Customs]. Hồ Chí Minh City: NXB Thành Phố Hồ Chí Minh.

Proschan, Frank. 2002a. "Eunuch Mandarins, *Soldats Mamzelles*, Effeminate Boys, and Graceless Women: French Colonial Constructions of Vietnamese Genders." *GLQ* 8: 435–67.

———. 2002b. "Syphilis, Opiomania, and Pederasty: Colonial Constructions of Vietnamese (and French) Social Diseases." *Journal of the History of Sexuality* 11: 610–36.

Rydström, Helle. 2006. "Masculinity and Punishment: Men's Upbringing of Boys in Rural Vietnam." *Childhood* 13: 329–48.

Schlecker, Markus, and Kirsten W. Endres. 2011. "Psychic Experience, Truth, and Visuality in Postwar Vietnam." *Social Analysis* 55(1): 1–22.

Soucy, Alexander. 1999. "The Buddha's Blessing: Gender and Buddhist Practice in Hanoi." Ph.D. dissertation. Canberra: Australian National University.

Taylor, Philip. 2004. *Goddess on the Rise: Pilgrimage and Popular Religion in Vietnam*. Honolulu: University of Hawai'i Press.

Taylor, Philip, ed. 2007. *Modernity and Re-Enchantment: Religion in Post-Revolutionary Vietnam*. Singapore: ISEAS.

Trọng Lang. 1935. "Đồng Bóng [Mediumship]." *Phong Hóa*, 164–68, 171–3.

VnExpress. 2006. "Lệch lạc giới tính ở thanh thiếu niên [Gender deviation among teenagers]," http://vnexpress.net/SG/Doi-song/2006/04/3B9E8A82/. Accessed January 29, 2011.

Yee, Jennifer. 2001. "'L'Indochine androgyne': Androgyny in Turn-of-the-Century French Writing on Indochina." *Textual Practice* 15: 269–82.

CHAPTER 8

The Blessed Virgin Mary Wears *Áo Dài*: Marianism in the Transnational Public Sphere between Vietnamese Catholics in the U.S. and Vietnam[*]

Thien-Huong T. Ninh

Introduction

"Just as Our Lady of Fatima had saved Russia in 1989, so too will she save Vietnam," said a priest in his Sunday Vietnamese mass sermon at the 2011 Annual Marian Festival in Carthage, Missouri. On the altar next to him and facing more than 5,000 attendees were statues of Our Lady of Fatima in a white robe and Our Lady of Lavang as a Vietnamese woman dressed in *áo dài*, a Vietnamese traditional costume. This was no ordinary Catholic event. The three-day festival attracted more than 70,000 people. They were mostly Vietnamese Catholics who drove from the two coasts of the U.S. to this small town of approximately 15,000 residents. Many flew in from other countries, including Vietnam, Canada, France, and Australia. They described themselves as the children of the Virgin Mary who have been dispersed throughout the world, isolated from each other, and have recently reconnected through her. They had come together to pray for her blessings, to heal the historical wounds that have fragmented their community and placed their country of origin under communism.

This chapter investigates how and why Vietnamese Catholics in the U.S. are motivated to maintain ties with coreligionists in Vietnam through the image of Our Lady of Lavang. In doing so, it aims to understand how Vietnamese Catholics in the U.S. negotiate with the meanings of religion in the private and public spheres of their new host society. While religion is often a family-based practice that manifests into public domains in Vietnam, it is a constitutionally protected individual right in the U.S. Therefore, it is common for Vietnamese Catholics, as well as their coethnics belonging to other religions, to come from a family of several generations of members professing the same religion. In contrast, nuclear families in the U.S. are unpredictably diverse in religious affiliation—a man may profess Christianity, his wife may follow Buddhism, and their son may be an atheist.

---

[*] This contribution is a revised version of a previously published article that appeared in Kato, Atsufumi ed. 2012. *Alternative Intimate Spheres for Women in Vietnam*, GCOE Working Papers (Next Generation Research) 71, Kyoto, Japan: Kyoto University Global COE Program for Reconstruction of the Intimate and Public Spheres in 21st Century Asia.

I argue that Vietnamese Catholics have resisted the reclusion of religion into the private, individualistic arena in the U.S., although this is their new host society and most do not see themselves returning to Vietnam. Through Our Lady of Lavang, they have interpolated their religious practices into the transnational public space. During decades of geographical isolation and separation from their homeland following the end of the Vietnam War, Vietnamese Catholics in the U.S. prayed to Our Lady of Lavang for hope, forgiveness, and solace. This cross-border, shared appeal mediated continuity and linkages between Vietnamese Catholics in the U.S. and coreligionists in Vietnam, breaking down the public-private barriers as these processes traverse through political, cultural, and economic domains. These processes have only expanded further since 1995, when the two countries established diplomatic ties. Today, Our Lady of Lavang has become synonymous with a global Vietnamese Catholic collective identity.

Mother Worship in the Transnational Public Sphere

Research on immigrants in the U.S. has discovered that Marianism exhibited in the public space often transcends national borders and is intertwined with ethnicity. In his study, Tweed (1997) has found that Marianism, through Our Lady of Exile, plays a crucial role in linking Cuban Catholics in Miami to their homeland. He observes that, through Our Lady of Exile, they create a "transtemporal" and "trans-locative" space at their church to reinterpret their history of displacement and envision a future in which they would return to their homeland. In doing so, Tweed argues that they transpose the conditions of displacement into survival and aspirations, reinterpreting their experiences of exile as hope and envisioning a future when they will return to Cuba. Similarly, Catholic and non-Catholic Mexican immigrants have evoked Our Lady of Guadalupe's image to appeal to a transnational ethnic identity (Horsfall 2000; Duricy 2008).

There is no current in-depth study on Marianism among Vietnamese in the U.S. However, observations of Mother Goddess worship among this population have found that this practice is also emerging into a transnational public sphere. Originally relegated to the private sphere, usually practiced individually or in small groups at home, Fjelstad and Nguyen (2011) have observed that the Mother Goddess practice has created a semiporous community and inspired many young Vietnamese adults to learn and maintain their Vietnamese roots, including traveling to the homeland for the first time.

How and why do immigrants in the U.S. look to religious mother figures to create a transnational public space that links them to ethnic coreligionists in other countries, particularly their homeland? As suggested by these studies, religious mother figures emerge most vividly in contexts of pain, suffering, and mourning associated with displacement, isolation, and migration. These are individual experiences, but spiritual mothers can conjoin immigrants in a public space by facilitating sympathy, acceptance, and solace among their followers. This shared public arena has no geographical boundary and, through cross-border outreach to countries such as the homeland, can inflect healing and reconciliation particularly unique to migration experiences. In particular, the ethnic underpinnings of religious mother figures, such as imagery and historical roots, can create, relink, and solidify blood, cultural, and physical bonds among members of a shared ethnicity.

Mother worship, therefore, is less bound to the commands of traditions than the demands of contemporary experiences and struggles. For Vietnamese followers in the U.S. and Vietnam, it has unshackled the full grasp of Confucianism that restricted women to the domestic sphere and assigned them religious and spiritual duties. In front of religious mother figures, both men and women could appeal for blessings, comfort, and guidance. This attraction across gender partly explains why the Mother Goddess tradition has experienced rapid growth in popularity within the past two decades in Vietnam and the U.S. Whether the goddess is the Liễu Hạnh of the North, Thiên Y A Na of Central Vietnam, or the Black Lady and Our Lady of the Realm in the South, she has summoned thousands of pilgrims from all over the world to her sacred homes in Vietnam (Taylor 2004; Fjelstad & Nguyen 2006; Pham & Eipper 2009; Endres 2011).

The transnational public sphere created by religious mother worship is a unique and rare intimate point of juncture between Vietnamese in the U.S. and Vietnam. However, this body of literature on religious mother worship is mostly concentrated on the Mother Goddess tradition and scantly considers (if not completely misses) other forms of mother worship. This chapter fills this gap with a case study of Vietnamese Catholics in the U.S. From issues such as ethnic identity, nationalism, citizenship, and womanhood, this paper hopes to contribute to the conversation.

Our Lady of Lavang: Her Apparition and European Image as Our Lady of Victories (1798–1998)

According to oral tradition, in 1798 the Virgin Mary appeared in a small village named Lavang, eighty miles north of Hue, the former capital of Vietnam

(Tran 2009). She comforted Vietnamese Catholics who were praying for protection from anti-Catholic persecutions. The Virgin Mary appeared three to four more times within the next twenty years and became locally known as Our Lady of Lavang. About a century later, on the occasion of the first Lavang Convention in 1900, Bishop Louis Casper placed a French-modeled statue of Our Lady of Victories (Notre-Dame des Victoires) in the first newly built church for Our Lady of Lavang. For nearly more than a century, this statue of a Western-looking Mary was associated with Our Lady of Lavang.

Although she gradually grew in popularity, Our Lady of Lavang was not as widely known among Vietnamese Catholics as Vatican-endorsed Marian figures such as Our Lady of Fatima and Our Lady of Lourdes until 1954 (Hansen 2009). During this year, communist North and anti-communist South Vietnam were divided at the seventeenth parallel, about twelve miles north of the Our Lady of Lavang sanctuary. This historic event forced approximately 60 percent of the million Catholics in North Vietnam to relocate to South Vietnam, where they would receive support from the US-backed Catholic Ngô Đình Diệm regime (Tran 2005, 427–49). While some of them traveled by plane or boat, many also migrated by foot to escape communist surveillance. Among these individuals, some resettled in the Lavang area between 1954 and 1956 (de Jaegher 1962, 8). They rebuilt their religious communities and often named them after Our Lady of Lavang. The Vatican expressed support for their struggles by elevating the Lavang sanctuary's rank to a national Marian center of pilgrimage in 1959 and to a minor basilica in 1961 (Tran 2009).

While Our Lady of Lavang symbolically united Vietnamese Catholics across the seventeenth parallel through her national status, she also reflected their struggles and hardships during one of the most violent periods in Vietnamese history. Between 1954 and 1975, the Soviet Union–supported North and US-supported South Vietnam fought over the unification of the country as part of the international Cold War. The war escalated to the "Red Summer Battles" (Chiến Thắng Mùa Hè Đỏ) of 1972, which nearly extinguished the Our Lady of Lavang sanctuary and killed a large number of Vietnamese Catholics in the surrounding area (Tran 2009). After the war ended in 1975, many Vietnamese Catholics fled the country.

Those that stayed in Central Vietnam slowly rebuilt the pilgrimage center and constructed another statue of Our Lady of Lavang, modeled after the image of Our Lady of Victories (Archdiocese of Hue 2009). Religious life gradually resumed and the number of pilgrims continued to grow, as reflected by the attendance of more than half a million people at the Jubilee Year closure mass in 2011 (*Union of Catholic Asian News* 2011). These collective acts of reconstruction and religious practices commemorated their history of suffering and separation. They also spoke volumes about the resilient faith of Vietnamese Catholics under continual harsh treatment from the new communist-led government and isolation from the Catholic Church outside of Vietnam. These locally situated meanings channeled the Vietnamese Catholic community toward its own distinctive trajectory of development, with tangential ties to the Vatican II transformations that fundamentally reinterpreted Catholic practices and beliefs in many parts of the world during the 1960s.

How Our Lady of Lavang became Vietnamese: The Virgin Mary, as a Symbol of Vietnamese Ethnicity on American Soil, Returns to Vietnam

The communist takeover of South Vietnam in 1975 forced more than 2 million Vietnamese to flee the country, not counting possibly another million who did not survive their flight (Tran 1997; Coughlan 1998, 175–201; Robinson 1998). While a small group of elites departed by plane, the majority fled in boats that left from ports along the Southwestern coast of Vietnam (Tran 1994, 299–323). In 1975, about 125,000 Vietnamese arrived in the U.S. (Zhou & Bankston 1998). This group included approximately 200 priests and 250 nuns (Luong & Hien 2011). By 1980, the Vietnamese refugee population had doubled (US Census Bureau 2011).

Among those who arrived in the U.S. during the 1970s, Catholics made up between 30 and 40 percent of this population (Chandler 1975). This overrepresentation, nearly four times their proportion in Vietnam, was likely due to the fact that many of them were associated with the former Catholic Ngô Đình Diệm government of South Vietnam. Moreover, some of the refugees had converted to Catholicism during the processes of flight and resettlement (Hoskins 2008), since Catholic Relief Services was the single largest sponsor for refugees. Today, the representation of Catholics is about 27 percent of the total 1.6 million Vietnamese Americans (Bankston 2000, 36–53).

While Orange County, California, has a comparatively higher proportion of Catholics than other counties in the U.S., with approximately one in three individuals claiming Catholic affiliation, it also has the largest Vietnamese Catholic community outside of Vietnam. In 1982, there were approximately 7,000 Vietnamese Catholics in Orange County (Vietnamese Catholic Center Booklet 1998). By 2010 this statistic had multiplied ten times and constituted 40 percent of the total number of Vietnamese in the region, according to the estimates of a church leader who works at the Orange Diocese (Father Long interview 2010). The Vietnamese population is the largest Asian Catholic group in Orange County, representing nearly 6 percent of the region's 1.2 million

Catholics. Although it is proportionally smaller than the percentages of Anglos (55 percent) and Hispanics (35 percent) among all Orange County Catholics, the Vietnamese Catholic group makes up nearly 30 percent of all priests in the Orange Diocese (Father Long interview 2011). As a result, many Vietnamese priests have to learn another language, usually Spanish, in order to serve non-Vietnamese Catholics.

From Exodus to Resettlement: Vietnamese Marianism Transplanted in US Soil (1975–84)

As they resettled in the U.S., Vietnamese Catholics continued to pray to the Virgin Mary and, arguably, did so more fervently because of their traumatic experiences of coerced displacement as refugees (Dorais 2007). However, there are no supporting records that they were devoted specifically to Our Lady of Lavang more than other Marian forms. Moreover, historical evidence has revealed that Vietnamese Catholics focused on Our Lady of Fatima in their homeland orientation. The popularity of Our Lady of Fatima—possibly more than Our Lady of Lavang—among newly arrived Vietnamese refugees in the U.S. may be because of the Vatican's official recognition of her apparition.

Beginning in their early years of arrival in the U.S., Vietnamese Catholics concentrated on homeland orientation and anti-communism in their Marianism. In 1976, they came together to pray for the freedom of Vietnam from communism after Our Lady of Fatima was reported to have appeared in Saigon (now Hồ Chí Minh City), although the Vatican did not verify the appearance (Tran 1994, 299–323). Since 1978, a larger number of Vietnamese Catholics across the U.S. also began attending the annual Marian Day to pray for Vietnam. The event attracted nearly 1,500 attendees during its first year and continued to grow in popularity, despite the fact that it is held in the isolated town of Carthage, Missouri, during the hot month of August (Phan 2005, 457–72). The organizers were priests and brothers of the Congregation of the Mother Co-Redemptrix, a religious order founded in Vietnam in 1941. They symbolically moved their religious headquarters to Carthage, Missouri after more than 50 percent of the group's members (175 brothers) fled Vietnam after 1975 (Beyette 1991). This refugee and near extinction experience has loomed large in the monastic practice of Marianism. Marian Day is not just another religious festival, but a collective grassroots political movement among Vietnamese Catholics to ask the Virgin Mary to save Vietnam and its people from communism. This is the grounding from which the patroness of the Congregation of the Mother Co-Redemptrix had been dubbed Our Lady of Global Peace. Our

Lady of Peace created symbolic connections with Our Lady of Fatima, who first received this title from the Vatican in 1952 in order to protect Russia from communism (Roman Catholic Saints 2011). It also alludes to another Marian statue in Hồ Chí Minh City (home of the largest number of Catholics in Vietnam) that was built in 1959 and was given the same title by the local diocese (Ngoc 2005).

The homeland orientation in Vietnamese American Catholic faith was marginalized by the u.s. Catholic Church's implicit policy of cultural assimilation. In Orange County, Vietnamese Catholics faced pressure from the diocese to assimilate into its structural organization. Despite sufficient funding, large numbers, and a clearly expressed desire, they did not receive permission from the Orange Diocese to establish their own ethnic parish. This disappointed them, since permission had been granted to the Polish and Korean Catholic communities during the 1980s (Krekelberg & Giacomi 2007). In 1983, Vietnamese Catholics were only allowed to establish the Vietnamese Catholic Center to hold nonreligious community functions. Meanwhile, they had to continue to hold masses at local parishes led by non-Vietnamese pastors, although Vietnamese Americans were significantly overrepresented among priests, brothers, and nuns.[1] These modes of coerced assimilation, with the Orange Diocese's aim of concealing and erasing the Vietnamese presence in the church, stirred resentment among many Vietnamese Catholics, who felt exploited for financial gain.

These experiences of marginalization resulted in Vietnamese Catholics mobilizing their ethnic representation outside of the local ecclesiastical hierarchy. In 1980, Vietnamese American Catholics established the Federation of Vietnamese Catholics, which expanded a clergy-based national organization founded in 1976 to include the laity (Phan 2000, 19–35). This grassroots organizing created networks among Vietnamese Americans dispersed throughout the u.s. and mobilized their representation within the Catholic Church (Father Lam interview, 2010). It occurred more than a decade before the Center of Pastoral Apostolate for Overseas Vietnamese was established by the Vatican in 1988 and by the us Catholic Church in 1989.

From these simultaneous experiences of exclusion from the u.s. Church hierarchy and organizational strength among Vietnamese American Catholics, Our Lady of Lavang emerged as a unique Vietnamese cultural representation by the early 1980s. She was not commonly known outside of Vietnam and her lack of recognition from the Vatican had restricted her popularity to Vietnamese Catholics. However, it is precisely because of these particular associations with

---

1 By 1978, four Vietnamese American priests had become pastors but, ironically, none served the largest Vietnamese American Catholic community, in Orange County (Tran 1994, 310).

Vietnam and Vietnamese identity that Our Lady of Lavang has become a symbolic ethnic marker for Vietnamese American Catholics to distinguish themselves from other Catholics in the U.S. As early as 1982, Vietnamese Catholics began using her name to label their ethnically based religious organizations (Dinh 1995). Within the next decade, Our Lady of Lavang's representation of Vietnamese ethnicity had achieved its full momentum, reaching beyond local recognition and toward international acceptance.

Our Lady of Vietnam: Ethnic Identity and Homeland Ties (1985–94)

In 1985, Vietnamese Catholics in the U.S. started to use their organizational prowess to globalize the status of Our Lady of Lavang. During this year, they received news from the Vatican that Catholics in Vietnam were petitioning for the canonization of 117 martyrs who had been persecuted in Vietnam (Tran 2009). Vietnamese American Catholics joined the movement and, for the first time in a decade, were reconnected to coreligionists in the homeland. While working on the canonization, Vietnamese Catholics in the U.S. and Vietnam also campaigned for the Vatican's recognition of the Our Lady of Lavang apparition.

As a result, Pope John Paul II publicly discussed the significance of Our Lady of Lavang with Vietnamese Catholics, for the first time in history, immediately after the ceremony of canonization for the 117 martyrs in Rome on June 19, 1988 (Tran 2009). During the same year, he established the Center of Pastoral Apostolate for Overseas Vietnamese to create an institutional bridge with the overseas Vietnamese community. The organization undoubtedly informed the Holy Father about the bicentennial commemoration of Our Lady of Lavang's apparition in 1998, and by the early 1990s, Pope John Paul II publicly referred to Our Lady of Lavang more frequently in anticipation of the celebration (Tran 1994, 299–323).

As the global popularity of Our Lady of Lavang grew, it further solidified ethnic pride among Vietnamese American Catholics in Orange County. However, her European image was incompatible with their yearning to integrate Vietnamese ethnicity into Catholicism. As a result, they constructed the first representation of the Virgin Mary with a Vietnamese face and costume in 1994 (Vietnamese Catholic Center 1998). The white statue, sculpted by Van Nhan and placed at the entrance to the Vietnamese Catholic Cultural Center in Orange County represents the Virgin Mary dressed in the traditional Vietnamese long tunic over silk pants (áo dài) with her head adorned by a saucer-like headdress (Figure 8.1). She holds a miniature statue of Jesus in front of her, "as if she wants to hand her most beloved child to the Vietnamese people in order to save them and their race" (Vietnamese Catholic Center 1998, 17).

FIGURE 8.1
Our lady of Vietnam (completed in 1995, Santa Ana, California)
SOURCE: PHOTO BY THIEN-HUONG NINH.

She stands on a grotto in the shape of an S that represents Vietnam and its mountainous ridges. According to a publication by the Vietnamese Catholic Cultural Center, this representation of Mary "guides the spirit of Vietnamese people to return to their homeland roots" and to pray for their coreligionists (17). Meanwhile, it also brings "peace and tranquility" to the Vietnamese faithful who are adapting to life in a new country.

Vietnamese American Catholics named her Our Lady of Vietnam to emphasize their lingering connections to the homeland as well as their cultural heritage. Moreover, they also informally referred to her as Mary of Global Peace. This created symbolic connections to other forms of Marianism that had also been associated with the same title by Vietnamese Catholics, particularly the statues of the Virgin Mary in Carthage, Missouri, and Hồ Chí Minh City, Vietnam.

Our Lady of Lavang: From a European Icon to a Global Symbol of Vietnamese Catholicism (1995–Present)

After Vietnam reestablished diplomatic ties with the U.S. in 1995, its economic integration and globalization created more channels for Vietnamese American

Catholics to reconnect to coreligionists in their homeland. For example, they could easily send remittances and fly directly to Vietnam on a US airline. Meanwhile, the government of Vietnam was also loosening restrictions toward religious practices as part of its agenda to create friendlier economic ties with Western countries (Bouquet 2010, 90–108). It formally recognized Catholicism as the second largest religious group in Vietnam, with a following of 6 million, or 7 percent of Vietnam's population in 2005 (Vietnamese Committee for Religious Affairs 2006).

Within the context of economic globalization and religious tolerance in Vietnam, Vietnamese bishops received news about the statue of Our Lady of Vietnam and wanted to replace the European statue of Our Lady of Lavang in preparation for the bicentennial commemoration in 1998. They were further encouraged by personal support from the Vatican. Between 1996 and early 1998, the bishops received many letters of blessings from Pope John Paul II in reference to the upcoming historic ceremony (Tran 1994, 299–323).

Consequentially, church leaders in Vietnam invited the Vietnamese American Van Nhan, who sculpted Our Lady of Vietnam, to create a statue of Our Lady of Lavang with Vietnamese features (Tran 2009). Like the image of Our Lady of Vietnam, the new representation of Our Lady of Lavang depicts Mary dressed in a white tunic (*áo dài*) and wearing a golden headdress (Figure 8.2). She also holds a statue of baby Jesus. However, it arguably portrays Vietnamese traditions much more poignantly than the former because of its added colors. The blue cloak that is on top of Our Lady of Lavang's white *áo dài* alludes to the conventional representation of the Blessed Virgin Mary. However, because the cloak is a Vietnamese traditional dress reserved for special occasions, such as weddings, the new image highlights important references to Vietnamese culture.

On July 1, 1998, this statue was blessed by Pope John II in Rome (Tran 2009). At this celebrated event, the Holy Father also proclaimed Our Lady of Lavang the patroness of the Catholic Church of Vietnam. Although this religious honor did not officially recognize the historical accuracy of the apparition of Our Lady of Lavang in 1798, it was a source of inspiration for Vietnamese Catholics throughout the world. For the first time in history, a Vietnamese icon of the Catholic faith was officially introduced to the global Catholic community. On August 13, 1998, two hundred years after her apparition, more than 200,000 attendees gathered in Lavang to worship Our Lady of Lavang represented as a Vietnamese woman.

Ever since, many sites have been constructed in the U.S. in honor of the Our Lady of Lavang. A church in Santa Ana, California, was completed in 2001; an altar inside the Basilica of the National Shrine of the Immaculate Conception in Washington, D.C., was completed in 2006. These developments are not simply

FIGURE 8.2
Our lady of Lavang as a Vietnamese woman (completed in 1998, La Vang, Vietnam)
SOURCE: PHOTO BY THIEN-HUONG NINH.

cultural representations for Vietnamese American Catholics. They also reflect, remind, and galvanize the continuing ethical responsibility of Vietnamese American Catholics to coreligionists in their country of origin. As citizens of the richest and most powerful country in the world, they have access to economic, political, and cultural resources to lobby for the religious rights of Vietnamese Catholics under communism in Vietnam. In 2010, Vietnamese Catholics dispersed throughout the world officially formed the twenty-seventh diocese of the Catholic Church in Vietnam. They were collectively known as the "Overseas Diocese," as engraved on a stone placed at the Our Lady of Lavang sanctuary on January 4 of that year (Publicity Committee for the 2010 Holy Year Mass 2011). On Marian Day in August 2011, a priest reminded more than 70,000 attendees (most of them Vietnamese) that if the Virgin Mary had freed Russia from the corruption of communism, then she would also do so for Vietnam.

Conclusion

This chapter reveals that Vietnamese in the U.S. have reestablished ties with coreligionists in Vietnam through Marianism in the transnational public sphere, evoked by the Blessed Virgin Mary as Our Lady of Vietnam and Our Lady of

Lavang. They resist nation-state models of integration and collectively work toward reconciliation through ethnic recovery. As the research has shown, the Blessed Virgin Mary in her indigenized Vietnamese forms intends to undo the erasure of Vietnamese Catholic history, memory, and experiences. At the same time, she alludes to the distinctive religious experiences of Catholics originally from Vietnam and now dispersed throughout the world. This uniqueness is an important ground on which Vietnamese in the U.S. and Vietnam forge a cross-border collective identity and heal through ethical responsibility to each other. By helping each other in terms of monetary, material, and spiritual support, they are relearning, recultivating, and rebuilding the basic principles of human relationship that have been damaged by coerced displacement, geographical separation, and continuing marginalized ethnic status.

The transnational connection among Vietnamese Catholics through the Virgin Mary reflects her symbolic role as a sacred mother who could sustain and mediate relations among her children who are dispersed throughout the world. Vietnamese Catholics have transformed her into their ethnic image in order to assert not simply cultural connections but also blood ties, as if she were their biological mother. They seek her to express pain and suffering as marginalized ethnic minorities with a long traumatic history of war and violence. She is their mother, who will listen to their cries and help them. It is precisely at this point of convergence that the Virgin Mary, in her various Vietnamese forms, has become a distinctively Vietnamese mother who can create reconnections between Vietnamese Catholics in the U.S. and Vietnam.

The mothering element of a female religious figure such as the Blessed Virgin does not conceal gender inequality or sexual marginalization. Rather, it complicates our understanding of these concepts in current literature on mother worship. Vietnamese women and men may be swayed by different reasons for seeking comfort and solace from goddess icons. However, they share the need and desire for a mother who will listen, accept, and understand their challenges and difficulties during a period of rapid cultural, economic, and political change. In this way, they have "hyper-gendered" Mother Goddess figures with certain conceptions of who and how a mother should be. At the same time, it is within this space of mother-children relations that Vietnamese men and women can redefine sexuality and gender in the U.S. and Vietnam.

References

Archdiocese of Hue. 2009. "Thanh Dia Duc Me La Vang" [Our Lady of Lavang Sanctuary]. http://www.xaydungbinhan.com/index.php?option=com_content&view=article&id=216:thanh-a-c-m-la-vang&catid=62:du-lch-ng-st&Itemid=91.

Bankston, Carl. 2000. "Vietnamese-American Catholicism: Transplanted and Flourishing." *U.S. Catholic Historian* 18(1): 36–53.

Beyette, Beverly. 1991. "Viet Seminary Transplants its Roots in Rural Missouri." *Los Angeles Times*, http://articles.latimes.com/1991-08-21/news/vw-1019_1_seminary-property.

Bouquet, Mathieu. 2010. "Vietnamese Party State and Religious Pluralism since 1986: Building the Fatherland?" *SOJOURN: Journal of Social Issues in Southeast Asia* 25: 90–108.

Chandler, Russell. 1975. "Familiar Landmark: Religion Vital to Vietnam Refugees." *Los Angeles Times* (1923–Current File), from ProQuest.

Coughlan, James E. 1998. "Occupational Mobility of Australia's Vietnamese Community: Its Direction and Human Capital Determinants." *International Migration Review* 32(1): 175–201.

de Jaegher, Raymond J. 1962. "Our Lady of the 17th Parallel." *Catholic Herald*, http://archive.catholicherald.co.uk/article/19th-october-1962/8/our-lady-of-the-17th-parallel.

Dinh, Viet Hien. 1995. "Vài Nét Sơ Lược về Công Đoàn Công Giáo La Vang" [Several Points about the Lavang Catholic Community]. In *Kỷ Niệm 12 Năm Thành Lập Công Đoàn La Vang* [Twelve-Year Anniversary of the Establishment of the Lavang Catholic Community]. Canoga Park, CA: Our Lady of Lavang Community of St. Joseph Parish.

Dorais, Louis-Jacques. 2007. "Faith, Hope, and Identity: Religion and the Vietnamese Refugees." *Refugee Survey Quarterly* 26(2): 57–68.

Duricy, Michael. 2008. *Black Madonnas: Our Lady of Czestochowa*. Dayton, OH: Marian Library/International Marian Research Institute, http://campus.udayton.edu/mary/meditations/olczest.html.

Endres, Kirsten W. 2011. *Performing the Divine: Mediums, Markets and Modernity in Urban Vietnam*. Honolulu: University of Hawai'i Press.

Fjelstad, Karen, and Nguyen Thi Hien. 2006. "Introduction." In *Possessed by the Spirits: Mediumship in Contemporary Vietnamese Communities*, edited by Karen Fjelstad and Hien Thi Nguyen, 7–18. Ithaca, NY: Cornell University.

———. 2011. *Spirits without Borders: Vietnamese Spirit Mediums in a Transnational Age*. New York: Palgrave Macmillan.

Hansen, Peter. 2009. "The Virgin Heads South: Northern Catholic Refugees in South Vietnam, 1954–64." Ph.D. dissertation, Melbourne, Melbourne College of Divinity.

Horsfall, Sara. 2000. "The Experience of Marian Apparitions and the Mary Cult." *Social Science Journal* 37(3): 375–84.

Hoskins, Janet. 2008. "Emigration, Exile and Exodus: Overseas Vietnamese Communities from the Perspective of Indigenous Religions." Paper presented at the International Union of Anthropological and Ethnological Sciences, Kunming, China.

Krekelberg, William, and Shirl Giacomi. 2007. *Diocese of Orange: Learning, Loving, and Living Our Faith*. Bowling Green, MO: Editions du Signe.

Luong, Dominic M., and Joachim Hien. 2011. *The Pastoral Care of Migrants and Refugees: Vietnamese*. Arlington, VA: Các Thánh Tử Đạo Việt Nam. http://www.cttdva.com/lichsu/USCCB_MRS.htm.

Ngoc Loan. 2005. "Nguồn Gốc Tượng Mẹ Nữ Vương Hoà Bình tại Sài Gòn" [The Historical Roots of the Statue of Our Lady of Global Peace in Saigon]. *VietCatholic News*, http://www.memedu.dk/hinhanhmevathanhdia/MeSaigon%202005/nguongoctu-ongme.htm.

Pham, Quynh Phuong, and Chris Eipper. 2009. "Mothering and Fathering the Vietnamese: Religion, Gender, and National Identity." *Journal of Vietnamese Studies* 4(1): 49–83.

Phan, Peter C. 2000. "Vietnamese Catholics in the U.S.: Christian Identity between the Old and the New." *U.S. Catholic Historian* 18(1): 19–35.

———. 2005. "Mary in Vietnamese Piety and Theology: A Contemporary Perspective." *Ephemerides Mariologicae* 51: 457–72.

Publicity Committee for the 2010 Holy Year Mass. 2011. "The 2010 Holy Year Mass." *Tổng Giáo Phận Huế*, http://tonggiaophanhue.net/home/index.php?option=com_content&view=article&id=3929:l-b-mc-nm-thanh-2010-ngay-trng-i-ben-m-la-vang&catid=71:be-mac-nam-thanh-2010&Itemid=120.

Robinson, Courtland. 1998. *Terms of Refuge, the Indochinese Exodus and the International Response*. London: Zed Books.

Roman Catholic Saints. 2011. "Our Lady of Peace." *Roman Catholic Saints*, http://www.roman-catholic-saints.com/our-lady-of-peace.html.

Taylor, Philip. 2004. *Goddess on the Rise: Pilgrimage and Popular Religion in Vietnam*. Honolulu: University of Hawai'i Press.

Tran, Dong Dang Dan. 1997. *Người Việt Nam ở Nước Ngoài* [Vietnamese Living in Foreign Countries]. Hanoi: Nhà Xuất Bản Chính Trị Quốc Gia.

Tran, Phuc Long. 1994. "Cộng Đồng Công Giáo Việt Nam Hải Ngoại" [The Overseas Vietnamese Catholic Community]. In *25 Giáo Phận Việt Nam* [25 Dioceses of Viet Nam]. Costa Mesa, CA: Self-publication.

Tran, Thi Lien. 2005. "The Catholic Question in North Vietnam." *Cold War History* 5: 427–49.

Tran, Quang C. 2009. "Trung Tâm Thánh Mẫu Toàn Quốc La-Vang" [The National Marian Center of Lavang]. *Tổng Giáo Phận Huế*, http://tonggiaophanhue.net/home/index.php?option=com_content&view=article&id=38:phn-1-s-tich-c-m-la-vang&catid=14:duc-me-la-vang&Itemid=99.

Tweed, Thomas. 1997. *Our Lady of the Exile: Diasporic Religion as a Cuban Catholic Shrine in Miami*. New York: Oxford University Press.

Union of Catholic Asian News Staff. 2011. "500,000 Attend Vietnam Jubilee Year Closure." *Union of Catholic Asian News*, January 7, http://www.ucanews.com/2011/01/07/about-500000-attend-vietnam-jubilee-year-closure/.

US Census Bureau. 2011. "The Vietnamese Population in the U.S.: 2010." http://www.vasummit2011.org/docs/research/The%20Vietnamese%20Population%202010_July%202.2011.pdf.

Vietnamese Catholic Center. 1998. *Vietnamese Catholic Center Booklet*. Santa Ana, CA: Vietnamese Catholic Center.

Vietnamese Committee for Religious Affairs. 2006. *Religion and Policies Regarding Religion in Vietnam White Paper*. Hanoi: Socialist Republic of Vietnam.

Zhou, Min, and Carl Bankston. 1998. *Growing Up American: How Vietnamese Children Adapt to Life in the U.S.* New York: Russell Sage Foundation.

Index

abortion   13, 103
Abu-Lughod, Lila   3, 13
academic attainment   116–8, 121–2, 127, 129, 134
administration   27, 31n7, 36, 37, 146, 150, 160
adopted child   62, 64, 70, 160, 187
adultery   7, 16, 89, 98–100, 102–4, 105–7, 110
affirmative action
    for ethnic minority   50
    toward women's political participation   35, 145
agency   2, 144, 191, 195
    of woman   viii, 1, 2–3, 4, 7, 9, 13, 14, 16, 17, 57, 156, 157, 168, 214
agriculture   15, 26, 32, 58, 107, 121, 125, 150, 157
    re-feminization of   12, 157
alumni association
    see same-age association
American War
    see Vietnam War
Amit, Vered   166
ancestral house
    see ancestral worship hall
ancestral worship   12, 15, 27, 28, 58, 61, 62–4, 66–9, 71, 72, 74, 75
ancestral worship hall   66–8, 72–5, 151
Andaya, Leonard Y.   201, 203
Anderson, Benedict   166
anniversary rice field
    see ky điền
Annual Marian Festival   218
anthropology   1, 9, 141
áo dài (Vietnamese ethnic costume)   18, 176, 218, 225, 227
Aoki, Atsushi   63
appropriation   2, 17, 143, 156, 157
Arendt, Hannah   7, 168, 189–90
association   4, 10, 15, 40, 45–6, 141, 143, 144, 148, 150–1, 155–6, 160, 162, 176n10, 224
asylum   15
asymmetry   5, 6
authority   6, 27–8, 87, 90, 118, 155, 170, 199
    village   6, 16, 168, 171, 182, 186, 187, 191

bà đồng (female medium)   196, 197, 199, 200, 202, 212–3
Bà Triệu   27n3
Bà Trưng   27n3
Bắc Giang   126
Bắc Ninh   25, 126
Ban Chỉnh Đạo Sect   167, 171, 172, 173, 174n8, 179
Bankston, Carl   222
Barbieri, Magali   3, 8, 12, 81, 88, 117
Barrow, John   26
Bát Tràng   27, 28, 32–3
Beck, Ulrich   10, 86
Becker, G.S.   94
Bedouin   3, 13
Bélanger, Danièle   3, 7–8, 11–12, 13, 33, 34n10, 39, 59, 81, 88, 116–8, 126, 131, 191–192
belonging   1, 7, 14–15, 17, 126, 171, 177, 183, 185–6
Bến Tre   173
bilateral kindred system   1, 7–9, 12, 27, 46, 58, 59, 65, 70, 75, 77
Bình dân học vụ (Mass Education Program)   160
Bình Dương   106, 126
birth control   146, 154
    see also family planning policy
birth rate   10
Blackwood, Evelyn   220–1, 203
Blanc, Marie-Eve   204n11, 205
Bloom, B.L.   95
Boddy, Janice   195
body   169, 189–90, 198, 202, 203, 204, 210n13, 211, 212
    commodification of   38, 39
    intervention into women's   3, 12, 25
Buddhism   50, 204n10, 212–3
Buddhist association   15, 45–6, 144
Buddhist temple   15, 27, 50, 145, 146, 170, 183
Bùi Thị Xuân   27n3
Burawoy, Michael   1
bureaucracy   27, 30, 36–7, 44–5
Butler, Judith   viii
bửu điện (palace)   176, 184

cá nhân (individual)   6, 88
   see also individualism
cadre   32, 120
   female   143, 147, 151, 152–3, 160–3
   good   6, 152
   local   144, 147, 155, 156, 158–9
   male   143, 147, 151–2, 153
campaign   27n3, 32n8, 38n14, 86, 146, 147, 148, 151, 154
   for "three responsibilities" (*ba đảm đang*)   11, 30, 145
   of five goods   145
căn đồng (destined aptitude or 'root' of mediumship)   194, 199, 200, 202, 204, 205, 207, 208
canalization   122, 128, 133
Caodaism (*đạo Cao Đài*)   167, 170–6, 182–3, 188
Caodaist Hanoi Temple (Thánh Thất Thủ Đô Hà Nội)   7, 17, 167, 173–4, 175
capitalism   3, 10
care   8, 10–11, 12, 30, 32n8, 35, 40, 41n16, 84, 103–4, 107, 169, 176, 177, 181, 187, 190, 210
   see also childcare, *lo lắng* (taking care)
   health   xiii, 12, 30, 39, 84, 86, 146, 154, 176
career   16–17, 28, 43–5, 119, 127, 134, 147
Catholic
   U.S.   18, 218–20, 222–9
   Vietnamese   18, 221–2, 227–9
   Vietnamese American   218–29
Center of Pastoral Apostolate for Overseas Vietnamese   224, 225
Central Vietnam   26, 34, 141, 187, 220, 221
   see also North Central Vietnam
centralized regime   10, 14, 118
Chakrabarty, Dipesh   vii, 3
Cham   8
Chang, Kyung-Sup   10, 85
chi (family branch, sub-lineage)   16, 61, 66–9, 71
chia sẻ (compassion)   17, 141–3, 151–3, 155, 156, 157
chiều (pleasing)   47
childcare   41–3, 49, 86, 89, 91, 100, 101, 104, 107, 150, 154, 157
child-rearing   31, 43–4, 47
China   10, 58, 61, 62–4, 70n25, 91–2, 130, 143–4
Chư Vị Cult   196–7

chung (general, for everybody)   6
   compare riêng (particular, separate)
citizenship   14, 17, 148, 154–5, 220, 228
civic organization   141, 143, 144, 156, 157
Civil Engineer Brigade   160
civil society   143–4
Cohen, Paul   166
Colclough, Christopher   117
Cold War   10, 221
collective   11, 143, 153
   agricultural   12, 14, 147, 150, 160, 161, 163
collectivism   86, 87–9, 93, 109, 110, 178
   see also tập thể (collectivity)
collectivization   1, 14, 28, 32n8, 144, 150
colonialism   vii, 1, 3, 8, 9, 11, 27, 28, 30, 57, 145, 196, 201
commercialism   3
commonality   143, 152
communal house (*đình*)   27, 45–6, 151, 171n4
commune
   see xã
Communism   151, 218, 223–4, 228
Communist Party   28, 30, 31, 35–6, 37, 121, 144, 145, 146, 147, 148, 150, 158–9, 160, 161, 162, 176n10, 182
community
   as intimate sphere   168
   as practice   166–7, 168, 173, 186
   ethnic   224, 225
   familial   175, 177, 179, 180
   local   1, 7, 10, 14, 15, 46, 65, 75, 87–8, 104, 144, 146, 156, 157
   of practice   17, 166, 169
   religious   50, 166, 167, 168, 169–70, 174, 175, 182–3, 187, 188–90, 219, 222, 227
   women's   1, 17
conflict   17, 83, 89, 93–5, 98, 100–1, 105, 106, 108, 110, 131, 141, 150, 152, 154, 179–81, 189
Confucianism   5, 6, 8, 12, 27, 32n8, 58, 59, 63, 70n25, 75, 76, 81, 86–7, 124, 170,173, 195, 197, 207n10, 208, 220
công (public)   5, 6
   compare tư
contraceptive   146
cooking   15, 41, 42, 186
co-residence   9, 27, 28, 34–5, 41, 46, 47, 84
corporate group   144, 150
court   5, 16, 82–3, 90, 93–4
Crawfurd, John   26

INDEX   235

credit   33, 150, 161, 162
Cuba   219
culture   1, 3, 8, 9, 13, 84, 87–8, 109, 121, 133,
    146, 206, 210, 227
    see also văn hóa
custom   57, 59n3, 60, 62n8, 75, 83, 118, 122,
    183, 202, 205

Dampier, William   26
dân công hỏa tuyến (volunteer army service
    crops)   158, 161
đạo ('way' or 'ism')   170, 172–3, 176, 177, 179,
    180, 185, 187, 189
    see also đạo mình, họ đạo
Đạo Mẫu (Mother Goddess Religion)   193,
    219, 220, 229
đạo mình (own moral)   18, 178, 180–1,
    188–9, 190
daughter   8, 12–13, 16, 25, 28, 33, 47, 58ff, 102,
    103, 105–6, 117–8, 119, 123–4, 126, 127, 128,
    129–31, 133, 134, 160
    see also factory girl
daughter-in-law   35, 46–8, 49, 107, 108, 110
death anniversary   71, 177–9
    goddess   184–5
deity   27, 171, 183, 184, 195, 203
    female   2, 3, 199–200, 202, 204n9
Delanty, Gerard   166
Deloustal, Raymond   57
demobilization   161
Democratic Republic of Vietnam
    see North Vietnam
demography   34, 81, 82, 119n1
Deolalikar, Anil   12
descent
    patrilineal   27
    bilateral   27, 46
developing country   12
devotion   11, 13, 151, 183, 223
Diaspora   1, 18
Diener, E.   86
Diêu Trì Kim Mẫu   172, 184
Difence Service   160, 161
diplomatic relationship   18, 219
distribution system   11, 122
divorce   9, 16, 81–8, 168, 174, 182, 197
    number of   91–2, 109
    procedure for   88–91, 93–4, 96–7, 110
    rate of   37n13, 91–2, 94–6, 109–11

reasons for   98ff, 109
doctrine   17, 170–1, 173, 175, 178–9, 189
Đổi Mới (Renovation)   3, 11, 12, 13, 14, 15,
    16–17, 30, 81, 85, 86, 93, 109, 110, 118–9,
    122–4, 126, 128, 133, 144, 145, 168, 171,
    192, 197
    as a gendered project   11, 17
domestic realm   4–5, 6, 14, 25–9, 31, 38,
    47–9, 220
domestic violence   12, 16, 89, 104–7, 110
domestic work   4, 5, 10, 11, 14, 28, 32, 33,
    35, 37, 41, 42n17, 43, 44, 46, 47–8,
    49, 50, 84, 86, 100, 102, 107, 130,
    154, 184
domestic worker   43, 49
đồng cô ('effeminate' male medium)   202,
    204–13
dòng họ (patrilineal kinship group)   16,
    60–62, 64–8, 70–6, 144, 168, 172, 182
    see also lineage
Đồng Lộc Junction   211–2
Đồng Nai   126
Đồng Ngạc   64–6, 70–2, 74
Doussantousse, Serge   205
Drummond, Lisa   32, 48, 168
Durand, Maurice   196, 202

East Asia   viii, 1, 7–8, 9, 10, 11, 27, 58,
    92, 117
Easterlin, R.A.   84
Eastern Europe   143
education   16–17, 85, 86, 92, 93, 94, 101, 107,
    117–20, 161
    moral   3, 11
    women's   1, 6, 11, 27, 28–30, 38, 40–1,
        46, 50
egalitarianism   7, 17, 85, 143
Eipper, Chris   220
Eisen, Arlene   168
elite   27, 76, 119, 222
Elson, Diane   118
Emotion   87, 105, 127, 130, 134, 147, 150, 157,
    169, 179, 180, 185–6, 190
employment   26, 39n15, 44, 86, 116, 125,
    133, 170
empowerment   vii–viii, 3, 4, 10, 14, 18, 85, 117,
    130, 131, 133, 151, 195, 214
    moment of   13, 16, 117, 129, 134
endogamy   46, 76, 146, 148, 150

Endres, Kirsten W.   2, 15, 18, 50, 145–6, 147, 154, 172, 193ff, 220
equality
   see also inequality
   gender   3, 6, 11, 35, 46, 50, 83, 84, 86–7, 92–3, 97, 105, 109, 118, 120, 121, 146
   of property rights   28, 58–61, 62, 64, 66–70, 71
Errington, Shelly   203
ethnicity   2, 8, 26, 39n15, 50, 51, 119n1, 122
   see also identity
exile   212, 219
experience distant concept   4
experience near concept   4, 5

factory girl (factory daughter)   13, 14, 117, 126–7, 130, 134
fairness   5–6, 190
faithfulness   11, 102, 131, 152, 226
familialism   9–13, 87–8, 98, 110
family   1–3, 5–8, 11, 13, 14, 57–60, 62–72, 74, 81–90, 117–9, 123, 125–7, 130, 134, 168–9, 172, 174–5, 179–180, 182–4, 188–9, 191
   Asian   8, 11
   cultured (*gia đình văn hóa*)   154, 165, 157
   see also Movement for Construction of Cultured Families
   extended   10, 47, 85, 88, 108
   modern   9–10, 11, 81
   nuclear   10, 47, 84, 86, 88, 218
   patrilineal   1, 7–8, 9–10
   premodern   7–8, 16, 75
   revival of   3, 11, 12
   traditional   6, 11, 29n4, 32n8, 65n16, 81, 104, 110
family branch
   see *chi*
family circle   9
family court   83
family meeting   89
family planning policy   3, 12, 118, 143, 154–5, 157, 162
   see also birth control
farming
   see agriculture
fate   13, 18, 116, 182, 194, 205, 208, 211
father-in-law   104, 182
Fatherland Front   159, 161, 174, 176

femininity   4, 15, 47–8, 117, 131, 133–4, 195, 201n7, 210n13
feminism   3
festival   14, 15, 66–8, 70–2, 151, 193, 218, 223
feudalism   50, 83, 85, 88, 151
fictive kinship   173
fire and incense
   see *hương hỏa*
Fjelstad, Karen   193, 219, 220
flexibility   viii, 6, 8, 9, 17, 59, 128, 200
fortunetelling   14, 15, 188, 202
Four Palace Mediumship   193–213
freedom   4, 5, 13, 16, 83, 85, 87, 93, 98, 120, 128–9, 134
French administrator   11, 57, 170
Fuess, Harald   104
funding   18, 146, 147, 161, 162, 176, 211–2, 224
funeral   15, 40, 66, 118, 150, 152, 185, 187

Gammeltoft, Tine   3, 11, 12, 13, 38, 46–7, 49, 88, 130, 146, 168, 173, 189
Geertz, Clifford   4
Geertz, H.   104
gender and mediumship   193–213
   see also spirit medium
gender androgyny   201n7
gender celibacy   197, 208
gender chastity   198, 202, 204
gender effeminacy   202–3, 205, 206–7, 208
gender role   12–13, 48, 81, 86, 119
gender studies   xiii, 3, 10, 12, 189
gender transgressive behavior   2, 18, 195, 200, 202–10
gender trouble   196
genealogy   58, 70, 72, 74
Giran, Paul   196, 197
globalism   3, 10–11, 25, 35, 40–1, 50, 86, 88, 93, 109, 117, 126, 219, 225–7
Goode, William J.   84, 94–5
Goodkind, Daniel   50, 81, 118, 123–4
gossip   50, 144
governance   14, 141, 145, 147, 153
government   12, 18, 30–1, 35–8, 41n16, 44–5, 50, 85–6, 89–90, 93, 110, 118, 120, 122–3, 125–8, 132–3, 146–7, 170, 174, 180, 193, 221–2, 227
grandparent   28, 43, 74–5, 182
Grossheim, Martin   154
Guan, Wen Na   62–3

Gunewardena, Dileni 44

Hà Nam 32, 34, 37n13, 82–3, 125
Hà Tây 32n8, 48, 49, 128
Hà Tĩnh 141, 146, 151, 211
Hà Văn Tấn 36n12
Hải Phòng 126
half-share law 63
hamlet
   see xóm
handicraft 26–7, 32–3
Hann, Chris 143, 144
Hanoi 26, 32, 37n13, 41, 49, 82–3, 101, 102, 103, 105, 116, 119, 128–130, 132, 134, 161, 166–9, 173–4, 175, 182–3, 187, 196, 205, 213
harvesting 67, 107, 148, 154, 156
hầu (to serve) 184
hầu đồng 193
   see also lên đồng
hầu thánh (serving the deities) 194, 202
Haughton, Dominique 81
Haughton, Jonathan 81, 84–5
Hayami, Yoko 9, 75–6
health 177, 184, 187
health expense 32n8, 40
health insurance 39n15
heavenly fairy (*tiên*) 203–4
heavenly principle 5–7
Heiman, Elliott M. 201
heritage 75, 81, 86, 193, 226
hermaphrodites (*ái nam ái nữ*) 200–3
heroine 18, 211–2
heterosexuality 195, 203, 208
Hickey, Gerald 170n2
hiền lành (living honestly) 19
hierarchy 7, 11, 27, 59, 81, 170n2
Hirai, Kyonosuke 166
Hirschman, Charles 34, 40–1, 81, 85, 93, 211
Hồ Chí Minh Trail 211–2
họ đạo 17, 170–5, 179–180, 188
Ho Tai, Hue-Tam 170
Hobsbawm, Eric 1
homeland 219–20, 223–6
hometown 16, 129–32, 134
homosexuality
   and spirit mediumship 199–200, 201, 203–10
   in French Colonial Vietnam 201
   perceived as a 'contagious disease' 206

Hồng Đức Thiện Chính Thư 60, 64
Hoskins, Janet 222
house 15, 62, 64, 66, 76, 82–3, 101, 102, 103, 106, 108–9, 127, 130, 160, 161, 171, 175–6, 182, 185
   as an inside space (*trong nhà*) 6–7
household 3, 11, 12, 14, 26, 27–8, 34–5, 39, 40, 57–9, 60, 61, 75, 81, 84, 145, 154, 168, 177
   division of labor in 32, 33, 34–5, 41–5
housekeeping
   see nội trợ
housewife 11, 12, 43–4
housework
   see domestic work
Houtart, Francois 32, 145
hot-temperedness (*nóng tính*) 47, 199
humanities 16, 116, 119, 128, 131–4
Humphrey, Caroline 143–4
Hưng Yên 126
hương hỏa (fire and incense) 59, 61, 62, 64, 75, 76
husband 11, 27, 33, 38, 41–2, 44, 47–50, 64–5, 68, 70, 75–6, 83–4, 86–9, 93–4, 96–7, 101–9, 116, 126, 133, 143, 153, 154, 160–2, 168, 174, 182–3, 187–8, 198, 202

identity 3, 117, 177, 213
   ethnic 1, 3, 5, 8, 18, 40, 219–220, 222, 224–5, 229
   gender 201, 205, 207, 208
   national 2, 3, 5, 8, 18
   religious 3
ideology
   gender 3, 11, 118
   state 6, 14, 17, 27–8, 31, 32n8, 40, 46, 156
ie 76
illness 39, 40, 49
   mental 155, 194, 195, 205
immorality 6, 13, 46, 102–3, 117, 187, 199, 209
income 12, 37, 43–4, 84, 107
independence 13, 37, 85, 86, 109
   national 1, 10, 28, 30, 93, 211
Independence Revolution, 1945 3, 11, 147, 150
individual 2, 57, 77, 85, 109, 119, 122, 127, 143, 166, 168, 169, 171, 173, 186
individualism 6, 7, 10, 16, 86, 87–8, 93, 94, 98, 101, 102, 104, 109–10
   see also cá nhân

industrialization 1, 10, 12, 16, 32, 37, 85, 86, 116–7, 126
inequality 4, 38, 50, 58, 105, 118, 189, 229
inheritance 8, 25, 27, 28, 33, 58, 60n8, 61–4, 70, 75
inner lineage
 see nội tộc
inside/outside
 see nội/ngoại
institutional capability 156
interaction 168–9, 175, 181, 186, 188
internal convention 17, 27
interpretation 17, 88, 143, 157, 189
 of policy 156
inter-subjective relationship 169, 190
intimacy 7, 17, 29n4, 87, 92, 93, 94, 108, 166, 168–9, 184, 188, 189–90
 see also thân mật
intimate sphere 166–9, 188–90, 192
 alternative 167, 169, 188–90
Irrigation Team 160, 161
isolation 7, 218, 220, 222
Ito, Mariko 7, 17–8, 50
Ito, Miho 6, 14, 16–7, 50
Iwai, Misaki 3–4, 8, 11–12

Jade Emperor (Đức Ngọc Hoàng Thượng Đế) 170–1, 175
Japan 7, 58, 61, 76, 88, 92, 104, 129, 152, 168
Jensen, A.M. 96–7
job 116, 129, 130, 132–4
job allocation system 17, 118–9, 122, 128
job selection 17, 133
Jones, Gavin W. 92, 93, 118
justice 5

Kato, Atsufumi 17, 46, 146, 176n10
Kawamura, Yasushi 61–3, 64n12
Kerkvliet, Benedict J. 144
Khmer 8
Khuất Thu Hồng 38–9
kindergarten 106, 161
kindred
 see bilateral kindred system
Kinh 88, 146
kinship 7–10, 13, 14, 15, 25–8, 31, 33, 34n9, 35, 39, 46, 50, 59, 88, 98, 117, 144, 146, 150, 166, 168, 169, 172, 173, 180, 182, 186, 188, 189–90

 see also lineage
 pre-modern Chinese 16
kitchen 144
Kleinen, John 15, 40, 118
Knodel, John 84
Koh, David W.H. 6
Korea 39, 58, 61, 88, 92, 224
Kwon, Heonik 210, 211
kỵ điền (anniversary rice field) 66–72

labor force viii, 3, 11, 12, 14, 32, 92, 120, 121–2, 124, 127, 145, 148, 169
labor market 38, 43–4, 86, 116, 118–9, 126, 134
Lambek, Michael 195
land 8, 16, 26–7, 35n, 57–8, 60n8, 68, 101, 107, 148, 150
land law 150
land reform 28, 161
landlord 65, 67, 170
làng 147, 148, 150
 see also village
Lạng Sơn 130, 207
Lào Cai 119, 122, 133
Laos 161
Lauser, Andrea 195, 221
Lavang 220–1, 227
law viii, 5, 6, 8, 28, 35, 38, 44, 57–60, 63, 75, 83–4, 92–3, 105
laywoman 169–170, 175, 177, 180–1, 183–6, 188, 190
Lê Anh Dũng 173
Lê Bạch Dương 39
Lê Code
 see Quốc Triều Hình Luật, the QTHL
Lê Duẩn 31–2
Lê Dynasty 58–60, 203n9
Lê Ngọc Hùng 30–1
Lê Ngọc Văn 42, 84
Lê Thị Nhâm Tuyết 27n3, 30, 83
leadership 6, 11, 25, 31, 33, 37, 44, 86, 89–90, 145, 147, 151–3, 155, 162, 175, 183, 187, 197, 222, 227
 see also cadre
Lee, Gary 85
Lemercinier, Genevieve 32, 145
lên đồng 193–213
liberal arts 16, 121
liberation of women 2, 3, 10, 12, 14, 104
libertarian regime 1, 17

life course   17, 81, 134
life history   2, 83, 147, 158–63, 187
lifestyle difference   16, 48, 87, 98–104, 108–10
light industry   121
lineage   58, 60–2, 64– 8, 70–6, 89, 110, 150, 151
    see also dòng họ, kinship, ngoại tộc (outer lineage), nội tộc (inner lineage), patlilineage
literacy   11, 62, 201n7
lo lắng (taking care)   160, 161, 162
loan   148–9
London, Jonathan D.   118, 124
Lộng Chương   199n5, 202
Lương Hồng Quang   40
Luong, Hy Van   ix, 4, 8, 11, 13, 15, 27–8, 35, 39–40, 41, 44, 46, 81, 84, 87, 118, 144–5, 150, 197, 222
Lusteguy, Pierre   57

Makino, Tastumi   57, 59
Malarney, Shaun   40, 150, 152, 193, 210, 211
manufacturing   26–8
Marianism
    see Virgin Mary
market
    local   15, 26, 144, 163
market economy   viii, 10, 36, 38, 39–41, 50, 85, 86, 109, 118, 123, 124
Marr, David   3, 11, 28, 118, 133
marriage   1, 6, 8, 11, 13, 16, 27, 58, 65, 81–90, 94, 95, 109, 118, 124, 126–7, 130, 161, 162, 163, 182, 210
    see also remarriage
    to foreigners   39, 50
masculinity   4, 15, 118, 195, 197, 200, 208, 213
Mason, K.O.   96–7
mass media   48, 96, 109
mass organization   2, 11, 14, 17, 45n18, 89, 110, 141, 143, 144, 145, 146, 148, 155, 156
maternity leave   38, 102
matrilocal residence   8
medical science   121–2
migration   13, 103, 106, 107, 183
    chain   3
    from the Ming dynasty   8
    to U.S.   219–20, 222–3
military   3, 14, 45, 158, 161, 170–1, 211
Ministry of Education and Training, Vietnam   116

misfortune   5, 210
Miyajima, Hiroshi   58
Miyazawa, Chihiro   6, 8, 15–16, 61, 87
mobilization   143, 144, 147, 171
    for military service   3, 14, 30
    of women   3, 32n8, 120, 121, 145, 154–5, 156, 157
    total   1, 11, 14, 17, 145
modernity   vii, viii, 1, 2, 9–11, 16, 92, 101, 168, 196, 209
    compressed   10, 29n4, 85–6
    shortcut   85–6, 88
    socialist   viii, 10, 118
modernization   2, 3, 16, 50, 81, 82, 83–4, 85, 88, 93, 101–2, 104, 108, 109–10, 119
Momoki, Shiro   57, 58, 76
Mông Sơn Ritual   211–2
Moock, Peter R.   117
morality   3, 13, 17, 38–9, 130, 141, 143, 155–7, 173, 183, 195, 197, 199, 200, 201n7, 205, 209, 213
    see also đạo mình
Morgan, Philip   102
mortuary   183–4, 186
mother   14, 48, 49, 61–2, 64, 65, 70, 71, 75, 76, 93–4, 103, 106, 109, 127–8, 133, 161, 172–3, 181–2, 184, 187, 220, 229
Mother Goddess   193, 219–20, 229
mother-in-law   35, 46–8, 49, 105, 107, 108, 110
mother worshipping
    see Mother Goddess, Virgin Mary
mountainous area   122, 183
Movement for Construction of Cultured Families   154
    see also cultured family
mutual aid   2, 10, 15, 17, 40, 141, 143, 155, 156–7, 177, 179
    see also support, tương thân tương ái
myth   8, 16, 60, 65

Nam Định   34, 126
nation-state   3, 10, 18, 229
National Assembly   25n1, 30, 31, 35–6, 38
national division   1
national integration   9, 18, 211, 229
    see also reunification
Neo-Confucianism   58

neoliberalism 10–11
Nghiem, Huong Lien 126, 130–1
Ngô Đình Diệm 221–2
Ngô Đức Thịnh 193
Ngô Tất Tố 5
Ngo Thi Ngan Binh 47, 49–50
ngoài (outside) 6–7, 25, 76
    compare *trong* (inside)
    see also *nội/ngoại* (inside/outside)
ngoại tộc (outer lineage) 65, 68, 70–6
    compare *nội tộc* (inner lineage)
Nguyen, Bich Thuan 134
Nguyễn Dynasty 58
Nguyễn Hữu Minh 34, 40–1, 81, 84, 88, 89, 105
Nguyễn Ngọc Huy 57–8, 59, 60n7, 61–2
Nguyễn Ngọc Thương 172, 177
Nguyen Quang Vinh 141, 144
Nguyen Tai Thu 58
Nguyễn Thị Hiền 194–5
Nguyễn Thị Vân Anh 33–4
Nguyễn Văn Huyên 36n12, 207, 208
Nguyễn Văn Khoan 196
Nguyễn-Võ Thu-Hương 48, 117, 189
nhẹ nhàng (toil-less) 128
Niida, Noboru 57, 59
Ninh, Thien-Huong 2, 5, 18
nội tộc (inner lineage) 65n16, 67, 68, 72, 74, 76
    compare *ngoại tộc* (outer lineage)
    see also patrilineage
nội trợ (housekeeping) 61
nội tướng (domestic general) 28
nội/ngoại (inside/outside) 6–7, 15, 76
    see also *ngoài* (outside), *trong* (inside)
norm 9, 13, 14, 16, 42n16, 44, 75, 173, 177, 189, 190, 196
    gender 11, 13, 17, 18, 27–8, 48, 116–9, 128, 130–1, 133–4, 157, 195, 197, 202, 207, 208, 210, 214, 220
    modern 82
    plural 2, 9
    public 2, 6, 17, 133–4
    social 117–9, 128, 130–1, 133, 134, 143, 196
    socialistic 124
    traditional 2, 10, 11, 81, 83, 109
North Vietnam (The Democratic Republic of Vietnam) 10, 83, 119–20, 122, 128, 133, 150, 151, 174, 221

Northern Central Vietnam 146
Northern Vietnam 4, 8, 15, 16, 33, 40–1, 46, 62n10, 146, 147, 150, 173, 213
Norton, Barley 194
nurse 28, 147
nursery 161

occupation 26, 30, 48, 49, 118, 122, 125, 128, 130, 133, 134, 203
    see also domestic worker, factory girl (factory daughter), nurse, teacher
Ochiai, Emiko 9, 10–11, 29n4, 85, 91, 92
Oi, Jean 144
one-or-two child policy
    see family planning policy
Open Door Policy 144
Orange County 222–5
Our Lady of Exile 219
Our Lady of Fatima 218, 221, 223–4
Our Lady of Global Peace 223
Our Lady of Lavang 218f
Our Lady of Lourdes 221
Our Lady of Victories 220–1
Our Lady of Vietnam 225–7, 228
outer lineage
    see *ngoại tộc*
own moral
    see *đạo mình*

Pastoetter, Jakob 205
parent-in-law 35, 47, 87, 89, 102–3, 105, 108
patriarchy 3, 6, 11, 15–16, 76–7, 118, 126, 133, 168, 190
patrilineage 7, 16, 25, 28, 33, 40–1, 58, 60–1, 74–6, 81, 168, 182, 189, 195
    see also ie, *nội tộc* (inner lineage)
patrilocal residence 8, 25, 27, 28, 34–5, 40–1, 46, 47, 84, 123–4
Patrinos, Harry Anthony 123
patriotism 8, 11, 174, 213
Peletz, Michael G. 200–1
Pelzer, C. 11, 118
Pendakis, Katherine L. 12, 13, 14, 116–7, 118, 126, 130–1
personhood 2–3, 44, 169, 173, 194
Phạm Nam Thanh 40
Phạm Quynh Phuong 15, 196–7, 220
Phạm Văn Bích 3, 28, 34n10

INDEX

Phạm Văn Đồng 120
Phan Đại Doãn 40
Phan Huy Lê 26
Phan Kế Bính 196–7
Phan Phương Thảo 26
Phan Thị Mai Huong 88
Phật Mẫu
    see Diêu Trì Kim Mẫu
phò loan 170
political arena 4, 28, 30, 35, 38, 145
political deliberation 5, 141, 144
political participation 30, 144, 145, 146
polygamy
    see polygyny, second wife
polygyny 28, 33, 107, 110
    see also second wife
Pope John Paul II 225, 227
popular organization
    see mass organization
post-marital residence
    see patrilocal residence
practice 17, 117, 166–70, 179–81, 188–91
    everyday 6, 141, 150, 166, 167n11, 175, 177, 186
    gendered 1–2, 157
    religious 170, 175, 193–214
pregnancy 84, 103, 108, 143, 153–4, 182, 187
premodern society 3, 4, 7–9, 12, 16, 57–8, 59–60, 62–3, 64, 65, 75–6
pre-revolution period 3, 59, 81, 87, 118, 147, 150
Preston, Samuel 211
priestess 169, 174–81, 183–5, 187–9
Princess Liễu Hạnh 203–4, 220
private vii–viii, 4, 7, 12, 15, 16, 17–18, 37, 57, 61, 66, 76, 89, 123, 143–4, 156, 157, 181, 187–8, 190, 196
    compare public
    see also public/private divide, *tư*
    as a local concept 5–7
    as an universal concept 4–5
private sphere 1, 2, 18, 57, 61, 143, 177, 214, 218, 219
private temple (*phủ*) 18, 193, 195n2
property 8, 14, 16, 26–2, 57–8, 59, 60–4, 76, 82, 83, 84, 91, 92, 94, 106
Proschan, Frank 201
prostitution 25, 37, 38–9
    domestic 38
public vii–viii, 2, 4, 5, 7, 13, 15–18, 75–6, 122
    compare private

see also *công*, public/private divide
    as a local concept 5–7
    as an universal concept 4
public authority 5–6, 27, 30
public dialogue 15, 32n8, 41, 144
public sector 13, 16
public service 28, 119, 154
public sphere 1, 2, 4, 7, 13, 15, 16, 25, 27, 28–9, 30, 31, 33, 36, 39, 40, 43, 44–5, 49, 50, 57, 61, 143, 144, 151, 169, 190, 193, 213, 214, 218–20, 228
    reconstruction of 1, 144
public/private divide 1, 2, 4, 5, 12, 15, 16, 17, 143, 157, 219

quan hệ (relation) 152
Quốc Triều Hình Luật (Lê Code, the QTHL) 31, 58–60, 76, 79

reconciliation 9, 82, 83, 89, 90, 93–4, 110, 220, 229
reconnection 2–3, 18, 218, 225, 227, 229
relationship among women 168, 188–9
    see also sisterhood (*chị em*)
religion vii, 1, 5, 6, 14, 15, 18, 46, 50, 60, 146, 151, 166–9, 170–1, 173, 174, 175ff, 193, 200, 201, 204, 214, 218–9, 220–1, 228, 229
    see also Buddhism, Caodaism, Catholic
religious organization 2, 6, 10, 14, 15, 17–18, 144–5, 174, 225, 227
religious persecution 221
remaking women 3, 11
remarriage 83, 160, 181, 202
Republic of Vietnam
    see South Vietnam
resistance 3
retirement 38, 39n15, 44
reunification 18, 93, 211, 221
    see also national integration
revolution 3, 11, 42n17, 146, 147, 182
    sexual 102
riêng (particular, separate) 6
    compare chung (general, for everybody)
Rindfuss, R. 81, 102
ritual 3, 17, 18, 40, 67, 68, 75, 171–2, 176–81, 183, 188, 191, 193–6, 197, 199, 200–2, 203, 208, 209, 210–3
Robinson, Courtland 222
romantic love 3, 11, 13

Rosen, Stanley 118, 133
rural area 12, 14, 15, 16, 34–5, 37, 41, 45–7, 50, 57, 76, 82–3, 84–5, 88–9, 91, 93, 94–6, 98, 102, 106–10, 116–7, 119, 120, 125–6, 130, 141, 143, 144–6, 154, 187, 193
  see also village
Rydström, Helle 3, 48, 90, 117, 130, 157, 168, 195

Saint Trần Cult 196–200
Saito, Junichi 169, 190
Sakurai, Yumio 151
Salemink, Oskar 15
same-age association 40, 45, 144, 150
science 121–2, 128, 130, 132
Schlecker, Markus 212
school 2, 14, 16–17, 29, 33, 38, 44, 48–9, 84, 105, 107, 117, 120, 122–3, 125–8, 130, 132, 160, 161, 162, 163, 175
Scornet, Catherine 12
Sechiyama, Kaku 10
second wife 9, 27, 33, 182
  see also polygyny
secondary education 124, 126
secondary group 14, 17, 141, 143–4
sect 167, 170–5, 179, 180, 188
  see also họ đạo
secularity 5, 177, 206,
self-determination 8
self-empowerment 151
self-fulfillment 119
sex worker 3, 36–7, 38, 39
sexual intercourse 13, 38–9, 47, 81, 107, 131, 187, 189, 197, 198, 204, 205–6
sexual sphere 13
sexuality 11, 102, 117, 130–1, 189, 195, 201n8, 207, 208, 209–10, 229
  see also homosexuality
sharing 152, 169, 173, 184, 186
  see also chia sẻ
Shimao, Minoru viii–ix, 58n2, 60n8
short 20th century 1
single mother 162, 187
sister-in-law 187
sisterhood (*chị em*) 7, 141, 143, 153, 155, 157, 172, 177
small business 8, 15, 163, 188
social benefit 147, 148
social evil 117
social network 14, 40, 46, 117, 143, 161, 168, 186

social organization
  see mass organization
social periphery 168, 189, 190, 199, 200
social prestige 84, 151, 152, 199–200
social relationship
  see social network
socialism 1, 3, 6, 85, 118, 119, 122, 124, 128, 133, 143
socialist regime 1, 11, 14, 17, 28, 31, 40, 87, 117–8, 121–2, 143
socialist transformation (*cải tạo xã hội chủ nghĩa*) 146, 150, 151
socialistic reform viii, 1, 10–11, 12, 14, 17, 50, 118, 174, 193
socialization 3, 39, 48, 157
  see also xã hội hóa (socialization)
society 2, 15, 18, 57–9, 64, 117–8, 121, 124, 128, 134, 166, 168–9, 187, 189–90
  see also xã hội
sociology of family vii, 1, 3
solidarity 7, 14, 86, 143–4, 148, 150, 152, 154, 157
son 27–8, 33–4, 41n16, 58–65, 67, 70, 71, 73, 75, 76, 81, 85, 117–8, 123–4, 127, 160, 168, 187
  not having 8, 12, 16, 27
Sơn La 127
Soucy, Alexander 197
South Vietnam (The Republic of Vietnam) 3, 36n11, 151, 221, 222
Southeast Asia vii, viii, 1, 2, 7–8, 9–10, 39, 91, 93, 109, 126, 200–1, 203
Southern Vietnam 4, 8, 26–7, 28, 33–5, 39, 40–1, 45–6, 48, 88, 107, 122, 126, 161, 163, 170, 201, 205n11, 220
Soviet Union 119, 143, 221
space 4, 5, 6–7, 13, 28, 40, 48, 134, 141, 144–5, 150, 151, 166, 168, 181, 184, 186, 196, 203, 208, 209, 214, 219, 220, 229
  alternative 2, 17, 141, 143, 145, 168, 186, 214
  of appearance 168–9, 189–90
  social 14, 120, 143, 146, 169, 174
specific other 169, 183, 186, 189–90
spirit medium
  female 196, 199, 202, 210–3
  gender-transgressive male 200–10
  initiation for 194, 195
  male 2, 196, 197, 199, 205, 208, 213
  master-follower relationship of 195n2

spirit possession 14, 15, 193–5, 196–7
spirit root
    see căn đồng
state 6, 35n9, 58, 59, 61, 65, 75, 118, 122, 124, 141, 143, 146
status of woman 1–4, 7–9, 12–13, 15, 16, 28, 51, 58, 85–7, 93, 97, 100–1, 107, 109–10, 145, 168
structure vii, 2–3, 4, 9, 11, 15, 28–9, 40, 58, 84, 88, 146, 170, 195
subject 3, 4, 169, 189, 190, 200
sub-lineage
    see chi
succession 57, 60, 76
Suenari, Michio 58n2, 64, 186
Sung Dynasty 58, 63–4
superstition (*mê tín dị đoan*) 14, 15, 193
support 126–7, 174, 181–2
    see also mutual aid
syncretism 170

Tạ Văn Tài 57–8, 59, 60n7, 61–2
tâm công 179
Tanabe, Shigeharu 166–7, 169
T'ang Code 59n3, 63
tập thể (collectivity) 17, 88, 141, 143, 144, 147–8, 150, 155–7
    see also collectivism
Tây Ninh 170, 173
Taylor, Keith W. 3, 59
Taylor, Philip 193, 201, 220
teacher 28, 30, 46, 49, 119, 122, 127–30, 132–3, 147, 160, 175, 176, 202
Teerawichitchainan, Bussarawan 85, 93
testament (*chúc thư*) 8, 16, 60–71, 75, 76
Thạch Châu 146, 147, 158–63
Thái Bình 26, 122, 132
Thái Nguyên 41, 122, 129
thân mật (intimacy) 7, 17, 167, 170, 180–1, 183–4, 188–90
thánh thất 167, 171, 173, 191
Thanh Thế Vỹ 26
Thaveerporn Vasavakul 144
Thích Nhất Hạnh 212
Third World 3
Thomas, Mandy 134
tín ngưỡng (belief) 15
tình cảm (sentimental relationship) 48, 152, 157

tình làng nghĩa xóm (sentiment and duty among villagers) 155
Tonkin 57, 66
total war
    see mobilization
trade 26, 32n8, 45n18, 49, 125–6, 174
tradition viii, 1, 2, 9, 10, 11–13, 18, 29n4, 32n8, 39, 40, 42n17, 46, 50, 57, 59n3, 70–1, 81–2, 83–4, 86, 87–8, 93, 101, 102, 104–8, 109–11, 133, 144, 151, 166, 168, 180, 190, 196, 202, 205, 206, 209, 218, 220, 225, 227
Trần Bồng Sơn 205
Tran Dinh Huou 81
Trần Dynasty 76, 77
Trần Giang Linh 39
Trần Hưng Đạo (Saint Trần) 196–8, 199, 200, 217
    see also Saint Trần Cult
Tran, Nhung Tuyet 3, 8, 16, 57–65, 75
Trần Thị Vân Anh 30–1, 44–5, 105
transgenderism 18, 200, 203, 207, 208, 209, 214
    see also homosexuality
    and ritual 200–3
transgression viii, 2, 18, 134, 195, 200, 202–10
transition 1, 10, 81, 84, 86, 88, 109, 110, 119n1, 143
Trinh Duy Luan 81, 98
trong (inside) 6–7, 25
    compare *ngoài* (outside)
    see also *nội/ngoại* (inside/outside)
Trọng Lang 202–3
Trương Hữu Quýnh 57
Truong Huyen Chi 32n8, 49
Tsuya, N.O. 86
tư (private) 5, 6
    compare *công*
tương thân tương ái (mutual love and affection) 17, 155
Tuyên Quang 128
Tweed, Thomas 219

unemployment 116, 133
unilateral kinship 9
United States 18, 92, 218–20, 222, 223–7, 228–9
university 14, 16, 116–8, 120–1, 122–4, 127–9, 130, 133–4
unmarried women 13, 63–4, 126, 148, 168, 174, 187

urban area   12, 37, 38, 42–3, 47–8, 49–50, 82–3, 85, 88, 91, 93–6, 98–102, 106–7, 108, 109–10, 117, 134, 193, 195–6
urbanization   84, 85, 93, 117, 131

văn hóa (culture)   17, 143, 154–7, 193
Vatican   18, 221–5, 227
Verdery, Katherine   1, 143–4
việc lớn (big issue)   4, 15
việc nhỏ (small issue)   4, 15
Vietnam War   30, 31, 85, 92, 120, 145, 151, 160, 168, 174, 176, 182, 187, 211–2, 219, 221, 229
village   3–4, 6, 7, 13, 14–15, 16, 17, 27, 32n8, 43, 46, 62, 67, 75, 76, 89–90, 110, 117, 120–2, 130, 146, 168, 171, 182, 186–7
   see also *làng* (village), rural area, *xã* (commune), *xóm* (hamlet)
   as a tentative living space   150
   male-centered order in   14–15
Vinh   160
Vinh Phú   33
Vĩnh Phúc   125
Virgin Mary
   statue of   2, 18, 218, 221, 224, 225–7
   Vietnamization of   2, 18, 225–9
virginity   13, 38–9, 168
vỡ lòng (literacy education)   160, 161
voluntary association   45–6, 141, 148
volunteer   17, 18, 155, 161, 186, 211
Vu Manh Loi   81, 84, 105

Walker, A.J.   87
war   3, 10, 11, 14, 32, 145
   see also Vietnam War
War against the United State
   see Vietnam War
war dead   18, 188, 211
wedding   15, 40, 83, 105, 144, 150, 152, 161, 201, 227

welfare   12, 157, 170
welfare state   10–11
Wenger, Etienne   166
Werner, Jayne   3, 7, 8, 11, 12, 13, 31–2, 35, 51, 108, 145, 170n2, 191
White, Lynn K.   94
widowhood   160, 161, 168, 174, 182, 185, 187, 188, 197, 202
Wiegersma, N   11
wife   3, 8, 14, 26, 27, 32–4, 38, 41–4, 48, 49, 62, 65–6, 68, 70, 76, 83–4, 87, 88–9, 96, 100, 101, 103, 104, 105–6, 107, 144, 147, 150, 202, 218
   see also second wife
Wischermann, Joerg   141, 144
womanhood   1, 2, 3, 9, 12, 18, 168, 180, 190, 220
women's sphere   6
Women's Union
   as a friendship association   143, 148, 156
   as an interest group for women   145
   as an official mass organization   11, 15, 17, 36n11, 45n18, 89–90, 141, 143, 145–6, 147, 148, 154, 155, 156, 158–9, 160–3, 176
Woodside, Alexander   151
workplace   11, 118, 122, 126, 129

xã (commune)   31, 32n8, 33–4, 36, 37, 41, 46n19, 89–90, 94, 110, 126, 146, 147
xã hội (society)   7, 25, 26, 151, 161
   see also society
   as the outside world (*ngoài xã hội*)   7
xã hội hóa (socialization)   157
xóm (hamlet)   41, 143, 146, 147, 148

yếu lược (elementary school)   158
Youth League   45n18, 150, 160, 161, 162, 182
Yu, Insun   3, 8, 57–8, 59